Daughters of

ZION

A Family's Conversion to Polygamy

A true tale of misguided faith, unholy violence,
and spiritual awakening.

Kim Taylor

ISBN: 978-0-615-25701-3

A Production of Rogue Hill Publishing LLC

To my children: Ryan, Jacob, Russell, Sarah, and Nathaniel. I did this for you.

Acknowledgments

To friend and teacher Nancy Allen for your willingness to share your incredible knowledge and love of the English language, as well as for invaluable time spent reading, correcting, gentle prodding, and advising (forgive the mistakes)...

To authors Mary Ann Cook and David Kupelian for your kind interest, welcome help, and wise counsel...

To my niece Elena Wariner for painstakingly transcribing my original manuscript, giving me the needed push to continue writing....

To Rhea Watters, Lauren Gardner, and Donna Goldberg for your enduring friendship and thoughtful reminders of times past...

To old friends Susan Schmidt and Irene Spencer, who graciously took the time to answer my questions...

To new "old friends" Susan Avalos and Lynn Wade for your encouragement and the simple eye-opening statement, "More dialogue..."

To cousin Alice Schack for your inspiring enthusiasm....

And to my beloved husband, Ron, for being always there to patiently help and believe in me, even when I didn't believe in myself...

Thank you.

Author's Notes

It is not my intention to offend the people of my past, many of whom I have fond memories, and still consider my friends. I have tried to objectively include both the good and the bad of what I saw and experienced during the part of my life I have written about here.

Neither is it my intention to insult the members of the modern-day LDS Church, some of whom are my family. I have deep respect for the strong family-based values and loving attitudes I have encountered amongst the "Mormon" people I have embraced in my lifetime.

While the events written about in this book are all factual, I have combined some of the less important ones to condense the length of the story. All conversations are not exact and are written to the best of my memory, as are minor details surrounding the events.

A few of the names have been changed.

Prologue

"Anyone who fails to fulfill their mission will get it right between the eyes."

> Ervil LeBaron -
> Infamous Polygamous
> Cult Leader

Rena Chynoweth stood nervously near the edge of the waiting room of Dr. Rulon C. Allred's naturopathic clinic in Murray, Utah. Inside the pocket of her blue parka clutched tightly in her hand was a .25 caliber pistol.

It wasn't long before the pleasant gray haired doctor came out of a back room and noticing the harmless looking woman nodded politely before disappearing into a small lab. He had been greeting patients all day, and still had others waiting to be seen before his busy workday was over.

It was the afternoon of May 10, 1977, and the time had come for the frightened but determined young woman to do the will of God as her husband—the Prophet—had commanded. Certainly dreading this moment, the wig-clad eighteen-year-old feared even more the consequences of death and damnation she had been promised if she should refuse her mission. There was no turning back.

~~~

My old friend Rena was the thirteenth wife of Ervil LeBaron, the leader of the violent polygamous sect to which she and her family belonged. A few weeks earlier at a somber meeting, her husband had told his followers in no uncertain terms, that the time had come for the wrath of the Lord to be poured out on Dr. Allred (who was at the time a polygamous leader of close to 3000 followers). For years the condemned man had refused to offer tithes in recognition of Ervil's God-given authority, and the Lord had finally had enough.

Ervil had accused Rulon Allred of engaging in psychological warfare against one of God's own champions of liberty, and now the time had come for this unrepentant religious rival to be blood atoned. At the meeting Ervil proclaimed that as one of the prettiest women in the church, the Lord had chosen his attractive youngest wife, Rena, to kill the doctor.

On that day in May when Dr. Allred walked back out of his lab, Rena lifted the gun from her pocket, aimed at the doctor's chest, and from only a few feet away, fired twice. The stunned and wounded man instinctively held up his hands in an attempt to protect himself. "Oh my God! No!" he cried. Fearing that she might leave her mission incomplete, Rena began shooting again, firing all five of the remaining bullets into the elderly man's body before calmly walking out of the office.

~~~

Inwardly I cried when I heard the terrible facts of that day. Yet it was only one of the horrors committed in the name of God by people whom I once knew and loved. At one time I had been a part of their lives—a sister in our common religion.

And Ervil! How well I remembered the gravely imposing Ervil. Years before I had even called this strange man with the distant eyes "Brother."

As I share my experiences in the unfolding chain of events that led to that terrifying day, I need to begin with a more innocent and much simpler place in time.

One

The Missionaries

The time was the summer of 1960. The place was the pleasant and flourishing town of Ogden, Utah. I was a pesky five-year-old who, along with my two older sisters, lived with my parents in our modest but comfortable home located in a peaceful middle class neighborhood. My oldest sister, Carolyn, was already married while Judy and Kathy, still living at home, were typical teenagers who attended the local junior high school.

Leo Wariner was my dad. He was an aircraft mechanic at the Hillfield Air Force Base, and my mother Tressie had found work in the linen department at a modern new department store in town named Sears and Roebuck. She seemed to be always busy - cleaning house, fixing meals, and doing laundry which in those days included ironing clothes. I don't think my mom knew the meaning of the word leisure.

Dad kept the outside of our home nice with dense green lawns covering the front and back yards. A tall camellia bush loaded with deep red blossoms spread its leafy green branches next to the front door in summer, and Dad was proud of his living bouquets of velvety irises that softened the edges of our simple white house. A gardener at heart, he was most comfortable working in the yard and repairing things around our full acre of property.

Besides the large weeping willow tree that grew in our front yard, my favorite place to play with my neighborhood friends was in our huge back yard. Dad even gave us permission to dig a hole, as wide and as deep as we wanted, out past the lawn where there was nothing but dirt and an old chicken coop.

Our whole family knelt at the living room couch to say bedtime prayers most evenings, and sometimes Dad would read to us out of the Bible or the Book of Mormon. I didn't understand most of what was being read, but as I sat beside him I put my head on his chest and listened to the deep vibrating sounds of his voice.

~~~~

I was a freckle-faced, reddish-haired kindergarten student with my first loose tooth when the missionaries came to town. These were not the familiar Mormon missionaries from our own church, but strangers who appeared cheerful and confident as they stood in the church parking lots passing out literature published by a church called The Church of the Firstborn of the Fullness of Times. The strangers had even invaded the Salt Lake City Temple grounds to distribute the urgent messages of their church leaders. The church, which appeared to embrace basic Mormon teachings, was based in Mexico.

My dad was an inquisitive man, and he became interested in one of the questionnaires he had found placed under a windshield wiper of our car. This was a simple flier titled *Priesthood Expounded* which contained forty questions that scripturally challenged the authority of the current Mormon priesthood. Dad was troubled when he was unable to answer the questions himself, so he gave a copy to his bishop and asked for help.

Not long afterwards he was summoned to a meeting with the local Mormon officials. The mood at this meeting was extremely solemn and its purpose was not to answer questions for my father, but to ask one of their own: was Brother Wariner questioning the authority of David O. McKay, the modern day prophet, seer, and revelator who represented the Mormon Church? I guess Dad gave the wrong answer, because not long afterwards he received a letter of excommunication from the church.

This came as a shock to our family, especially Dad who was deeply committed to Mormon doctrine. My oldest sister, newly-married Carolyn and her husband Bill, were already beginning to take the teachings of the new missionaries to heart. It was only a matter of time before Dad concluded that his excommunication was actually an answer from God. He committed himself to the Church of the Firstborn of the Fullness of Times.

I would later learn that the name of the founder of our new church was Joel F. LeBaron and that, like David O. McKay, he was considered to be a prophet by his followers. He had the reputation of being a peaceful man who emphasized what he called the "Civil Law" which was based on the Ten Commandments as an important part of his teachings.

I don't remember Joel coming to our house in Utah, but his brother Ervil, a prominent church leader himself, impressed me as a child. He was a huge man at six foot five, and to a young child like myself he seemed a broad-shouldered giant. His neatly-cut dark hair above deep set eyes combined with a handsome square jaw made him even more impressive.

One morning I stirred on the couch where I had slept while my mother, smartly dressed for work, rushed busily around the crowded house, her cut and permed blond hair already neatly in place. Ervil, who was in town doing missionary work, had slept in my twin bed the night before.

"Kimmy, it's time to get up and get ready for school," Mom's voice urged me cheerfully, but I lingered lazily. My muscles were sore and tired from a weekend of rambunctious playing.

"Come on, little girl - you need to get up!" she called again, this time from the kitchen as she expertly cracked eggs into the hot black cast iron skillet and pulled a glass milk container from the fridge.

Still lying on the couch, I had just completed a good stretch when I suddenly found myself bouncing up and down like a limp rag doll. Looking up, I saw that Ervil stood over me pushing up and down on the couch springs with his mighty arms, a broad smile on his face. "This will loosen up those sore muscles," he teased, giving me a few more firm bounces before straightening up to his full height. "Get up now, Sleepy Head," he said gruffly. The corners of his mouth barely turned up but his eyes were smiling.

This was not the first time that my parents hosted Ervil as well as several different Church of the Firstborn missionaries in our home during those early years. I was always a little nervous around these strangers, especially this big important man so strangely named Ervil - yet I found myself giggling and whooping the few times that he grabbed and tossed me effortlessly into the air, catching me neatly in his giant hands. One day I heard that Ervil had a "presumptuous attitude." I learned the meaning of these big words when Mom complained to my older sisters and father about him.

"He seems to think he should have the best of everything at other people's expense," she fumed after Ervil had finally left our home after a few days' stay. "I couldn't believe how that man followed me around the grocery store and, without a word threw expensive things into my cart. Then when we got to the checkout line, he let me pay for everything without offering one red cent!"

Hospitality ran deep in the roots of my mother's family. She had been raised in Oklahoma by hardworking generous country folk. Grandpa and Grandma Flowers were self-sufficient people who had survived the Great Depression by farming the land with horses and plow, along with raising their own meat and milking a small herd of cows. They had always welcomed their visitors wholeheartedly, sharing the best of their hard earned food and supplies with appreciative kinfolk and friends. Although Mom certainly knew the difference between gracious giving and being taken advantage of, she held her tongue and treated the traveling Church of the Firstborn missionaries who came to our home in the cordial way she had been taught.

My mother was skeptical, but soon our family was being swept along with other Mormon converts in a swelling current of excitement that was beginning to surround the Church of the Firstborn. My father and sister Carolyn shared in this dream of religious fulfillment and change in a new "Promised Land" in Mexico where people would strive to work together, live God's laws and be free. Although Colonia LeBaron was the official name given the young colony, our new church leaders referred to it as Zion.

Many traditional Mormon followers were shocked when an entire group of twelve respected missionaries, of both men and women, had converted to the Church of the Firstborn following their return from a mission in France. A small exodus into Mexico had begun.

My sister Carolyn, her husband Bill, and their new little boy were the first of our family to leave behind the life they knew to settle in Colonia LeBaron. Within a few years, Dad himself bought property in the colony and over Mom's vigorous objections sold our family's home in Utah.

"I'm sorry, Kim won't be able to come to the children's class tomorrow," I heard my mother speaking politely into the receiver of the black, rotary dial phone that hung on our kitchen wall. Apparently my Sunday School teacher at the Mormon church had called to inquire about me. "She is busy sorting her toys because we will be moving soon," Mom added with resignation.

Moving. This was a word that I did not fully understand as I cheerfully helped pack my toys and belongings.

It was on a lovely spring day that we stood in the front yard beside our loaded station wagon and said goodbye to our friends and neighbors. My mother and sisters were tearful at this parting, especially sentimental fourteen-year-old Kathy who had grown with her friends since early childhood. But I could not comprehend that we would not be returning to this happy and familiar place. This was the only home I had ever known. My last memory of Ogden would be of my best friend Debbie's sad smile, her wispy pale blond hair moving in the breeze as she stood waving goodbye under the old weeping willow where we used to play.

Two

Colonia Le Baron

We traveled many miles from Ogden to our new house located in the small church colony in the Mexican state of Chihuahua. Although this was an entirely different world from our old one, our first impression of the colony was not unpleasant.

We discovered that Colonia LeBaron had a certain open country charm about it – especially in the springtime. Dirt roads ran along ranches and farms separated by acres of pecan orchards and fertile fields. Nearby to the east, were hills of green scattered with rocks, cactus, and occasional wild flowers. To the west the land was flat for as far as the eye could see to the distant blue mountains.

In the spring of 1962, the main street of the colony was lined with a few houses, a church, and a single tiny store named after its owner " Maudie," which housed the only telephone in the colony. There were numerous houses scattered over many acres of land within the colony, belonging to Mexican and American families who had converted to the Church of the Firstborn. A few of the houses were comfortable with bathrooms and running water, but most were simple adobe structures with bare cement floors and outhouses and wells in the yards. Only a few families who could afford generators enjoyed the use of electricity.

I did not understand why my sister Carolyn and her husband Bill had now disappeared from the little house where their last two children had been born. I knew that Carolyn had given birth to two babies within eighteen months of arriving in Mexico, and I had even overheard my mom describing to Judy and Kathy how my brother-in-law had passed out on the kitchen floor as his wife lay on the table giving birth to a breach baby boy. Mom had been both amused and disgusted that the colony women in attendance were forced to temporarily divert their attention from Carolyn to assist the traumatized man.

Now that we had arrived in the colony I had expected to meet their entire family - but they were nowhere to be seen. During this time of new experiences and discovery, I was not one to ask many questions, preferring to watch and learn things for myself.

Our own house was a small one located on the main street not far from the church and store. It consisted of two bedrooms, a living room, and a kitchen. Outside, the adobe walls were covered with stucco and painted white while the inside stucco was an unpainted and rough gray, matching the bare cement floors. I was fascinated by the small red hand pump that protruded from our kitchen floor allowing us to pump water directly into the tiny room.

"Let me try it!" I begged as I eagerly tackled the challenge of pouring water into the top of the pump while frantically working the handle up and down to "prime it." I remember the sense of satisfaction I felt when the pump handle offered resistance and fresh, clear water gushed noisily into the metal water bucket. Mom, who was tackling the dusty floors with a damp broom, paused to give me a smile. Standing over me, Dad gave me a pat on the shoulder. "You did it, Sis," he mused happily. "You surely did."

I believe we all secretly enjoyed the new ritual of lighting the strong-smelling, old-fashioned kerosene lamps. Carefully, we would replace the fragile glass chimneys over the softly glowing wicks as darkness fell over our cozy house. There was no television to watch, and most of the radio stations were in Spanish, so after we had run out of things to talk about, we would blow out the lamps and snuggle down under the familiar blankets in beds we had brought from home.

One night my sister, sixteen-year-old Judy, slept in the twin bed next to mine. She must have sensed my unspoken homesickness. "Close your eyes and we can go on an adventure," she had said in a mysterious, soothing voice. "We can go anywhere you want to go. Picture the mountains and the rocks as we fly over them on our magic carpet." I tried to stay awake for the adventure, but soon found myself falling asleep as she guided me through imaginary new places and far-off lands.

Yet there would be other nights when I would remember the green lawns of Utah, and in my dreams would run to greet my old friends. It was then that I would wake up in the darkness with tears on my face and long for home. When morning came, my happiness would return as I watched the free-roaming cows graze contentedly on the tall green weeds that dotted our yard in the pleasant morning sunshine. Soon, even the dreaded trips to the smelly outhouse didn't seem so bad.

I met new friends – American girls my own age who, to my surprise and envy, chattered away fluently in Spanish. I was proud to learn my first Spanish word and used it as often as possible. "Sí!" I would exclaim happily to every Mexican child I encountered.

It wasn't long before I also learned something even more surprising and slightly disturbing about my new friends and their families: their fathers had more than one wife! I got to know two sisters whose family had also come from Ogden. Brown-haired, lightly-freckled Fara was my age, while the fair-skinned and blond-haired Susan was a few years older. They explained reverently to me that this was an important, but almost secretive, part of my new religion. In fact their father had already taken a Mexican woman for a second wife since moving there.

"Your dad will probably marry another wife too," Fara informed me as we walked towards the front door of their small adobe house one pleasant day. "Then your mother will have a sister-wife like our mother does." This information brought me to a sudden stop my in my tracks. I had to think.

"It's okay," I finally responded resuming my steps, "I know we will always be special to him because we're his main family."

Fara brought me to another halt with her admonishing tone, "That's not the way it's supposed to be," she said shaking her head. "He's supposed to love all of his families the same."

I don't remember discussing it, but my sisters and I eventually came to accept this curious new idea as normal. Even though our own father would never enter into a polygamous or "plural marriage" as it was often called, he did accept that it was an original teaching of church founder Joseph Smith.

It wasn't long before I discovered why Carolyn was no longer in the colony. It seemed that living in Zion and working in Zion were two different things. There were no jobs there - no way to earn an income on which to survive. My sister's growing family had moved to El Paso, Texas.

One day I learned that another American family was living just a few houses down the dusty road from us. My parents remembered them from Utah, and Mom made arrangements for me to go over and play with their two oldest daughters one day.

Ralph, their father, was off working in the United States, but their mother, brilliantly red-haired Rosemary, welcomed us with a soft smile and gentle voice. I had packed a little cloth toy case with some American candy to share and a few of the toys I had brought in my toy box from Utah.

The friendly but shy girls, named Janice and Sherry, greeted me as their three younger siblings stood in the background watching us. Janice had long dark straight hair and was a little more talkative while, Sherry, like her mother Rosemary, was soft-spoken and had thick red hair and pale lightly-freckled skin.

I was slightly uneasy as I looked around me at the sparse surroundings of their home. They had very little furniture and there was no comfortable place that I could see to play. The walls separating the rooms of the house appeared to be made of large bed sheets stretched tight on long wires that ran along the floors and ceilings. After my mother left, we sat down on the cold hard cement floor in the living room and I got out my toys.

"Do you want to play?" I asked shyly, feeling pressured to break the awkward silence. But- where were their toys? They seemed not to have

7

any. The older girls handled my dolls with longing in their eyes and eagerly took the candy that I handed out to them and the younger children. Their faces were grateful - too grateful. I struggled with a sensation of sadness in the pit of my stomach. This wasn't the way it was supposed to be at play time. Yet it was with a growing sense of mutual affection that we made the best of our time together that day.

When my mother came to get me several hours later, I turned to give each of the girls one of my tiny plastic dolls with a simple dress. Their eyes shone with happiness and I wanted to do more. I dumped my other belongings onto my lap, presented them with a jump rope and a few other odds and ends before leaving with my remaining toys clutched in my arms.

I would only have a few more opportunities to visit Rosemary's house to play with Janice and Sherry after that. "Where are we going to now, Mama?" I asked resignedly as we prepared to leave our little Mexican home. It had been only a few short months since our arrival and already we were moving. "Moving" - a word that I was beginning to understand the meaning of all too well.

"We're going to live in El Paso where we can earn some money," Mom responded, not too cheerfully herself.

Three

Growing With the Church

We locked up our little house, climbed into our white Chevy station wagon, and made the four hour trip north to El Paso where we would live while my parents struggled to earn a living for our family managing the Texas Motel. Our residence would be the house- sized apartment section of this rather run- down facility located on a long stretch of nearly-deserted highway.

I entered second grade in the middle of the year. How badly I now began to miss Utah! My life seemed a boring, lonesome burden as I trudged through each day with no friends at school and no one to talk to at home. Mom and Dad cleaned motel rooms and did laundry for our few motel guests while my sisters watched T V and vegetated. Kathy soon dropped out of the ninth grade at the public school. The stress and cruelty that my shy sister experienced as a new student there had broken our parents' resistance to the idea of her quitting. My whole family seemed depressed at this point.

Mom had tried to break the ice for me at my school by planning a birthday party and giving me invitations to pass out to the girls in my class. On the special day I watched and waited. Nobody came. I wondered - what was wrong with me? Was the rejection just because I was the only new girl in school? Was it because I was one of the few Caucasian students in a class made up mostly of children of Mexican-American descent? I didn't understand. I noticed that, except during class discussions, most of my classmates spoke to one another in Spanish. Their world seemed to be one into which I could not fit.

With a growing loss of self-esteem I continued to study in school, returning from my class each day where, except for a few kind words from my teacher, no one had spoken to me, and I would look around the barren yard for something to do. Using my sister Judy's idea, I would escape for hours into my imagination.

...I was exploring an exotic land on the other side of the rainbow. Not only were there bright flowers and trees of all sizes scattered everywhere, but a carpet of brilliant green grass stretched for as far as the eye could see. And the houses! They were made of real gingerbread, which could be nibbled on anytime one became hungry.

"Kim where have you been hiding?" Mom seemed a little irritated yet concerned as she stood looking at me standing next to the garden tools that hung in the storage building that smelled of old gas and oil.

"We couldn't find you anywhere," she continued sounding tired, "come on in the house and get your dinner."

The spell was broken and I was momentarily overcome with inner pain as I looked around at my dreary surroundings and saw what was really there. That night I dreamed of Utah again. This time it seemed so real that I ran crying into the arms of my old friend Debbie. "Pinch me," I begged her. "Pinch me so I know that this is real." There was no feeling of pain from her pinch, and I awoke once again with tears streaming down my face.

A new pattern had begun in our lives- an unwelcome pattern that would be repeated during the next five years of my life. We moved often to new places where my parents could find work and where there were other church members nearby. After giving up their disappointing efforts at the Texas Motel, my parents invested in a small two bedroom trailer house that could be towed behind a large pickup truck, and from El Paso we moved to Las Vegas and back again, always parking our trailer in an inexpensive trailer court where we lived. Except for in El Paso, where apparently there weren't enough church folks living, we attended local church services regularly at the homes of other members. We spent our vacation and holiday time in Mexico in our otherwise abandoned house.

We also attended church conferences which were usually held in the colony. On these occasions I took happy solace with the other youngsters of the church. Fara's older sister, Susan, taught me to play duets on the piano in the house of Bill Tucker while we sat with some of his young children while he and his wives attended the meetings.

Brother Tucker was a well-admired young Mormon convert who was extremely articulate and intelligent. A rather short man, what he lacked in height was more than made up for with his muscular build and strikingly handsome face.

For lunch at the Tucker house, we served coarse and crumbly homemade whole wheat bread spread with butter, then savored the dried, leathery apple slices we found kept in a tightly-sealed jar in a cupboard. There were no refrigerators in most of the colony homes, including Brother Tucker's. Outside the snug dwelling we could hear the wind murmuring gustily as it stirred up fine dirt to toss against the thick, semitransparent plastic stretched over the wooden window frames that took the place of glass.

Sometimes after meetings there would be large community meals served up buffet-style in a community kitchen. After sitting through hours of religious sermons, the adults would visit and laugh as they worked and ate together, and when we younger children had finished eating the food that had been prepared, we ran outside to throw a fat, bouncy ball back and forth over the roof of the building, shouting, "Ollie, Ollie over!" until we were hoarse and tired and it was getting dark.

On one of those happy evenings, Sarah, the pre-teenaged daughter of Ervil, and some of her friends took turns playing with me. Grabbing my forearms, they spun with me wildly, until my feet would shoot out behind me, and I would be flying round and round in a dizzying, exhilarating circle. Finally pausing to regain balance, the laughing, out-of-breath girls continued to show genuine interest in me, asking questions and indulging me with conversation. Here, I thought gladly, was where I really belonged.

These conference meetings also played an important role for our parents, providing the opportunity for social and religious fellowship and uniting members who sometimes traveled from long distances to attend. As the years passed and I grew older, I would often get a chance to hear our prophet Joel speak. He was always scheduled as the last and most important speaker at these events which convened for several days in a row.

I was too young to understand everything that the prophet said, but the subject was usually the Civil Law. "I don't care what a person believes in or how he worships," Joel would emphasize, jerking his head to the side and bringing his arm down on the pulpit. "They can worship an old yellow dog, if they will join us in respecting the rights of others." This respect would be manifest, he taught, in the lives of people who would embrace and live the moral and civil code embraced in Judeo-Christian ethics. Of course the freedom to practice polygamy was an important part of Joel's Civil Law.

"Let me show you something, Sister Wariner," he said one day to my mother as he was traveling with our family from Colonia LeBaron back to the United States. It was very common for Joel to catch rides with church members after a conference when they were traveling in the direction that he needed to go.

Sitting in the front seat with my parents, he opened the Bible which he knew my mother was partial to because of her Southern Baptist upbringing. She had not really relinquished her old beliefs when she agreed to follow the Mormon religion of my father's family after marrying him.

"See what it says right here in the Old Testament?" Joel pointed to Exodus 21:10 as he read it out loud. " Do you understand, Sister Wariner?" He spoke to my mother in a friendly and gentle manner, as if he understood her doubts about our religion. "This scripture is saying that God allows a man to marry other wives if he doesn't take away from the needs of the ones he already has." Joel smiled encouragingly, and his voice sounded pleased, as though he had just given Mom a pleasant surprise. My mother nodded her head slowly, not knowing what she should say in return.

By this time all of our family, except for our mother, had come to fully accept the teachings of our religious leader. Truly, Joel's gentle magnetism held powerful sway over us and the vast majority of his other followers. There would be times in the future when it was all we would have to cling to.

On one trip to Colonia LeBaron we were saddened to discover that our little Mexican house had been broken into and most of our possessions from Utah had been removed. It was during this same visit that I overheard a shocking conversation between my parents that made my stomach tight with confusion. The news disturbed me more than even the loss of our belongings.

"I don't know, Tressie, I don't understand it," my dad was saying, sadly shaking his head and looking down at his upturned hands spread out in front of him on the table - one of our few remaining pieces of furniture.

"How has Ervil ended up with Rosemary's family, Leo?" I heard my mother's voice say, pressing him in confused disbelief. My ears perked up.

"And Anna Mae - she and Nephi had four children together. That man's heart must be broken. He has lost everything to Ervil. Please, please tell me how Joel can allow this. How can Ervil still be in good standing in the church? Leo, he is going after other men's wives." Mom ended her tirade in a tone of helpless frustration. " That man is crazy - you know it, and I know it."

I was in instant conflict. The smiling giant of my youth, turned prominent church official, had now turned destroyer of families. What would happen to Ralph and Rosemary's children? I couldn't bear to think of my shy and insecure friends losing their father.

Although I would learn later that divorcing Ralph to marry Ervil had been Rosemary's idea, Anna Mae, a short, maternal redhead that I had noticed mainly for her strong singing voice in church, had married Ervil while her husband, Nephi, was simply out of the colony on business for a short time. She considered a hushed religious ceremony to be all that was necessary to leave behind simple and hardworking Nephi for the handsome and powerful church leader.

Joel was distressed with what his brother was doing, but Ervil was careful to pursue his selfish interests in these and other ways while Joel was away from Colonia LeBaron. My parents shared a question with other members of the church who were aware of this unfolding, unsavory drama: Why was our religious leader apparently doing nothing to put a stop to his younger brother's actions that undermined not only church doctrine, but his own authority?

The dream of a thriving community governed by mutual respect for others, that had lured my parents from our comfortable home in Utah, was becoming more and more elusive in spite of Joel's captivating personality and lofty teachings.

Four

Joel and the Le Baron Brothers

As a young man Joel had broken away from the Mormon church choosing instead to remain faithful to the old church doctrine of polygamy. This belief had been instilled in him since early in his youth by his father Alma D. LeBaron, who was called by his middle name, Dayer.

Dayer had himself been a polygamist who believed as did many others of his time, that the leaders of the Mormon church had betrayed a fundamental part of their religion when they declared in a manifesto that polygamy would no longer be tolerated within the church. Like many others of his time, Dayer had rebelled, firmly instructing his sixteen children in the traditions of many of the original church fathers.

By the spring of 1951 Joel's father was dead. Joel and his mother would one day claim that the weak and frail old man had sent for Joel shortly before his death. They claimed that when summoned to his father's side, Dayer conferred a mysterious blessing of religious authority upon his son.

It was in the year of 1955 that Joel claimed to have climbed upon a mountain in Utah to seek God's direction in his life, vowing not to leave the mountain until he received an answer that he knew to be from God. Here Joel claimed to have been visited by heavenly prophets of old and that the Lord himself had spoken to him and instructed him in the way he should go about exercising divine authority to fulfill the important mission of setting His house in order. The goal of this mission involved establishing a church priesthood directly answerable to the Almighty, and a church colony where the laws of God would be established to serve as a model of freedom and virtue for truth seekers all over the world. Colonia LeBaron was to be Zion.

Joel claimed to hold the highest office of priesthood once held by Joseph Smith and the biblical prophet Moses. To the office just under his own, which he referred to as the Aaronic priesthood, he had appointed his younger brother Ervil. I rarely saw Ervil any more except at church meetings, or coming and going with one of his many wives. Even in the limited amount of time that we were now in the presence of this impressive man, I could plainly see that the friendly giant I remembered from Utah seemed to be a different person as he aggressively embraced his religious authority with a growing attitude of self- importance.

Truthfully, he *was* admired for his incredible knowledge of verses from the Bible and from Mormon writings, and he possessed the uncanny ability to recite scriptures from memory that always seemed to prove his point. He was an effective but long-winded speaker and teacher of church doctrine who would impress and convert several Mormon intellects with his writings. In fact, many of the church pamphlets we had received in Utah were written by Ervil. He was so good at what he did that Joel eventually offered to support his families with church funds so that Ervil could dedicate himself to writing and teaching.

Yet with all of his intellectual know-how, Ervil's ability to appeal to others on a personal level could not compare to Joel's humble charisma. For Ervil was obviously a proud man who expected to be pampered and catered to, and any type of physical work was something he made obvious efforts to avoid.

Another church leader was Joel's brother Alma, who was the oldest of the LeBaron men still living in the colony. Alma shared his father's first name which originated as the name of a prominent figure in the Book of Mormon. I remember Alma for his strict diet, and the modest dress code he imposed on his families. Garlic played an important role in his diet, and it was not unusual to notice a faint garlicky odor when in his presence.

I eventually became friends with Alma's daughter. Rosa, who was about my age, was a beauty, yet seemed unaware of it. I often wondered how she could be so sweet and friendly instead of vain with her lovely Latin face and tall graceful figure. As Alma's oldest daughter she worked hard at cooking and cleaning - always helping her mother with the care of the large family.

I once heard Alma speaking from the pulpit about the importance of disciplining children. "It doesn't take a lot of discipline to teach your children well," he said speaking almost conversationally as he proceeded to bring up a case in point. "One day my son disobeyed me one time too many. I took him to the mountains alone, where no one could hear or interfere, and I disciplined him there. That was the last time he ever disobeyed me in his life." He didn't describe the method of discipline he used, and I remember shifting uncomfortably in my seat as I involuntarily imagined what had happened to Rosa's brother on the lonely mountain.

As I reached my early teens, I was astounded to hear that my childhood friend Sherry, Rosemary's red-headed daughter, had married Alma who seemed more like a strict grandfather in her soft and childlike presence. There was in reality a huge age difference between them and it seemed to me that she had been snatched way from a hauntingly unhappy childhood into an adult world of thankless hard work and childbearing. I was too young to understand the need to reach out to her, and she never sought the friendship or help of others. After many years of marriage, the quiet and unassuming woman suffered the tragedy of a nervous breakdown.

As he grew older, Alma would have trouble holding on to most of his wives. Some would claim that his dictatorial style was too much for even a woman of the church to live with.

Perhaps on the opposite extreme there was the ever friendly Floren LeBaron. Floren was one of Joel's younger brothers – an adventurous dreamer who was known for his pioneering spirit as well as his wanderings throughout Mexico and Nicaragua. It was said that he was in search of lost sacred Mormon writings.

Maybe this was the reason that he had only three wives, one of them being Rosemary's other daughter, Janice, who seemed to be in a more tolerable position than her younger sister Sherry. Yet Floren's travels were a source of obvious misery to his families as they struggled to survive without him in his frequent and long absences. Floren was not seen as often in the church colonies as his brothers even though he too held an office in the church.

Youngest of the LeBaron brothers was tall, blue eyed Verlan. Even with his dark hair thinning, his thick lashed expressive eyes and masculine jaw gave his face a handsome quality. Next to Joel, Verlan was the most popular LeBaron brother, possessing a certain boyish, friendly charm. Besides being very outgoing, he had an unusually good sense of humor.

One day I overheard him laughingly telling another church member of a time when, as a young man, he had worked at a grocery store as one of his first jobs. A lady had approached him to ask where she could find the sanitary napkins.

"I don't know how sanitary they are," he had answered innocently, "but the napkins are right over here, Ma'm." He had been eager to politely guide the bemused shopper around the corner to where packages of paper dinner napkins neatly lined the shelf.

Verlan's first two wives were half sisters, sharing a father who had been married to both of their mothers. They too were born into a polygamous family which had rebelled against the Mormon church's manifesto prohibiting their ancestors' lifestyle.

First wife Charlotte, whose long dark hair was always pulled back into a bun on the back of her head, was tall, quiet and dignified, while second wife, talkative Irene, possessed a rosy complexion, and always wore her light brown hair in short modern cuts. How she loved to make people laugh with the colorful stories of her life.

Charlotte and Irene easily won my affection with their warmhearted kindness. Even though they had not been especially close as sister-wives, they stood firmly in the traditions of their ancestors looking on bravely as their husband took one new wife after another until he had eventually married ten women in all. My childhood friend, pretty blond-haired Susan who taught me to play my first songs on the piano, eventually became Verlan's youngest bride at the age of fifteen.

The sacrifices that Verlan's wives made hoping to earn heavenly blessings for their husband and his families were many. I'm sure that Charlotte, Irene and the other families were honored when the office of the Presidency was bestowed upon Verlan, but they must have discovered it to be a heavy burden because of the demands made on his precious time - for this was the third most important position in the priesthood following the offices of Joel and Ervil. Even without attending to the varied needs of a growing church, these men already had very little time to spend with their large families.

Along with Joel's brothers, many other converts were placed in offices of the church priesthood. All of the men who had been former French missionaries for the Mormon church were rewarded with various positions of authority.

Our family would become well acquainted with some of these men over the years. In fact, my sister Carolyn would become the fourth wife of Steven Silver, a cheerful, energetic and intelligent French missionary who was a full foot shorter than herself. Carolyn and Bill, her first husband, had struggled in their marriage and finally divorced, and Bill had left the Church of the Firstborn sometime after the birth of their third child. I never really understood the reason for their split, and only gradually realized that my sister's husband was no longer a part of our lives.

Of the many people we came to know like family, none became more familiar to us than the prophet himself: Joel F. LeBaron. The very mention of this name evoked feelings of love, respect, and admiration within the hearts of most of his followers and his families.

At the time we came to know him he was a tall, lean, balding, brownish- haired man who had been rather handsome in his youth. We were impressed by his unpretentious attitude and down-to- earth qualities. His manner was disarmingly simple and direct and, even under the most trying of circumstances, he always seemed good-natured, calm, and unruffled.

To those who knew him, Joel appeared to be a hardworking man who had managed not to have let being a prophet of God go to his head. It was not unusual to see him building windmills, planting trees, or making adobes in the hot summer sun to help Zion to flourish.

He had also won the respect of many poor and humble citizens of Mexico who were well acquainted with him. As a result of his father's outlawed polygamous lifestyle, Joel had spent most of his life in Mexico and had been very poor himself. He seemed to truly understand and identify with the Mexican people. The wife of his youth was a Mexican lady named Magdalena. Although Magdalena was raised as a Catholic she would begrudgingly remain loyal as Joel courted and married other women of the church.

It was Joel's desire to deal with others in what he believed to be a Christlike manner. To him that meant putting others first and forgiving people when they did wrong. We would understand later that this was one reason that he did little to challenge his brother Ervil or other men of the church, even when they were guilty of outrageous offenses by almost any religious standards.

In spite of Joel's kind attitude and personal magnetism, my mother always told us that there was something about his eyes that bothered her. "He won't look at you in the eye when you talk to him," she complained to my father one day. "Sometimes it scares me--- it's kind of like looking at the eyes of a snake." My mother was terrified of snakes.

Mom suffered alone with her doubts, often feeling isolated from her own family and other church members who saw her as being negative if she voiced her opinion. Although she was not happy with many things about the church, she would certainly not abandon her family.

To maintain her sanity, and because she was a naturally kind-hearted person, Mom maintained a friendly and hospitable manner with other church members and, if Joel himself was passing through our area, she always made sure that he was given good meals and a clean, comfortable bed. I also remember watching my dad, who had trained as a barber at one time, getting out his clippers to give our busy leader haircuts.

Within a few years of founding the church, Joel and his brothers had established Colonia LeBaron with around five hundred believers coming and going from the settlement. Except for a few men who managed to remain in the colony by carving out a living ranching and farming, the community would continue to consist mostly of women and children. The husbands and fathers traveled north to work at various jobs in the United States, or south where a few jobs could be found in the good-sized Mexican city of Chihuahua- for some of the men had mastered the Spanish language. One of the former French missionaries had even found a job as a teacher there.

One day, news of an encouraging nature came to my parents and other church members. Using church funds Joel had managed to obtain 8,500 acres of property located on the Mexican peninsula of Baja. The extensive parcel was two hundred miles south of the California border and lay over the hills just outside a small Mexican town stretching west to the beaches of the Pacific Ocean. Joel's dream of establishing a second church colony was on the verge of becoming a reality.

Five

Kathy

My sister Kathy was the next to the youngest child in our family. She was seven years old when I was born. According to my mother, Kathy was the most temperate, least demanding child she had ever raised. Kathy rarely complained about anything.

As she grew older she developed a very witty sense of humor, and was known to be a terrific dancer, yet she was still easily pushed into the background. This did not seem to affect her popularity among the close friends she grew up with in Utah.

Kathy was only two years younger than our outgoing and talkative sister Judy who was the exact opposite in many ways. Judy was a pest. Besides constantly begging for and demanding things from our mother, she actually had me believing she was a vampire! I was probably the only first grader in my school who feared her older sister might be interested in a sampling of blood. When we were alone Judy would stare into my eyes as a slow wicked smile spread across her face, sending me flying out the back door into the safety of daylight.

After Mom learned that Judy was secretly opening and then re-wrapping her Christmas presents while our parents weren't at home, new gifts were hidden in secret spots throughout the house. Mom's efforts were in vain. She always knew well before Christmas what she and everyone else would be getting. Although I suspect that the witty and precocious Judy was his favorite, I think my easy going dad unconsciously tried to just stay out of her way.

It must have been hard for mild mannered Kathy - being sandwiched between a confident older sister and a much younger, rather spoiled little sister. Although she and I usually got along well, I remember times when I wanted to play the piano and she wanted to listen to records. Being the youngest, I almost always got my way. Dad, who was wonderful with us as small children, seemed bewildered about how to relate to his family of girls as we grew into teenagers. He usually sided with the youngest and, until the grandchildren came along, that was me.

For some reason, during her preteen and early teenage years, Judy took devilish pleasure in teasing our quiet sibling. I don't remember the special irritating words she chose for her weapons, but I do remember Kathy finally becoming incensed and there would be a stampede down the hallway to the back bedroom where Judy would slam the door in

Kathy's face and lock it to protect herself. Heaven help her if Kathy caught up with her. Kathy was strong for her age and, using her knuckles, she knew how to give punches to Judy's arms that would leave bruises.

Because both of our parents worked, I was frequently left in the care of my two older sisters. I much preferred the company of Kathy who, I was certain, was not a vampire. And, lucky for me, she was the conscientious sister who looked after me most often.

It was Kathy who taught me how to lay the towel on the edge of the bathtub and dry each foot as I carefully stepped out onto the linoleum, and it was she who spread the first layer of peanut butter on my pancakes introducing me to a lifelong habit.

One day while our parents were out, Kathy stood brushing my hair as I sat in a chair in front of her. I was squirming and complaining about the tangles left behind by the rubber band that had come out of my ponytail, and we began calling each other silly and insulting names.

"Dummy," Kathy said in between hairbrush strokes.

"Stupid," I had replied.

"Silly," was Kathy's next insult.

"Bastard," I retorted.

This was an interesting new word I had overheard our sister Judy calling one of the neighbor boys down the street, and now had seemed like the perfect time to use it.

There was a gasp and I felt the hard edge of the hairbrush strike me across my bony chest. "Where did you learn that word?" Kathy demanded several times. Tears filled my eyes as, embarrassed and subdued, I refused to answer.

Though most people would not imagine it, Kathy was extremely sentimental. At a surprise birthday party thrown for her by some friends in Utah, she had buried her face on Mom's shoulder and sobbed. That would not be the only time she would cry on her birthday, for she would often weep emotionally when we sang Happy Birthday to her even into adulthood.

I suspected that she suffered terribly after our move from Utah - maybe more than any of us, but she never complained or shared her feelings. Once, when my parents let her take a Greyhound bus from Texas to stay with one of her old friends in Utah for a week, I had peppered her with questions about the trip.

"You know what I did when the bus got close to Ogden and things started looking familiar?" she had asked me with an embarrassed little smile. "I cried." With that simple two word sentence, my quiet sister had revealed her sadness to me.

By 1963, we had left Utah-- lived for awhile in, and then moved from the colony. After our parents had given up managing the Texas Motel, they had worked hard at various jobs in El Paso, and had saved enough money to buy their own small business. It was then that we hitched up the small trailer house we were living in, and made the move to Las Vegas where there were other church members living and working at the time.

After enrolling me in the third grade, my parents took over as owner operators of the Super Sonic Hamburger Drive-in which was attached to a busy car wash of the same name. To the amusement of my older sisters, I came up with my own name for our little enterprise, always referring to it as "The Malt Shop."

Here my life would not be as lonely or boring as it had been in El Paso. I loved the smells of fresh bread, frying hamburger patties, and sliced onions combined with the more subtle scents of chocolate, strawberries and vanilla that filled our cozy, modern shop with the shiny tiled floors. My mother was happy to fix me up a hamburger any time I wanted and I soon became a milk shake connoisseur.

Yet after school and on weekends there were times that I would play by myself for hours on a large old boat, complete with a rusty steering wheel, that seemed to have been abandoned in the field in back of the car wash. This provided a new outlet for my always active imagination - my adventures would now take me to faraway places on a stormy sea filled with helpful dolphins, giant whales, and of course friendly mermaids.

Mom and Dad flipped burgers and drained sizzling fries while Kathy and Judy took orders and served up milkshakes and malts mostly for hungry car wash customers and employees during the busy lunch and dinner rush hours. Kathy had grown into a quiet but friendly blond-haired, trim and attractive sixteen-year-old who was appreciated by our regular customers for her ability to make a mean chocolate malt.

One day, she had been thrilled when the recording star- turned-Las Vegas entertainer, Wayne Newton, stopped by while his car was given the royal treatment at the Super Sonic Car Wash. He came to the window that opened into the car wash lobby and gave Kathy his order. As she handed him his change he flashed his famous smile and winked at her.

It was at the impressionable age of seventeen that she quit working at our hamburger business after landing a job as a telephone operator, providing her with the opportunity to make new acquaintances. There were young people's dances in Vegas, and Kathy enthusiastically accepted the invitations to join her friends at the popular events where she picked up the latest moves easily, wowing her companions with her natural grace and rhythm.

One night after a dance Kathy woke me up as she got ready for bed before crawling in next to me. "Guess who I saw tonight?" she asked almost laughing with excitement. I opened my eyes and stared at her sleepily. "I saw President Johnson," she continued smugly without waiting for an answer.

"The President of the United States?" I asked in disbelief now fully awake. "Where did you see him?"

"His car was coming down the street real slow and he was waving at people," Kathy continued, grinning from ear to ear, "and suddenly he just jumped out of the back seat and came right into the dance floor, smiling at everybody and shaking hands. It was pretty neat. I guess he had just been giving a speech over at the Convention Center," she added before reaching over to turn out the light.

On another night Kathy and her friends went to The Flamingo Hotel where Fats Domino would be performing. The girls were too young to attend the nightclub act, but since he had been one of Kathy's favorite singers before leaving Utah, her friends stood with her in the lobby where they had been told that they might catch a glimpse of him. After milling around for what seemed like a long time the group was becoming restless when to Kathy's utter delight she turned to see, larger than life and smiling at them, the legendary, piano playing rhythm and blues singer himself as he exited the show.

"He actually stopped to talk to us," Kathy gushed to my parents the next day. "He even invited us up to his his room." She paused, taking in the displeased looks on our parents' faces. Kathy rolled her eyes. "Don't worry...of course we didn't go," she added in exasperation.

Up to this point, Kathy had dated several young men from our church, but these were simple and sometimes backwards young men, some of whom already had jealous wives. It was in the dusk of a summer evening in Colonia LeBaron when a petite, young Mexican woman scampered up to splash a large can of kerosene onto the parked car in which Kathy sat talking to a friendly fellow named Joseph. Joseph was the woman's husband. In his wife's hand was a box of matches which she proceeded to use, trying to set the car on fire. Her simple strategy worked amazingly well. Not only did the alarmed and flustered Joseph scramble out of the car as if it really was on fire, but I don't think Kathy chose to see much of him after that.

Obviously, such experiences could not compare to the excitement and glamor that Kathy was experiencing in glittering Las Vegas. Her group of acquaintances was rapidly expanding and she found herself coming more and more under the influence of a few older and wilder friends, and faced with many new temptations.

In spite of our religious upbringing and our parents' concern, she began experimenting with life in the fast lane. The carefree dances were gradually left behind as wild parties moved in to take their place. At some point, the husband of one of her new friends began making unwelcome intimate advances behind his wife's back. This was a line that Kathy was not willing to cross. Even though she had been raised to accept the idea that it was normal, even respectable, for a man to marry numerous women, betraying the trust of an unsuspecting friend was completely foreign to her nature.

It wasn't long after this that the dark side of Las Vegas seemed to weigh heavily on my sister's conscience, and she began the struggle of taking back control of her life. It was at this point that she decided to commit herself completely to the Church of the Firstborn.

To our mother's dismay and in spite of her objections, Kathy, who until recently had been the most practical of her daughters, decided now to go to the opposite extreme. Kathy announced to our parents that she would marry the church prophet, Joel F. LeBaron, who was twenty-five years her senior.

I don't remember Joel ever courting my sister, and it was Kathy who had gone to him. This was not uncommon, for in our church girls and women sometimes claimed to have inspiration and even revelations, about whom they should marry. These choices were usually respected. The wedding was hurriedly scheduled to take place in Colonia LeBaron. Young Kathy would be Joel's fifth wife.

It was on a pleasant evening in the year of 1965 that Kathy was married to Joel in the colony church as most of the colony residents, including several of Joel's other wives, looked on. For some reason, my parents chose not to have me attend the ceremony which was performed by Joel's brother, Ervil, but Mom had been willing to describe the event and answer my questions about it.

Instead of purchasing a traditional wedding gown, Kathy chose a light green modern but simple dress from her closet. Her hair was done in an unflattering style by one of the women of the colony, but few people noticed – for she appeared blissfully happy. A lovely wedding cake standing three tiers tall, scattered with icing roses and topped by small wedding bells within a heart, was baked and decorated by some of the well- wishing women of the colony.

After the ceremony, Kathy was congratulated by family, friends, and strangers and given welcoming hugs from some of Joel's more friendly and accepting wives. After the serving of the wedding cake, the marriage was celebrated into the night by young and old, rich and poor, Mexican and American at a big Mexican style folk dance.

That night, the newlyweds retired to a room that had been specially prepared for them in the large home of Joel's mother, Grandmother

LeBaron, so called because of her many children and grandchildren. One precious night was the extent of Kathy's honeymoon, for Joel was an extremely busy man.

The next day, Joel accompanied our family on the trip back to Las Vegas where Kathy would continue to live at home for awhile. Although the wedding bliss was quickly fading, something had changed within my sister. She had come home not only as a married woman, but as the wife of a man who hundreds of people followed and revered as a prophet of God.

Joel shook hands with my father and gave my mother a friendly hug as he prepared to leave. "Take good care of her for me, Brother Wariner. Goodbye Sister Wariner. Young lady..." he said turning to give my hand a firm shake.

Outside in the yard, next to the small mobile that was our home, Joel fondly kissed his new young wife goodbye. "I'll be back as soon as I can, Darling," he promised, giving her one last hug. Then he was gone to attend to pressing church business – and to his other wives.

Six

The Flowers

I was now the only child at home and it was time to move again. At the age of ten I found myself living with my parents, for the second time, in the city of El Paso after the sale of our successful little business in Las Vegas.

I honestly don't know how we ended up in El Paso again and I didn't bother to ask why. Why did we do anything? What were my parents searching for? If Joel was our Moses, we certainly seemed to be wanderers in the wilderness in search of our promised land. Even at the young age of ten, I could see that the religious fulfillment my parents had longed for since leaving our home in Utah had been mostly a chain of confused events so far.

The following year in El Paso turned out to be an especially unpleasant one for me. I was once again in the minority, and this time I was not only picked on by a few older girls, but ridiculed occasionally by a cruel teacher. There were a few bleak days when I experienced sudden blinding headaches from the accumulating stress, and would have to be escorted from my class to the school sickroom. I didn't understand why the Hispanic and Caucasian races did not intermingle in my community in El Paso. In Mexico, I was always treated kindly by the Mexican children and their families.

One day, as I began the long trek from school to the dusty and depressing trailer park where we now lived, I looked up to see the first black girl I had ever noticed in our neighborhood, walking a little ways ahead of me. This must have been her first day. I felt hope rising in me. Maybe I could catch up and befriend her.

She walked quickly with her head down, focusing on the sidewalk in front of her. As I drew closer I understood why. A group of preteen Hispanic boys trailed close behind, jeering and making taunting remarks. "Hey, Hershey Bar!" I heard one of them shout as his friends whooped with laughter.

My heart sank and I slowed my pace as the noisy group moved out of earshot. I was afraid of becoming the next target if I caught their attention. As I lay in my bed that night I remembered the blush that had stained the girl's dark cheeks and the wounded look in her unblinking eyes. I cried for both of us. Ashamed that I had been afraid to call out to her, I promised myself: *tomorrow I will find her and treat her as a friend.* But I never saw the girl again.

Never had I been so lonely. It was at this young age that I even entertained thoughts of suicide. To make matters worse, my parents and I didn't talk much during this unhappy and distressing time. They were unaware of my misery, and although I knew that they both had jobs, I didn't even know what they did for a living. I didn't ask and they didn't bother to inform me. In fact, they never told me anything. Was the lack of closeness that I felt coming about because they too were depressed? I think deep down I knew the answer.

For whatever reasons, I certainly wasn't disappointed when Mom and Dad made the unexpected decision to move from El Paso all the way to Sacramento, California where Grandma and Grandpa Flowers had lived for many years.

This surprising news caused vivid memories of the happy times we shared with my mother's parents to flood my senses. I could almost hear Grandpa humming as he brought in chairs and benches from every room in the house to place around the expanded kitchen table laden with steaming platters of fragrant foods and freshly baked rolls that Grandma cheerfully placed before her children and grandchildren during our holiday visits. Mingling with her best china on that bountiful table, were colorful shiny metal cups for us kids, and not far away, cooling on the kitchen counter, a hot blackberry cobbler could be seen and smelled, waiting to be smothered in home-made vanilla ice cream that Grandpa was churning on the patio.

As a young child, I had wondered if there was a mysterious reason that my grandparents shared the wonderful last name of Flowers. It fit them perfectly. Grandma loved flowers, and in her front yard surrounded by perfectly trimmed hedges, she tended large multicolored rosebushes that grew alongside bold blue and pink hydrangea blossoms that were amazingly giant and round.

Behind the tidy yellow house, my cousins and I would run through a tall cascading sprinkler that slowly swayed back and forth spattering water on our dripping heads and the soft green lawn where we played. Nearby, sitting in lawn chairs under the lacy shade of Grandpa's room sized grape arbor, our elders visited and drank coffee out of Grandma's delicate china coffee cups. Above their heads masses of delicate young vines, leaves and tendrils wove a living canopy that moved in the breeze and cooled them with its shadow, allowing only a few tranquil specks of light onto the cement patio.

This would be the first time in my life that we would be living in the same city as my kindly Baptist grandparents. It was also the farthest I had ever been from fellow church members or the colonies.

I'm not sure why my parents chose to live so far from the colonies and activities at that time, but they had both found good jobs working for the government at McClellan Air Force Base. Next, they decided to buy a comfortable two bedroom mobile with an expanded living room in a pleasant trailer park almost within walking distance of their new jobs. After living for so many years in the same cramped trailer, and sleeping in a bed that people brushed by on the way to the tiny bathroom, it was a luxury for me to have my own room complete with two twin beds.

I was registered to begin sixth grade in an elementary school in Sacramento that fall. As always, I had been terrified on my first day at a school in a new city. I was even more worried than usual because I had grown tall and developed a more mature figure over the summer. People who didn't know me were mistaking me for a high school teenager. Painfully I realized that I would be as tall as some of the teachers, and almost certainly taller than most of the other students in my class.

I was right. But I was soon to discover that this was to be a pleasant reprieve from my past experiences in El Paso. My classmates weren't unfriendly and our easygoing middle aged teacher, Mr. Engels, in his characteristic dark-colored ties and rolled-up white shirt sleeves, proved to be not only interesting, but funny.

A girl named Lauren sat in the desk directly behind mine. She was a porcelain-skinned girl with large, sparkling blue eyes and amazingly thick, wavy chestnut hair exploding towards her shoulders. Our eyes met when I turned to pass her a paper, and we smiled. We began chatting during recess and after school and soon became friendly enough to exchange phone numbers.

"Mom, can I go to my new friend's house after school tomorrow?" I asked breathlessly one day, tossing my schoolbooks onto the kitchen table. My mother, who was already home from work and starting dinner, smiled at me.

"She lives right near the school," I continued without pausing. " We can play for awhile and she says she can walk me part way home."

"Are you sure her parents won't mind?" Mom asked.

"Her mom already said yes."

Mom, looking pleased to see me so excited, had been easy to convince. "Okay. You can go if you're home by dinnertime."

After that Lauren and I were at each other's house or talking on the phone almost constantly. To her, I was another typical American girl. I kept my silence about our unusual religion as did my parents. Even Grandma and Grandpa Flowers thought we were still an average Mormon family.

Mom and Dad didn't seem concerned at all if sometimes Lauren and I joined Grandma and Grandpa for Sunday services at their church. Out of the corner of my eye, I could see Grandpa's strong bespectacled profile as he leaned forward listening intently to the preacher, his long masculine fingers laced tightly around his knee.

Grandpa cleaned the church every week and sometimes I would help. In the large quiet room of worship where tall gold-colored windows reached solemnly towards the high ceiling, I would dust off the rows of sturdy wooden pews and replace hymn books in their holders before running a vacuum over the carpet in the tight space between each row.

Then I would sit at the piano on the raised platform near the stately wooden pulpit and breathe in the indescribable smells of the open sanctuary. I could hear Grandpa humming lively tunes in a rich, clear baritone as he characteristically breezed through his work - cleaning bathrooms and straightening the Sunday school classrooms in the far parts of the large church.

One day while helping him, a sense of peace settled over me as I placed my fingers on the smooth cool keys of the piano to play the familiar chords I remembered from our own church hymns. The reverent melodic notes did not seem out of place. But how different this church seemed compared to our unadorned cinder block colony church with its uncarpeted cement floors, hard metal folding chairs, and flies that buzzed through the open doors and around our heads.

How different also was the focus of the lives of my grandparents. Grandpa, who believed that serving God meant first fulfilling his commitment to his wife, his home, and children, still took time to serve his church and help his neighbors. I was aware that for years before I was born he had worked relentlessly in the fields of Oklahoma from dawn until dusk, even in ill health, using only his hands, simple farm tools, and horses and plow in every type of weather.

Now my ever observant eyes watched as he poured himself into his present chores with a cheerful heart, never once complaining about the hard times of the past. In the present Grandpa took time to enjoy simple pleasures and the fruits of his labor - but nothing seemed to give his life more happiness than spending time in the company of his growing numbers of grandchildren.

One day he called me to the kitchen table where he had spread a few old pictures taken of the farm in Oklahoma. In one of them I saw the faded image of a rather plain looking woman in a simple cotton dress, standing outdoors next to two young children in front of a rough wooden wall. "Who is this in front of the barn?" I asked innocently concentrating on the picture in my hand.

Grandpa looked over my shoulder and I felt a burst of silent laughter. "That's not the barn," he finally exclaimed still chuckling, "that's the house, you nut!" Embarrassed, I gave him an apologetic smile. Grandpa shook his gray head in amusement, put a firm hand on my shoulder and pointed to the tiny figures in the picture. "This here's your Grandma," he said speaking softly now, "and these little girls are your Aunt Opal, and your Aunt Ruby. Your momma and Aunt Joyce wasn't born yet."

Over the years Mom had shared stories with me of the many times Grandma had tirelessly cared for the sick and dying in her younger days in Oklahoma. Mom described hearing the creaking wheels of a wagon bringing her home in the early morning hours. Aside from these absences she had been the ultimate stay- at -home, hard working mother. Now I sensed the joy Grandma found in tending her flower beds and working in her clean and productive kitchen.

In the summer days following our arrival in Sacramento, I developed the habit of lazing around on the springy grass next to the sweet smelling honeysuckle vine growing up the side fence in my grandparents' backyard. Here I sometimes visited with my Grandma as she hung out cold damp sheets that appeared dazzlingly white in the morning sunshine. Behind the glasses that perched on her nose, her eyes smiled at me.

Grandma, who was not a big talker, liked children and cheerfully made down- to-earth conversation, listening carefully to my responses. I'm sure she was aware of the feminist point of view that was gaining popularity in our society, but she never said a word about the modern women who might regard her life as trivial or unliberated. She didn't have to. The unspoken message of her life said everything: Why would she want to be liberated from the home and family she loved?

Although my grandfather occasionally asked me about the religious teachings of the Mormon church, during the many times I now visited with them, Grandpa and Grandma Flowers never preached. Perhaps they were afraid of alienating me from the comforting relationship that I so desperately needed. Yet their actions and attitude told me everything they believed -everything I wanted to know about them. How simple life seemed in their presence.

As my teenage years approached, I found myself diving enthusiastically into what seemed to be a different world, now wonderfully enriched by my loving grandparents and Lauren - my first real friend outside the church.

Seven

Los Molinos

A t the time of Kathy's marriage, there were other church members already living in the newly established colony in Baja named Los Molinos, which in Spanish means "The Windmills." Like Colonia LeBaron, Los Molinos was to be not only a location where God's laws would be established by His people, but it would also be another place of peace and safety for those who would flee the wickedness and eventual destructions of "Babylon" - another name for the United States.

For the time being, however, Los Molinos, with its uninhabited, undeveloped land was sorely in need of pioneers to help make this exciting vision a reality. Soon a small tent city sprang up, followed by trailers and a few houses. Joel began moving most of his wives, including Kathy, into the windy colony.

Judy, who had become the third wife of a Mormon convert from Utah named Paul, and our oldest sister Carolyn, had also relocated to the budding community. Carolyn's new husband, Steven Silver, was given the responsibility of creating a colony school for the youngsters to attend and had thrown himself into the task with his usual enthusiasm and ingenuity

I was excited to learn that my parents were planning a trip to the young colony of Los Molinos during Easter Vacation. I would be seeing this new Zion for the first time and I was eager to spend time with my sisters and their children. I'm sure that Mom and Dad were anxious to check on their daughters and grandchildren and see for themselves what direction Joel's vision of the church was taking. Could the new colony somehow truly fulfill their hopeful expectations in a way that Colonia LeBaron did not? We explained to my grandparents and Lauren that we would be visiting family "near San Diego" for the holiday.

At last the day of departure arrived and we were on our way. After two days of traveling, we found ourselves crossing the border at Tijuana, then driving along the Mexican highway right next to the Pacific Ocean. For several hours I looked out of the car window, comfortably mesmerized as the morning sun brilliantly lit up the white-capped waves crashing onto alternating rocky cliffs and flat shores.

We passed the tourist town of Ensenada and the road narrowed as it turned inland and became more like a two lane country road. A few hours later the pavement was gone altogether and we were bumping along on a wide dirt road still heading south.

This was much slower traveling and very tiresome. The scenery on either side was not much more than scrub brush and dry brown earth. We had not seen many cars during this part of the journey, but after about another hour, traffic was suddenly at a standstill and backed up. Dad got out to investigate.

"The road is flooded ahead," he announced in his calm manner, sticking his head into the rolled-down window on Mom's side of the car.

Using this as an opportunity to stretch, Mom and I got out and joined the group of Mexican travelers who stood staring at a sudden deep dip in the dirt road that had what looked like, a small muddy river rushing across it. On the other side we saw a small propane business at the edge of what appeared to be a tiny community. There were people stranded on that side staring back at us, and at a car that sat stuck in the middle of the swirling water that rose to just below its doors.

"What do we do now?" I wailed above the rush of the moving water.

It was then that we saw another American waving to us across the watery gulf. It was Harold. Harold was a middle-aged, outgoing member of our church - a successful businessman known for his friendly, can-do attitude. It wasn't long before he had spoken to the owners of the propane business and was sitting next to one of them in a large, old flatbed truck used for delivering propane tanks as they slowly drove into the rushing water.

"They're going to help the car that's stuck!" Mom cried out as we watched the men tie a rope around the bumper and slowly pull the car to safety. Then amidst shouts of encouragement the truck moved carefully again into the swirling water, this time not stopping until it had reached us where we stood on the other side.

"Well, hello there folks!" Harold's smiling bespectacled face was a welcome sight as the dark haired man jumped down from the cab of the truck and firmly shook our hands. He cheerfully welcomed us to the little town of Guerrero.

"You're not far from the colony," he promised, "not far at all. This is where we come to get our supplies. Los Molinos is just beyond those small mountains there on the other side of town." Our eyes squinted in the noonday sun as we stood looking in the direction where his outstretched hand pointed.

"I could see that there were some shallow spots in the water as we crossed over," he continued confidently. "How about if we get this fella to tie a rope around your bumper," he tied an imaginary knot in the air, then gestured towards the smiling driver. "If your car stalls he can pull you on across."

Dad hesitated only for a moment as he stood looking at the flood. He shrugged. "I guess we'd better give it a try," he answered with resignation.

We could hear the water rushing against the lower sides of the car as we slowly followed the truck's path across. I instinctively raised my feet from the floorboard expecting to see the brown, wet stuff filtering in any second as we reached the deepest part. We were relieved and amazed when we suddenly emerged on the other side where we offered the friendly man a small sum of money for his help and waved goodbye.

Full of excitement and anticipation we followed Harold past the town where a few small stores and a gas station lined the dusty street, and turned off the main highway a few miles later onto a rutted dirt road that ascended a large hill. Then we were there, looking down into the colony at the bottom of the hills before us.

Instead of having one main road, straight dirt roads divided the rather barren scrub land into large rectangular blocks where a few scattered windmills turned slowly in the wind amidst older mobile homes and a few adobe and conventional houses that spread out over the even land. From the high spot of the hill just before descending, we could see expansive salt flats glistening in the sun on the edge of the settlement. Beyond them in the distance stood tall sand dunes guarding the edge of the world's largest ocean which was visible to us as only a glimmer.

Harold led us past one of the nicer adobe houses, freshly painted white, which he stopped to identify as the home he had just built for his first wife, Betty. Then he guided us on to Kathy's place on the far side of the colony. I would realize later that no vehicle came over the hill and into the colony without being noticed by its residents. My sisters already knew we were there.

A windy breeze blew Kathy's long blond hair away from her beaming face as she hurried to meet us outside the door of what appeared to be a mid-sized older camping trailer. As she gave us all welcoming hugs, I noticed that she appeared thinner than I could ever remember seeing her. Yet when we embraced I felt an unfamiliar fullness around her waistline and suddenly realized that she was wearing a loose fitting blouse that could have been a maternity smock. I suddenly felt shy and awkward. Why hadn't someone told me that she was pregnant? Did Dad and Mom know? Not knowing what to say, I bent over to scratch a sudden itch on my ankle.

Kathy chuckled. "Uh-oh," she said with a smile, "you just got a flea bite."

I bent to scratch again. "I have two bites," I corrected as I rubbed them briskly, trying to stop the irritating itch.

"What do you mean fleas?" Mom asked in surprise. "I thought fleas only bit dogs."

"Not these kind," Kathy lamented no longer smiling. "They live in the sand and they bite humans. I guess you get used to the little creeps because after awhile, they either stop biting you, or you just don't feel it anymore." She turned to walk towards the trailer.

"C'mon in, Kim," she said, "and I'll put some wet soap on the bites to help make them stop itching."

Because her trailer was so snug, Mom and Dad took a quick look around and then stood waiting outside as she wet a piece of soap using a long-handled dipper to scoop water from a large metal bucket on the counter. She rubbed the brown slippery bar onto my ankle and blew on the wet spot to dry it. Like magic, the itch was temporarily gone under a dry film of soap.

As we rejoined my parents outside, Dad was already walking towards the car. "Hop in, Kathy," he called, motioning towards the front door, as Mom and I climbed into the backseat. "How about showing us where Judy and Carolyn live?"

It turned out that all three of my sisters were living in trailers about a mile apart from one another. In each yard was the familiar sight of an outhouse standing well away from the living area in plain brown dirt yards. We were surprised to learn that, as of yet, none of them had wells of their own. For all of their needs - drinking, bathing, cooking, and laundry - they had to laboriously haul buckets of water from the properties of their good-willed fellow pioneers.

Carolyn now had four children, three boys and one girl, and Judy had a little dark haired brown eyed girl - a toddler who was joyful at seeing her Grandma and Grandpa again. Except for Judy's husband, Paul, all of my brothers-in-law were missing from our little reunion. We assumed that Carolyn's husband, Steven, was either busy with one of his other wives or working on planning the colony school. Always on the move and busy, Joel was not even in town. Perhaps he was visiting his other families and taking care of business in Colonia LeBaron.

Paul was a friendly man with thick, wavy dark blond hair and the squarest jaw and chin I had ever seen. Athletically built, he stood six feet tall and was handsome enough to be a movie star. I wouldn't learn until later that Paul had left behind his first wife and their Mormon family in Salt Lake City when he joined the Church of the Firstborn. I never understood if his wife had refused to join the new church or if he had simply abandoned her and their three young children. At the time, I only knew that he was my sister's new husband who seemed pleased to welcome us to Los Molinos. "Come on, Judy," he said enthusiastically, " let's all take a walk and give your family a tour of the colony."

After admiring a few of the many rows of small fruit and eucalyptus trees that Kathy and others had helped Joel plant throughout the colony, we marveled at the deep unfinished well that Judy and her husband Paul had been tediously digging by hand with the help of his second wife Rosalinda.

With some input from Judy, Paul explained the laborious process. Using a ladder, the three of them would take turns climbing down into the bottom of the hole using picks and shovels to fill large buckets with dirt. The person standing at the top of the hole would then drag the buckets up by rope and empty them onto growing mounds of dark damp earth. They hoped that soon they would be rewarded for their backbreaking labor with a sweet water well of their own. This was no sure thing - some colony settlers had gone to all of this work only to discover useless salt water on their property.

"Rosalinda and Paul do most of the digging," Judy said in conclusion. "Rosalinda is strong," she added with her familiar teasing smile. "I think Paul might be a little afraid of her."

Paul grinned back a little sheepishly. " I try not to make her mad," he said with a wink in our direction. I had seen the twenty-something tan and striking Rosalinda who was almost every inch as tall as Paul. She was one of Joel's nieces and possessed a sturdy, healthy beauty that made me think of a princess of the Amazon.

Next we walked to take closer looks at the wooden windmills that Joel had spent many days erecting with the help of his hardworking wives and followers. These were like giant flat pinwheels whose tips almost brushed the earth before rising almost twenty feet into the air. Kathy, we were told, had often stood at the bottom of the massive structures to maneuver needed materials to where her husband balanced precariously on the edge of a giant wooden blade that had been stabilized with ropes. Now the windmill that we stood looking at turned slowly in the light wind, bringing forth water from a deep well.

We had been so absorbed with the new sights and familiar faces greeting us on our expedition that it was mid-afternoon before we noticed that we were becoming very hungry. My parents and I hadn't eaten since breakfast at a restaurant on the other side of the border far to the north of where we now stood. Since Judy's trailer was really a two bedroom single wide mobile, and actually big enough to hold all of us, we returned for an early dinner there.

Here I was reminded once again of Colonia LeBaron where meals had to be adapted to foods that didn't need to be refrigerated. Judy, who had a knack for cooking, made spicy enchilada sauce from canned tomato juice, chili powder and garlic thickened with flour. Working quickly, she layered fried corn tortillas dipped in sauce and sprinkled with Mexican cheese on our plates, topping each stack with a fried egg. Because all of the seats were taken, some of the children took their food outside to sit on the steps and I stood at the counter to eat.

The first bite made my eyes water. After the second bite my nose was running too. I looked around urgently for a napkin. Paul, who had been watching my face, broke into an amused smile. "Too spicy?" he asked before taking another large bite himself.

"Just keep eating," Judy prompted, reaching into a cupboard to hand me a piece of tissue from a toilet paper roll for my nose. This was the closest thing my sister had to a napkin. " The first bite numbs your mouth and then they start tasting pretty good." I followed her advice and found that after a few bites, although I reached for new tissue several times, the enchiladas tasted surprisingly delicious.

Even though it had been a long day, we decided to take a hurried look at the ocean before dark. I could feel myself becoming weary as we drove across the expansive white salt flats and climbed to the top of a tall sand dune. There we stood in dusky darkness, gazing over a deserted cold and windy beach. The sun had already set, and stretching before us was the sight of a never ending expanse of foaming gray water crashing powerfully onto the shore. I wondered: Did salt have a smell? For I certainly imagined that I could smell it in the wet air.

Somewhere near the edge of the world, a deepening gray sky rose– stretching itself endlessly upon the water, over the earth, and above our tiny figures standing on the giant dune. The mighty roar of the ocean seemed to drown all thoughts. No one said a word. We held our jackets close as one by one we slowly turned to make the descent from our sandy perch to seek the comforting warmth of our waiting cars.

After returning to the darkened colony, we split up and I joined Kathy to spend the night in her little trailer. Since her useless tiny bathroom had been turned into a closet, I dipped a cup of water from the bucket and stood outside in the pleasant stillness looking around at the faintly- lit residences in the distance as I brushed my teeth, spitting into a prickly weed. The wind had died down, and after Kathy lit her own kerosene lamp, we breathed in fresh damp air as together we took the usual evening stroll to visit the outhouse, using a flashlight to illuminate our way.

Next Kathy lit the propane cooking oven to warm the chilly trailer and placed a small metal bucket on the stove top burner to heat some of the water Dad had hauled for us in the car. We poured the precious soothing warm liquid into wash basins for our sponge baths before retiring.

The next morning I helped cut up potatoes for our breakfast, while Kathy heated a cast iron skillet. Then she stood beside me, coaching as I clumsily used a spatula to flip two wiggly fried eggs to eat with our potatoes. So began a new day before leaving the little trailer on foot to visit with our family and friends.

Our limited time in the new colony passed quickly and soon it was time to make ready for our journey home. This trip would be the first of many. On each visit I became closer to the young people already living in the colony, and eventually befriended others who were still moving into the small community, as my sisters' families grew and their lives changed.

Kathy, who was only nineteen years old and beginning her first pregnancy, seemed happy and adventurous as we celebrated that Easter together, hiding colored eggs in the bushes of the flat colorless landscape while the children covered their eyes, laughing and shouting in the distance. Yet she seemed so alone as we said our goodbyes. I'm certain that my parents' hearts were heavy as we began the return trip to our very different lives in Sacramento.

Eight

The Road to Heaven

As the prophet's new wife, Kathy was soon immersed in her religion, living and practicing church doctrine each day. She found herself believing, along with the other women of the church, that the road to heavenly exaltation was paved with personal sacrifice. She must suffer to prove her faith and in the end, sacrifice would be rewarded with a crown of glory in the highest realm of heaven: the Celestial Kingdom. Over time, I watched as my sister began not only to conform, but to transform into the person who she believed she should be.

It was after our first visit to the colony that Kathy would learn the true meaning of suffering for her religion as a full fledged plural wife and pioneer of Los Molinos. In our absence, she became heartbreakingly familiar with poverty, physical hardship, and loneliness on her barren piece of land with no well or electricity. Like most of Joel's other wives, my sister had no car, so using a child's hand wagon, she continued throughout her pregnancy to haul water from a well nearly a mile away on the far side of the colony. Often she did not see Joel for weeks, sometimes months.

Joel did not consider it beneath himself to work in the United States doing construction work or painting houses, but the money he earned was never enough to support his large families and the growing church. In years past he had made serious efforts to embark on several different business ventures, including a sawmill that he hoped would employ church members in Mexico, but in the end it and all others had failed miserably, usually losing money.

"That man has absolutely no business sense," Mom would complain in exasperation. "I would make a better businessman than him." This was almost certainly true. My mother had inherited her father's keen horse-trading sense.

Without a regular source of income except for what was contributed by one of Joel's other wives who had gone to work as a waitress in San Diego, things became very bleak during that first year in Los Molinos. Many years later, Kathy would tell our parents of a time that she and other women of the colony were forced to find food in an old shed. There they discovered an old sack of beans on which they and the children could survive. My parents, busily working in Sacramento, had no idea of the trying circumstances their daughter had been facing. And it was into this dismal situation that Kathy's first baby was born.

Audrey was a full term baby but weighed only four pounds. She was delivered with Joel present in Kathy's little trailer, by Jeanine, Joel's second wife. There were no apparent complications, but several years later we would discover that Audrey was mentally disabled.

It was not until the spring following Audrey's birth that my parents were able to take enough time off from work for us to make the long trip south to visit our family once again in Baja. Although unaware of all that had taken place during our absence, some changes were obvious. Judy was expecting another child, and her husband Paul had taken another wife, a Mexican woman named Ramona.

Ramona was not exactly a church convert. In fact, I was told that she had gone into a mild state of shock and smashed her hand through a glass window after meeting Paul's other wives, even though she had known that her new husband was a polygamist before their marriage. It was my impression that she had been smitten by the handsome American who had taken her from her home some distance away, and into a lifestyle that she was unable to understand and did not believe in. Probably not even twenty years old, she was confused - and she was homesick.

Paul, who was becoming fluent in the Spanish language, was clearly delighted with his new wife. He believed that the Mexican people of North America were descendants of a man named Laman spoken of in the Book of Mormon. It was the teaching of our leaders that these people, referred to as Lamanites, would one day be blessed when Caucasian bloodlines would combine with their own, creating a unique new race.

I was introduced to Ramona, and in spite of our language barrier found her eager to be friends. "Would you like to take a walk with me?" she asked cordially, speaking in slow Spanish for my benefit. For awhile we were both quiet as we walked along a deserted dirt beach road just outside the colony, heading nowhere in particular. I decided to make a self-conscious attempt to converse by complimenting her on the lovely earth toned bandanna she wore folded and wrapped about her head. The cotton material pushed dark thick hair away from her forehead, fully exposing high, flat cheekbones. I smiled and pointed to the bandanna.

"This is very pretty," I said, using my best Spanish accent.

She stopped and smiled warmly. "Do you like it?" she asked, removing the bandanna from her head. Reaching for my wrist, she pressed the folded cotton material firmly into my open palm. "It's yours," she said graciously.

During this visit to Los Molinos, I could see that my sister Judy and her friendly sister-wife, Rosalinda, were unable to effectively reach out to their husband's new wife. Below the surface of their attempts to be cheerful and accepting, ran an unmistakable undercurrent of unspoken sorrow on their part and a coolness on hers.

Attractive and very vulnerable, Ramona was for the time being, the apple of their husband's eye. Paul was unabashedly protective, attentive, affectionate, and unable to suppress the strong attraction he obviously felt towards his newest wife. This would be one of the first instances where I became aware of the pain endured by women who lived "the Principle" as polygamy was sometimes called.

Later that day, I learned that Kathy had also experienced a new aspect of plural marriage during our absence. "Isabel hit me," she confided as she struck a match and held it to the propane burner on the stove in her little trailer where we sat visiting. Isabel was one of Joel's Mexican wives who Joel had married before Kathy, and she had a reputation for being extremely jealous.

My mouth dropped open and my eyes grew wide. "You're kidding," I responded incredulously. "What happened?" I asked, eager for the details. "Did she hurt you?" Young girls of the church were rarely given inside information of this nature.

"She came and looked through my window and saw Joel kiss me while I was folding laundry," Kathy responded in a matter-of-fact tone of voice as she placed a metal dishpan of water to warm on the stove.

"What did you do?" I asked, feeling rather uneasy about her explanation. What was the Prophet doing kissing my sister in the middle of the day anyway?

"I hit her back," Kathy said, unable to suppress a half grin. "It looked like she was getting ready to swing at me again, so I gave her another punch. I had laundry in my hand so it didn't hurt her much," she continued dryly. "Then Joel got a hold of her and took her home."

Kathy, who seemed to accept the fact that Joel would never be hers alone, had sounded amused by the experience. In my youthful ignorance, I failed to consider how hard it must have been for Isabel to watch her husband kiss another woman. I giggled at the thought of my easy going sister being forced to defend herself. Remembering my two older sisters fighting in Utah, I realized that Isabel had fared much better than Judy.

The sound of a high pitched wail came from the small bedroom at the back of the trailer where Kathy's seven-month-old baby had been napping. To me, the cry sounded different from the cries of my other sisters' babies - somehow more desperate and unrelenting.

"She's still so tiny," I observed as I sat on Kathy's couch holding the warm little bundle dressed in a well worn flannel gown. Audrey was a darling child with a very round, fuzz-topped head and chubby cheeks. Large blue eyes stared into my own.

Kathy sat down next to me and gently squeezed the baby's hand. "She was the size of a doll when she was born." Smoothing the fine blond hair on the baby's head she continued, "She doesn't cry as much as she used to, but she still cries more than she should. Joel thinks I spoiled her."

It wasn't until a few days later that I felt very disturbed about the way my sister was learning to deal with her infant daughter. Someone had instructed Kathy to simultaneously cover Audrey's mouth and nose with her hand if her cry should become too annoying. The baby would begin to suffocate and would have to stop crying.

My parents were present on that day. When Kathy couldn't quiet the screaming Audrey, she tried placing her in the small porta crib in the cramped bedroom. There the high pitched crying continued, becoming more intense. Finally Kathy brought the squirming child back into to kitchen area and stood with her hand pressed tightly over the tiny nose and mouth. I looked anxiously at my parents, wondering if one of them would intervene.

"Kathy, you shouldn't do that to that baby!"our appalled mother cried out sternly. "Babies don't cry for the heck of it, they cry for a reason."

"Oh, Mother," Kathy responded defensively, "it's good for the baby. The Indians used to do it all the time to teach their babies not to cry." For a moment I wondered - *could it really be all right for her to do this?*

The procedure didn't work right away. It took several times before the baby became still, looking exhausted from the struggle to breathe and confused by the fear of crying. Dad frowned and shook his head in disapproval.

"I don't care what anybody says, you shouldn't do that to a baby," Mom repeated grimly. Silently, I agreed with her.

But Kathy, whose husband supported this sort of discipline for a young child, truly believed that she was dealing correctly with her crying infant. "Don't worry," she said, smiling at our squeamishness and apparent lack of understanding. "See?" she added, holding the silent infant towards us. "She's okay. She's being a good girl now."

~~~

It was a few months after returning to Sacramento that we learned that Kathy was pregnant again. As with her first pregnancy, she was doomed to struggle along mostly alone, only now she must care for Audrey and occasionally one of Joel's other children whose mother was working in the U. S. to help support the family. Kathy took some comfort from the presence of our two older sisters still living in the windy little colony, and she shared something in common with them. Judy and Carolyn were also expecting babies, due at around the same time as Kathy's.

By the the eighth month she had managed to gain more weight than with her first pregnancy, but her diet had still been very limited. It was on a winter evening in January, a full month before her due date, that Kathy struggled in vain with an excruciating headache. For some reason our sister Judy had decided to spend the night with Kathy perhaps to help or keep her company.

With Judy's daughter sleeping soundly on Kathy's couch in the cramped front room of the trailer, and Audrey in her small crib crammed next to the only bed, Judy watched helplessly as Kathy took aspirin after aspirin and walked the floor in desperation late into the night. Nothing seemed to relieve her pain. Suddenly Kathy stopped pacing. "These aspirins are worthless sons of a gun!" she cried out before dissolving into tears of anguish.

It was in the wee hours of the morning that Kathy lay down on the bed and lapsed into unconsciousness. Her body suddenly became tense and jerked in what would be the first of many convulsions. Our terrified older sister ran on foot across the still-dark colony to the home of our friend Harold, where he and his first wife Betty slept.

"Harold! Help me – please I need help!" Judy cried as she pounded on the wooden door. Harold thought quickly as he listened to Judy's frantic narrative of the night's events.

"Let's get Brother Dambacher to get her to a hospital in his car," he said as he and Judy rushed out into the chilly darkness of the quiet colony.

After rousing Ray Dambacher, one of the other few men residing full time in Los Molinos, a stop was made at the home of Verlan LeBaron's second wife, Irene. Together they rushed to where Kathy still lay convulsing. Irene was horrified at the sight of bright red blood squirting from her mouth as Kathy clamped down on her tongue in the midst of yet another seizure.

"Hand me that piece of wood!" Irene cried pointing to a small triangular chunk lying on the windowsill. Using a butter knife Irene pushed the wood between Kathy's teeth prying and holding them open, preventing further damage to her already deeply-bitten tongue. Then the small group of people worked quickly to place her awkwardly in the back seat of Brother Dambacher's car.

Irene, who had already instructed one of her children to come to Kathy's trailer to care for the children who slept there, finally climbed into the backseat to wrestle with Joel's rigid and unconscious young wife, tackling the nerve wracking task of trying to keep her from completely biting off her own tongue.

Kathy convulsed continuously kicking at the windows and jerking, while Judy sat in the front seat watching and weeping. "She's dying, I know she's dying," she cried desperately as a particularly violent seizure took hold.

Brother Dambacher sped along on a harrowing journey to Ensenada. Adding to their misery, came the winter rains and rockslides covering part of the road slowing the normally two and a half hour trip to almost four hours.

At the hospital, Kathy was rushed into the operating room where an emergency cesarean section was performed to save her unborn child. Her body continued to jerk convulsively throughout the operation. Into an operating room buzzing with tense, frenzied activity, a howling, premature little boy was brought forth and rushed off for treatment to save his life. As for Kathy, the diagnosis was acute toxemia. As blood poured from the catheter meant to drain her kidneys of toxins, the doctor turned gravely to Judy and Irene. "She's dying," he said sadly, "I'm sorry."

~~~

The phone rang early that morning in our quiet mobile home in Sacramento. From my room I could hear Mom crying and talking brokenly to Dad. "You're not going to school today," she told me through her tears when I appeared in the living room. "Kathy's in the hospital in Ensenada. They don't think she's going to live."

Grief stricken and stunned, I could hardly comprehend that my older sister Kathy was probably dying in a Mexican hospital hundreds of miles away. We threw a few things into the car and sped frantically towards the Baja peninsula stopping only for gas during the entire trip. It was in the early dawn of the next morning that the three of us anxiously made our way to the hospital entrance in Ensenada, famished, numb and exhausted - not knowing if we had arrived too late.

We stood in the small hospital room looking solemnly down at my sister who lay swollen and unconscious, connected to an array of tubes that carried fluids to and from her body. Her face looked waxen and was as white as the sheets around her. A swollen, gashed tongue protruded grotesquely from her mouth, and one of her upper front teeth was chipped. I was given a cup of ice and shown how to use the ice to swab out her dry, bloodied mouth. I did so, inwardly flinching as I ran the ice over the half-inch long cut that opened the side of her tongue.

The busy hospital staff also instructed us to roll Kathy onto her side and to pound her on her back to keep the fluids from settling in her lungs. Kathy, whose abdominal incision was held together by metal clips, would cry out and struggle in pain against the unwelcome movement. Soon, a nurse entered the room with a syringe, which she prepared to inject into Kathy's hip.

The thought of another needle piercing my sister's traumatized body was more than I could bear. "No..." I murmured weakly as I rushed blindly from the room with my heart pounding in my ears. Darkness had almost overtaken me when someone guided me into a chair and instructed me to put my head between my knees.

For three days our family took turns keeping a constant vigil by Kathy's bedside. As a sign of encouragement, the catheter that at first had carried only blood was now filled with dark green toxins. Each day gave us hope that she would survive, yet the doctors informed us that there was a 70 % chance that she would suffer from brain damage if she did.

Along with other church members some of Kathy's other sister-wives came to see her, sadly shaking their heads and offering us encouragement before leaving. Late one night as I slept in our motel room near the hospital, Joel's youngest brother Verlan arrived. After offering words of comfort to my parents he said a prayer and gave my sister a religious blessing before leaving. A short time later, my parents looked up to see Verlan returning once again to the room.

"I got in the car but I just couldn't leave," he explained. His voice was full of sadness and concern as he laid his hands once again upon his unconscious sister- in-law's head, "I would like to give Kathy a second blessing before I go."

It was on the fourth day while I was resting in our hotel room, that Kathy suddenly awoke. She looked dazedly around the room and seemed surprised to see my parents.

"Where am I?" she asked dreamily looking at our mother. "What are you and Dad doing here?" She had no memory of becoming ill. Mom and Dad were overcome with relief.

"You were very sick, little girl," Mom explained, gently stroking her forehead and struggling to hold back grateful tears. " But you have a new baby boy," she managed to announce with a wet smile. Puzzled, Kathy shook her head in disbelief.

Later that day, Joel finally arrived to find his wife fully awake and recovering – still unaware, herself, of all that she had suffered. The tiny premature baby, who Kathy soon named Lynn, was now also out of danger and well on the road to recovery at the home of Lucy, Verlan's third wife who was living near Ensenada.

The next day, Joel sat behind Kathy on the hospital bed and, using his pocket knife, went to work on the massive rat's nest that used to be her long, thick hair. As he cut through the tangles, he spoke glowingly of Kathy's unexpected recovery. "We almost lost you, Sweetheart," he mused tenderly, " but your mission on Earth wasn't complete. Don't you see that the Lord has used you to give us a miracle to strengthen our faith?"

As if to fulfill her husband's words, Kathy went on to recover quickly from her life threatening sickness. Her story was repeated throughout the church as one of miraculous recovery, inspiring and encouraging others on their own difficult journeys. Soon my sister was well enough to continue on in her mission of bearing children to be raised in the church.

Nine

I Never Promised You a Rose Garden

They live what?" Lauren's expression showed confusion as we sat talking cross-legged on her bed in the part of the garage they had converted into her bedroom. Lauren's parents had five children, and she loved the feeling of independence the informal room provided. She had decorated it to her liking which included a box springs and mattress that sat directly on the floor, and an old wooden stereo on legs that usually played selected albums by the Beatles or the soulful sounds of Motown.

We were teenagers. Together we had moved through childhood, sharing secrets and dreams as we eagerly grew into young women. Yet in all this time, I had been reluctant to share one secret with my good friend. Up until now, she still knew nothing about my religion.

For the first time in my life, I had attended school in the same city for three years in a row. As my final year in junior high school came to an end, I had become acquainted with a few other girls, but Lauren was still my closest and best friend outside the church. Now the time had come that I would be leaving my parents' home in Sacramento to live in the colony of Los Molinos. I wanted Lauren to know the whole truth about my life.

"It's called polygamy or plural marriage," I tried to explain. "It's a part of our religion. It's where a man can have more than one wife."

"Why would a man want more than one wife?" she asked with a frown. Then smiling, she asked brightly, "Can a woman marry more than one husband too?"

This was going to take more explaining. So was the fact that I was leaving. The move had been my own idea, and it had taken awhile to win the approval of my parents.

"Things are different in the colony," I told her. "I know it sounds weird for women to marry the same man, but the teenagers don't use drugs, or have abortions, or smoke - they don't even drink. And the colony we live in is right by the beach - we get to body-surf almost everyday, sometimes at night we make big bonfires and play games there."

My time spent with my sisters and friends in Los Molinos had provided a contrast to the things Lauren and I saw happening in the lives of many of our peers. Drinking, smoking marijuana, and casual sex were becoming more common for youngsters even at my junior high school. Although Lauren had not been brought up with any type of religious instruction, as we approached high school age she and I shared the same sense of right and wrong.

Unfortunately, the truth was that I was finding it harder each day to deal with the corrupting pressures and various temptations that now assaulted my teenage sensibilities. It seemed that my parents and grandparents were unable to protect me from a dark side of society that was so different from their own life experience, that they were simply not aware of it.

I had experimented with smoking myself, and Lauren and I now both found ourselves dealing with interested members of the opposite sex.

Although I knew that I was no beauty (I sometimes complained bitterly about inheriting my Dad's unattractive nose), there were some who found me attractive. I had been told by my friends that I had pretty eyes and a nice smile.

Now at the age of fourteen I was taking phone calls from a twenty-year-old man who had asked my schoolmate's older sister for my number. The answer to my dilemma seemed obvious to me; I could live in the colony like my sisters and their children. There I could enjoy the innocent socialization of my friends, and still come back to Sacramento to visit my parents, grandparents and Lauren. I would have the best of both worlds.

Over the years I had noticed that when Lauren's father wasn't working, he spent almost every waking hour in an easy chair placed in front of the television with a can of beer at his side. In the time that I had know them, I don't remember seeing him even once interact with his children.

As I grew older I came to understand that my friend's father was an alcoholic. Although Lauren's mother was very friendly and did the best she could, I could see that my friend was pained by the lack of awareness on the part of both of her parents. "Do you ever wonder if you're adopted?" she asked me one day. "I think I might be," she said hopefully. "I don't feel like I belong to my parents."

During the time we lived in Sacramento, Kathy, Judy, and Carolyn came to visit every year, giving Lauren the opportunity meet my sisters and the ever- expanding circle of children in our family. I'm sure that my Grandma and Grandpa Flowers wondered why their granddaughters' husbands were always absent from these visits, but my parents could honestly say that their sons- in-law were too busy working to join us.

On one exciting evening, Mom and Dad sat with the grandchildren while Judy took Lauren and me to an enchanting live performance by the original Supremes in downtown Sacramento. It was in a dreamlike atmosphere that we watched the three beautiful mahogany-skinned women in long shimmering gowns moving in unison as Diana Ross crooned the words to hit songs like "Baby Love."

Through our friendship, Lauren had found a certain sense of security with my family. Ironically, it seemed that my parents had provided a backdrop of stability for her life, as my grandparents had for mine. It would be hard to say good-bye.

Mom and Dad were torn. They wanted me to live with them and finish school, but I could sense the discomfort they felt around some of my new friends, and they appreciated the fact that I wanted to be close to my sisters and help with their families.

It was during the previous summer, which I had spent in Los Molinos, that all three of my sisters had encouraged our parents to allow me to make the move. "Kim is getting old enough to come under the wrong influences now," Carolyn had pointed out. "With both of you working, and her having too much free time, it could lead to trouble. Remember what Kathy went through in Las Vegas," she warned.

They took the entire following school year to think about it, but by the next summer the decision was made. Instead of entering the high school I was scheduled to attend, my parents enrolled me in a high school correspondence course and moved me and our small pet dog named Lady into a house they had decided to buy in Los Molinos. Mom and Dad remained in Sacramento, where they continued to work not only to support themselves, but to help with some of the growing unmet needs of their married daughters and their families. Judy, like our oldest sister Carolyn, now had four children while Kathy had three.

Kathy's third child was a little boy she named Luke who was delivered in a cesarean section operation that was performed in a San Diego hospital without complications. Although he was a strong and healthy baby, he too was later diagnosed as having slight brain damage. The exact cause of his handicap was never discovered.

Unbeknownst to Kathy, she was now the mother of two mildly mentally disabled children. It was not until Audrey and Luke were well into their toddler stages that we began to realize that first Audrey and then Luke had learning disabilities - although Grandma Flowers had been the first to notice something amiss in Audrey's behavior while she was still an infant. "There's something different about that baby," she had warned my mother in private.

The house that my parents purchased in Los Molinos was one of the nicer homes in the colony - in fact it was the very house built by Harold for his first wife Betty that we had seen on our first visit there. It contained three large bedrooms and, instead of the usual bare cement that I saw on the floors in the other homes, actually had gray tiles and painted walls inside and out. It even had an inside bathroom with a toilet that could be flushed using a bucket of water hauled in from the well. The large wire-fenced yard was cheerfully dotted with the multicolored blossoms of ice plants planted by Harold's first wife Betty, before moving with her family to San Diego.

Even though I felt safe in my new home in the windy little colony with my little dog Lady at my side, when darkness approached and the dim glow from the kerosene lamps cast eerie shadows throughout the quiet rooms, I would find myself struggling with uneasy thoughts and loneliness. Often, I spent nights at the homes of my sisters and friends.

Joel's youngest brother, Verlan, had relocated all of his families to Los Molinos and already built houses for his first three wives there. I was delighted to be welcomed into the fold by the oldest daughters of his first two wives, Charlotte and Irene, both of whose houses were on the same side of the colony as Kathy's trailer.

Although there were other young people living in the colony, the three friendly girls named Rhea, Laura, and Donna seemed most happy to have a girl close to their own age to become better acquainted with. I discovered that like Alma's daughter, their cousin Rosa, they were extremely attractive yet unpretentious and sometimes even a little shy.

I noticed that Charlotte's oldest daughter, Rhea, who was two years older than me and less talkative than her sisters, took in everything with her beautiful sultry brown eyes. I would later learn that the friendly girl was an excellent basketball player with superb coordination and a high level of energy. Her younger sister, Laura, was my age and, to my delight, was just as tall as I was. Thick and wavy golden brown hair draped luxuriously over her shoulders to her waist, while a confident smile flickered easily across her naturally tan face. Born only a few weeks earlier than Laura was Donna, the daughter of Verlan's second wife. Donna, whose cute baby face was framed with masses of glossy honey blonde hair, was a chatterbox like her mother, Irene.

I found myself marveling at the down-to-earth qualities of my rediscovered friends. It had been my experience in the schools of the United States, that girls with this type of beauty were usually placed on pedestals and were often snobbish with the more average looking girls like myself. But here I was treated like a sister by the attractive and friendly girls whose mothers graciously accepted me into their already full houses, where they shared not only food with me but, on nights that I found particularly lonely, would squeeze me into one of their already crowded beds.

It wasn't long after moving to the colony that I discovered what would be expected of a young single girl of the church. It seemed that my sisters weren't the only women who were in desperate need of help with growing children of all ages.

"Kim, will you come and help me take care of Carla's kids today while she goes into town for supplies?" asked Tina one morning soon after my arrival. Tina was an outgoing teenager who like myself had no little brothers or sisters that needed caring for at home. I walked with her to the residence of Carla who was married to Steven, my sister Carolyn's husband. Apparently Carla and Steven had already started a good sized family before Carolyn had joined them.

Tina and I went to work caring for a roomful of small children who ran and played in the large wooden structure that had been added onto an old mobile home. It seemed more like an uncomfortable noisy nursery than a family's home. Some of the children played on the dusty cement floor, while a toddler sat bouncing her head over and over against the back of an old cushioned wooden chair where she sat. A blond-headed baby, who sat nearby in a highchair, watched us with interest as we took over duties.

Working as a team we changed diapers, washed hands and faces, and tried to keep the children entertained which wasn't easy to do with almost no toys or things to interest them. At lunch time we fried canned meat and boiled rice that came in containers that said something about being provided by the Department of Agriculture in California. I would later learn that this was "welfare" food. Then it was time to wash dishes, sweep the floors, clean up the children and change diapers again.

After a boringly stressful day, I was relieved when Carla returned that afternoon to set us free. "How does she handle all of those kids on her own?" I asked Tina as we walked along towards her house. Tina, who was the youngest girl in a family of thirteen, shrugged. "It's hard," she said matter-of-factly, "but women who answer this calling get used to it."

~~~

One day Kathy approached me about caring for her children while she went to pick pine nuts with Joel and some of his other wives in the high mountains of Nevada. This had become a lucrative yearly tradition for many Church of the Firstborn members who set up various camps for young and old to join. At least half the church went to work picking and gathering the valuable little brown nuts to sell.

I knew that many of my friends including Rhea, Laura, and Donna were excitedly making their own preparations to join this massively-organized camping trip, and looking forward to earning money for some of the small luxuries that teenage girls of the church usually went without. Unlike some of the other fundamentalist Mormon groups still practicing polygamy, girls from our church were allowed to dress modestly modern and wear a little makeup - if they could afford it.

"I can pay you because I'll be earning good money," Kathy continued, "and I'll only be gone for a few weeks."

Knowing that this would be a rare opportunity for my sister to spend time with her husband while earning much needed money, I naively agreed. I had already spent so much time with Audrey, Lynn, and Luke that I was certain that I could easily handle things on my own.

On the first night, I got a taste of what the next few weeks would be like. I kept the two youngest, Lynn and Luke, in the double bed with me, which at the time was the only bed in the house, while Audrey slept on the couch. Lynn, who was a precocious two-year-old little boy at the time, was the first to wake up crying in the middle of the night which woke up eight-month-old Luke. I soothed Lynn and fixed Luke a bottle, but we had barely gone back to sleep when I felt something warm and wet spilling out of the plastic pants that covered Luke's cloth diapers onto my pajamas.

Wearily, I turned up the wick on the low burning kerosene lamp. Now Luke and I and the bed all had to be changed which of course woke up Lynn again. I couldn't believe my bad luck. It was past midnight and both boys were wide awake.

What to do now? I wondered helplessly. Certain that the children were uneasy about sleeping in a new place and were missing the presence of their mother, I decided to move them into the living room where I began sweeping and cleaning purposefully to distract myself from the intense frustration I was experiencing. They sat on the couch near where Audrey slept, and watched me work, as if mesmerized by all these unusual late night activities.

"You guys getting tired yet?" I asked as I emptied the dust pan into a wastebasket. Their little eyes blinked at me sleepily. After an hour or so, the boys were beginning to doze and I moved them gently into the bed. I held my breath and slowly crept in between them, letting out a gentle sigh of relief before relaxing and finally welcoming the sleep my body craved.

The next day held new challenges. I became worried about four-year-old Audrey, who simply stared at the food I placed in front of her. "Come on, Audrey - don't you want to try a bite? You must be hungry, sweetheart," I coaxed. She did not seem ill, but had no appetite. I had to feed her mostly by hand. I decided to try being firm, as I knew some of the women in the church might be. I grabbed her arm roughly. "Audrey, you pick up that spoon and start eating right now!" I demanded in a gruff voice. She only stared back at me blankly, leaving me overcome by a hopeless feeling of guilt.

By the end of the first week, I was used to doing some of my housework in the middle of the night but, thankfully, Audrey was beginning to eat on her own. When Kathy returned a week later, the children had finally somewhat adjusted to her absence, but I was one happy teenager to be released from the full-time responsibility of three children.

The stress and loneliness of the past few weeks were soon forgotten as my friends returned a few at a time in good spirits with new clothes, make up, and extra money in their pockets. Who cared about the sticky pine tar that had ruined their old clothes and had to be cut out of their long hair? It was a merry homecoming and I for one was grateful that life was returning to normal.

When we were not busy caring for children or helping with housework, my friends and I would sometimes ride our bicycles out onto the expansive salt flats that stretched just beyond the colony. Then on hot afternoons, we would walk to the tiny family-owned store, which was really the front room of a house, where we purchased many a warm soda pop from a smiling Mexican youngster who lived there.

One day I waited in the gray-stuccoed house of Verlan's first wife Charlotte for Rhea and Laura to join me for a walk to the beach. My friends finished sweeping and mopping the floors while their mother bustled about the kitchen putting loaves of whole wheat bread into the oven to bake. Their brothers were busy at work outside, and the younger girls swept the braided living room rug and polished sooty glass lamp chimneys before replacing them on the old-fashioned kerosene lamps.

As I watched, there was the sound of a tinkling crash as one of the chimneys slipped, falling onto the concrete floor. I looked around, waiting for someone to react - but to my surprise, there was no pause in the various activities, no admonishment to be more careful from Charlotte or the older girls, and not even a word of frustration passed from the lips of the young girl who cheerfully grabbed a broom and dustpan to sweep up the tiny fragments of glass.

This home was an exemplary one. I have never, before or since, seen such purposeful varied activities organized so efficiently and performed so calmly and cheerfully. It seemed to me that a spirit of serene order reigned in Charlotte's home.

"Let's go get Donna," Laura said as she finished brushing out her long hair. She pulled it over her shoulder and began expertly working it into a thick braid in preparation for our upcoming adventures in the rushing ocean waves that would otherwise leave her massive locks hopelessly tangled.

"We'll be back in a few hours," Rhea called cheerfully as we walked out into the bright day letting the screen slam behind us. "Don't let the kids eat all that bread Momma, save some for us!"

As we approached Donna's house, I could see that Irene was busy doing the wash out in the yard using her old-fashioned gas-powered wringer washer. This was no small task for a women with twelve children. She smiled and waved. "Hi kids!"she shouted over the noisy roar of the machine motor. Donna's mom was an amazing bundle of energy. Somehow, in spite of the heavy burdens she carried, she still managed to go out of her way to help others. Irene also had been wonderfully gifted with the ability to cheerfully encourage those who were less able to tolerate the hard work, poverty, and never-ending stress.

We lingered to help Donna hang mounds of freshly-washed pants, shirts, towels, bedding, and diapers on rows of clotheslines that stretched from one end of the yard to the other. Then Donna, who was Irene's oldest child and biggest helper, joined us to make the rounds gathering our other friends for the long walk to the beach. With us, we carried large precious pieces of styrofoam someone had ingeniously rescued from an old ice chest to be used for body surfing.

On other less pleasant days, I worked with Kathy helping Joel while one or two older children of the colony watched her children. "I think my back's going to break," I complained to Kathy one day when Joel was out of earshot. For hours, we had been loading countless heavy adobes from their frames on the ground into the back of Joel's pickup only to have to unload them at another building site.

"Here," said Kathy as she passed me the old work gloves we were sharing, "put these on for awhile so your hands don't get too sore." But well before the end of the day, both of us had sore hands, bruised and raw, from handling so many of the bricks made from rough dried mud and straw.

Much more enjoyable were the days when Kathy, myself, and sometimes others of Joel's wives rode in the back of the same pickup next to large metal barrels of sloshing water. Joel would drive slowly around the colony stopping at each newly-planted tree onto which we would pour a bucket of water dipped from the barrels, laughing at each other's soaked clothes as we bumped along. "How come I always get the wettest?" I complained in mock annoyance as I made squishing sounds against the floor of the pick up with my soggy tennis shoes.

"La Cucharacha, la cucharacha, ya no puede caminar," I sang, practicing the words to the song that Joel had taught Kathy and she in turn was teaching me. "I think it's nice how Joel always calls you 'Dear' and 'Darling', I said heaving a bucket out of the barrel only to splash more water onto my shoes.

"Are you kidding?" she laughed heartily. "That's his way of not having to remember all of our names. He doesn't deny it." She wasn't angry. That was Joel for you.

One day after completing our work, we relaxed with the children on the orange vinyl covered cushions of the sofa in Kathy's small trailer.

One of her most valued possessions was a battery operated record player and radio that my parents had supplied her with some time ago. As we listened to her prized collection of albums and 45 records, we talked and ate our usual refried beans and tortillas. Suddenly one of the songs caught my attention and I stopped to listen to the lyrics. *I beg your pardon, I never promised you a rose garden.*

"Did you hear that?" I asked my sister gleefully. "That should be Joel's theme song!"

Looking amused, Kathy chuckled and nodded her head in agreement. "I think I really will have to play that song for Joel." Later on she did.

Ten

Coming of Age

In the evenings it was not unusual for a large group of young people to gather in one of our homes to sing, make candy and play games. A new girl our age named Deanna had recently moved into the colony with her family from the state of Washington. She was a girl with an unusual sense of humor who like myself loved dancing. Together we took to choreographing modern dance moves for a large group of girls in my living room to the sounds of Credence Clearwater Revival.

One night after an evening of fun with my friends, Irene was in the mood to tell us about the interesting experiences of her life. The woman had the darndest way of making some of her past unpleasant experiences entertaining and even funny. This time she shared her experience of being in the tiny colony store where she had laid her infant down in his seat for a moment to look around. She saw Verlan come in, but her husband didn't see her. He stopped to admire the child. "What a cute baby," he told the storekeeper. "Whose baby is this?"

He was startled to see Irene appear as if out of nowhere shouting furiously, "It's yours, you idiot!"

Now we all laughed, including Irene. I guess we accepted the fact that with thirty or forty children a father couldn't be expected to recognize all of his children all of the time. And I knew that Verlan took pride in the daunting feat of remembering the many birthdays of his entire family.

I was already aware that Irene's husband wasn't the only one who had trouble recognizing a family member. Her story reminded me of a day when, along with one of my sisters, I visited with a family who was sharing a house with some of Ervil's wives in San Diego. As I sat in a comfortable rocking chair with my back to the hall, Ervil himself suddenly walked up behind me and boldly began to massage my shoulders.

Without a word, I fairly shot out of the chair, landing somewhere over on the nearby sofa. Ervil gave the roomful of us an embarrassed smile. "I thought you were one of my wives," he told me gruffly.

After listening to more of Irene's anecdotes, I was invited to sleep over with her daughter Donna that night. This was not unusual. Although Irene barely had enough beds for her own large family, she would always cheerfully scoot over to the edge of her own double bed to make room for Donna and me to squeeze in beside her. Looking back it almost seems impossible - but I came to expect to find a baby, and sometimes even another of Irene's children, crammed in beside us, when I awoke the next morning.

On this particular night Irene stopped me in the hallway next to the bedrooms to hand me a small brown paper bag. I looked at her curiously as I pulled out a box of chocolates and a card that said something about "Thinking about you." It was signed by Verlan, Irene's husband.

Perhaps noticing my confusion, Irene patted my arm. "Verlan just wanted you to know that he thinks you're a very sweet girl," she said quietly before turning towards the kitchen to retrieve a kerosene lamp that had been turned down low for the night. I retreated to the bedroom where I slid the package under the bed to hide it for the time being before sitting down on the edge of the mattress to think.

So Verlan thought I was sweet. I was a little flattered by the idea - but then again, how could he know? I couldn't remember even bumping into him in any of the homes of his wives - I was more likely to see him at church or in a car traveling from one place to another. I was almost surprised that he even knew who I was.

I was only fifteen. This was the first time that a man of the church had shown interest in me. I chose not to talk to my parents or friends about Verlan's gift and since I so rarely saw him, it had been easy for me to simply eat the chocolates, stash the card in my drawer and push the incident aside, as I forgetfully immersed myself in day-to-day life in the colony. I was very much enjoying the company of Verlan's daughters and my other friends. Courtship and marriage were the last things on my mind. I naively thought that the subject would stay closed. But I was growing up - and the fact that I looked older than I actually was didn't help.

It was only a few months later following a conference meeting in Los Molinos, that my parents had joined us to attend, when my father pulled me aside one day in our front yard as we returned home from the church house. "Alma talked to me about you today," he said sounding uncomfortable. "He was interested in courting you. When I told him you were too young for him, he said that he would be happy if you would consider being courted by any of his sons." Dad paused and shrugged his shoulders uncertainly, "I told him that would be up to you."

I knew most of Alma's sons and, in fact, was fairly good friends with several of them. I instantly concluded that if any of them was interested in me, they could approach me for themselves. I was anxious to put this awkward conversation behind us. "Okay, thanks for telling me, Dad," I said politely as I looked longingly towards the house. My father seemed as happy to change the subject as I was. Relieved to have our talk over with, we turned and walked through the front door of the house together.

The best thing about the conferences in Los Molinos were the dances that were planned for the first or second evening after meetings. The chairs in the church house would be arranged against the walls, and one of Joel's wives would usually play the church piano for a big community square dance. At first I had been horrified at the unfamiliar moves I saw the dancers executing, but little by little my fears gave way to enjoyment as my friends coached me through the different steps and turns that the caller announced.

The dance following this conference was proving to be one of the best ever. I no longer needed coaching, and my friends and I laughed and danced merrily with Alma's and Verlan's older sons who had been working in San Diego, as well as other young men of the church who had come to join us from long distances including Colonia LeBaron.

Sometimes the music would change to a waltz or other slow type of dance. It was during one of these songs, while sitting on the sidelines with my friends, that a familiar plaid shirt-sleeved arm appeared extended in front of me. I looked up to see the Prophet himself smiling into my face as he stood offering me his hand. I stood up, almost trembling with embarrassment, and walked with Joel onto the dance floor.

He held me politely, a comfortable distance from himself; yet - as I stared numbly at the walls beyond his tall shoulders, I felt myself stumbling and stepping on his feet as we moved about the room, vaguely aware that we were being watched. *Which dance was this anyway? And why was I doing it with Joel?* It was to my relief that the dance finally ended. I felt myself blushing and nearly tripped again as he escorted me back to my seat.

Looking around I saw people staring and smiling. *What was the matter with them? He was my brother-in law, wasn't he?* Yes, that was it he was my brother-in-law. I had been dancing with my sister's husband. I pushed all other thoughts far into the back of my mind.

I reminded myself that soon most of the men would leave. They would go back to their jobs or Colonia LeBaron, or wherever it was that men of the church went, and I would continue to be a relatively carefree, innocent teenager enjoying my sisters and their families, and playing happily with my friends on the deserted beaches near the colony of Los Molinos.

My immediate future did indeed hold many enchanted summer evenings. We would joyously build bonfires and sing in rounds before joining hands to play crack the whip, yelling and laughing across the massive, moonlit sand dunes. Afterwards, we sat in happy exhaustion, breathing in the salty air as we perched on a dune, transfixed by the sight of the relentless glowing white-capped waves of a silver ocean. At this time of my life I was not particularly inclined to question my lifestyle or my religion.

Eleven

Mark

J ust down the dirt road that ran past my parents' house, there lived a young man named Mark Chynoweth. Until I saw his name written somewhere, I always referred to him as Mark Shanoff, for that was how I thought I heard others pronouncing his last name.

Mark was an extremely talented and handsome eighteen-year-old who had been a member of a popular rock band in Ensenada before moving into the colony along with his parents, a younger brother named Duane, and Rena, his little sister. His older sister Lorna had married Ervil LeBaron while still a teenager some years earlier.

I always felt a little self conscious around Mark - almost considering him too cool and superior to relate to. He reminded me of the elite older guys in Sacramento who would date cheerleaders or a prom queen in their spare time. In fact Mark had already been involved with at least two of the most attractive and sought-after girls in the church. One of them was Joel's stepdaughter - a friend of mine named Lillie.

Feeling like an awkward kid in the presence of these two beautiful popular people, I had suppressed my girlish attraction and watched from the sidelines as their romance ignited and burned brightly only to gradually flicker and fade. I think it is safe to say that most of the girls I knew had developed a crush on Mark at one time or another.

Perhaps, as one of the few young men living full time in the colony, he was becoming lonely or bored, because a year or so after my arrival Mark began attending the church dances and inviting the young people of the colony to sing-alongs in his home, where he would play the guitar and teach us some of the modern songs he had arranged himself.

Mark's easy-going brother Duane, who was only a year younger than me, didn't seem interested in sharing the limelight with his older brother - or singing. He steered clear of these occasions, preferring to work alone in the shop on the dune buggy he was transforming from two older French Citron vehicles. Rena, the cute pre-teenaged baby of the family who was learning to play the piano herself, would sometimes join in the singing - but usually the quiet youngster would be busy at work around the house or watching passively from the side.

Soon I not only found myself feeling more comfortable around Mark and his family, but looking forward to these visits which were quickly becoming my favorite pastime. Mark, who enjoyed giving us different parts to sing, made learning fun with his incredible musical talent and easygoing personality. I found it exhilarating to hear our voices weaving and rising together to practice one of our best songs made popular by The Mamas and The Papas called "California Dreaming." The fact that Mark seemed to instantly know how to play on the piano or guitar any song we asked for made our get-togethers even more entertaining. When the rest of us tired of practicing, we would relax and listen while Mark took our requests.

At some point, Tina and some of the more confident teenagers decided to turn one of Mark's favorites, the "Ballad of Rocky Raccoon" taken from an album by the Beatles, into a comedy play complete with props. To my amusement they cleverly acted out the silly lyrics that Mark expertly sang as he played the guitar. We all agreed that this would be great entertainment to provide for members of the church who would be attending the next big conference, and it ended up being just that.

It was on a dreary winter day, as I was working alone around the house, that I looked out of the kitchen window to see the Chynoweth's family pickup spitting out clouds of cold exhaust, and coming to a stop just outside the gate of our yard. Mark, in his usual blue jeans and cotton shirt covered by a warm jacket, climbed out of the driver's seat and held his raised hand in a fist ready to knock on the door when I unexpectedly opened it.

"Hi!" he said, smiling brightly.

"Hi," I said smiling back. There was a pause.

"I was just on my way into town," he said, as if suddenly realizing that he needed to explain the reason he was standing in my doorway. " I thought I'd stop by and see if you wanted to come over and sing tonight."

"Sure," I said, obviously pleased with the idea. "What time?"

"Hmmm, let's see," he said rubbing, his chin absently. "Just come over at about seven," he decided before turning towards his still- running pickup.

That will give me plenty of time to make the rounds and let everyone know, I thought as I stepped out into the yard and returned his wave goodbye. As he drove away I wondered why he decided to tell me first this time. Then again - why did it matter? We hadn't been singing together as often after the last conference, and this would be a welcome diversion for all of us since it had been too cold to go to the beach.

That evening, what turned out to be a large group of mostly girls gathered in the nearly finished living room of the A- frame house that the Chynoweth family had been patiently building over the last year. As usual, our several hour long songfest was fun and lively, but as I prepared to exit through the kitchen door, Mark unexpectedly stopped me. "Let me give you a ride," he said, reaching for the keys to the pickup.

There was an awkward silence as we bumped slowly down the road towards my house. To my surprise, at the gate Mark turned off the engine and faced me. "You know how I asked if you wanted to sing tonight?" he asked gently. I nodded blankly. "I only meant you - I didn't mean everybody."

I stared at him, at first not comprehending his words - then my eyes grew wide. "Oh, I - I thought you meant, you know - everyone," I stammered in bewilderment. "Like we usually do."

"I noticed," Mark said, with an amused smile.

Suddenly envisioning the small crowd of people I had just invited to the Chynoweth home for the evening, I turned away from him and slumped down in the seat. "I blew it," I said lamely, staring out of the front windshield. "I'm sorry."

Now Mark laughed outright. "It's okay - it's okay," he said soothingly. "It was fun, right? You can come over tomorrow. I have some songs that we can work on that I think would go good with your voice. I'll pick you up after dinner, okay?"

"Okay...." I responded, nodding my head slowly, and not feeling at all okay about singing alone with Mark.

I made it through our first session, but I had been as nervous as a child in a doctor's office for the first time. Mark, sitting at the piano, turned to see me perched stiffly behind him in a chair halfway across the large room that had been deserted especially for us. For a moment, he looked as though he wanted to say something, then changed his mind. Instead he began playing a song on the piano that I instantly recognized.

"Do you know this song?" he asked as his fingers smoothly pressed the keys. "It's by Dusty Springfield," he added before singing the first few lines himself: *The look of love is in your eyes, the look your heart can't disguise...*

I picked up easily where Mark left off, for this was one of my favorites and suited my voice comfortably. Without pause Mark moved into the next song. "Let's try something by the Carpenters," he said, once again singing alone as he waited for me to take over the lead before joining in with the harmony. For the rest of that evening, I stubbornly remained in my seat, straining to hear his voice from where I sat.

The next night Mark brought me to his house to practice again. This time he gave me a stern look as he exaggeratedly placed a kitchen chair next to the piano. I frowned and begrudgingly sat down, but when our eyes met we smiled. I was surprised by the realization that this was beginning to be fun. As it turned out, it was also the beginning of an unusual relationship between an ordinary young girl, with a lingering inferiority complex - and a confident, teenaged heartthrob.

That winter passed quickly in Los Molinos. Singing with Mark and working on the dance I was creating with my other friends kept me well-entertained. I had become friendly enough with Mark that he always offered me a ride home after the fun and games that took place in the various young people's homes. Often he would leave the pickup running for heat, and linger - never asking to come inside. We would talk and joke sometimes for well over an hour, eventually bouncing our ideas, problems and dreams off each other.

There were times that Mark would seriously lecture me about my lack of confidence, and one night a trauma from his own past invaded our discussion. As I listened sympathetically, I came to the realization that, even with all of the attention that so naturally came his way, Mark was still lonely. Perhaps sensing that I expected nothing more than his friendship had freed him to reach out for just that.

I didn't see Mark on the otherwise ordinary day that I heard electrifying news that had just reached the residents of Los Molinos. My sister Carolyn had paced into her living room to face a few of us youngsters visiting there. " I just got word that Brother Joel has removed Ervil from his office in the priesthood," she announced grimly. Although her face was expressionless, there was an unmistakable undercurrent of excitement in her voice. "Kim, you look after things while I go out for awhile," she said before hurrying out the door. I assumed that she was going to meet with other colony dwellers to discuss the details that she had just learned about this shocking development.

Mark stopped by my house early the next morning. "No singing practice tonight," he said, looking a little stunned. "My family is going to spend the day in fasting and prayer for Ervil." I was not surprised; after all Ervil was Mark's brother-in-law, and I knew that Mark's mother, Thelma, admired him deeply. "We're afraid for him," Mark continued, "we don't understand how this could've happened."

Throughout that winter information about the events that had taken place in Colonia LeBaron had gradually trickled down from the men of the church, to the women - and finally - to the young people. We heard rumors that Ervil had taken tithing money for his own use, and that one church member claimed Ervil had cheated him out of his house and property in Colonia LeBaron.

One thing was unmistakably clear - over time Joel's influential brother had grown tired of being second in command. In Joel's frequent absences, he had begun to override some of the prophet's decisions and teachings with his own, and at the time of his removal from office, had even begun taking steps to enforce his version of the Civil Law.

Ominously, his version of this standard would one day include the death penalty. Ervil foresaw the government that he planned to establish and oversee as one day ruling the entire earth.

He had also become obsessed with the possibility of obtaining a large sum of money with which to carry out his schemes, by recruiting developers to transform the church-owned Baja beach frontage into a tourist resort. Joel, who had purchased the property to be used as an *"ejido"* for agricultural purposes, mainly by and for the growing numbers of Mexican church members, was soundly against the idea. This enraged Ervil who was becoming accustomed to having his own way.

Months of heated debate followed, with Ervil becoming increasingly bold and antagonistic, while Joel tried unsuccessfully to keep the peace. Finally the day came when it was no longer possible for Joel to overlook his brother's persistent undermining of his own authority. Perhaps realizing that ignoring Ervil's insolence was only serving to make him more brazen, Joel's hand was forced. It was with a heavy heart that he made the difficult decision to remove Ervil from his elevated position as Patriarch of the Church of the Firstborn.

Surprisingly, I was told that Ervil had been humbled by the move, even weeping and asking for forgiveness. But many church members, including some who had already left Colonia LeBaron because of Ervil, felt that the decision had come much too late.

Twelve

Lauren's Summer Visit

M y second spring in the colony of Los Molinos was mostly untouched by all of these developments as my friends and I continued life as usual, a good distance away from Colonia LeBaron. While, what I considered to be unpleasant adult problems were being discussed by our elders, I had been working on a childishly bold scheme of my own. I missed my friend Lauren, who was just completing her sophomore year at a high school in Sacramento, and I wanted her to join me in the colony for the summer.

After writing numerous letters to both my parents and Lauren, the plan was actually beginning to take shape. Lauren handled the details with her parents, conveniently forgetting to mention that the colony she would be visiting was populated by polygamists, and it was finally decided that after my parents' summer visit, I would ride with them back to Sacramento to spend a few weeks and visit my grandparents. Then Lauren and I would take a bus to San Diego where we would catch a ride with someone traveling to the colony. I was certain that the plan would work, and it did.

On the bus ride to San Diego, I told Lauren many things about the colony and the people she would meet there, but because I had grown used to it, I failed to adequately prepare her for the difficult living conditions that the women and children of the church endured.

Lauren was shocked. The lack of simple modern comforts and conveniences at first seemed overwhelming to her, and suddenly, I was seeing our community through her eyes. No running or hot water, no electricity, no heating or cooling, no cars. And not a single telephone was to be found in the little colony she had traveled so far to visit.

There were no lawns, plants, or flowers, and the only trees were the hardly- noticeable ones we had been watering that had barely taken root. My heart sank when I realized she would soon experience the people-biting fleas.

But Lauren, who was no whiner, was soon busy helping me with my chores and enjoying meeting the friendly youth that resided in our not-so-perfect paradise. For my part, I was thrilled to have my good friend participating in the different activities that had bonded the young people here so closely. As I had hoped, my friends were becoming hers.

On Sunday we attended church. I wondered what Lauren would think of this service that was so different from those we had attended with my grandparents. The meeting began with a hymn led by Mark's mother Thelma, who stood at the front of the room beaming with a broad smile as she raised her arm, moving it enthusiastically in time to the music.

Following a prayer, we sat to listen to the words of Brother Perez spoken in Spanish and translated into English. The subject was an interesting one that covered the eternal nature of intelligence, and the existence of spirits before birth. Our leaders referred to this as "the pre-existence." At the end of his talk, he asked if anyone would like to come forward to bear their testimony.

After a short pause, Verlan's first wife Charlotte rose and walked slowly to the front of the room to address us. She was a quiet woman and I had never heard her speak about our religion. I leaned forward and listened closely.

She began by telling us about her dramatic conversion to the the Church of the Firstborn. It seems that Charlotte, who was born into a polygamous family, was already living the "Principle" of plural marriage herself when her husband's brother Joel began making his claim of religious authority.

Charlotte had been willing to consider and study his teachings, but when she was unable to either reject or embrace his claim she had eventually petitioned God for divine help. She asked Him to make her ill as a sign of the truthfulness of Joel's teachings. Soon after, Charlotte not only became ill - she became sick enough to have to be carried to the water for her own baptism.

Continuing her testimony, Charlotte moved on to the subject of humility. "Some people ask that their children be successful and rich in life," she said in closing, "but me, I ask the Lord to give my children the suffering and poverty needed to keep them humble and give them compassion for others." Her words coming so sincerely from the heart were tinged with emotion. I believe that, without realizing it, Charlotte was clearly emphasizing the philosophy and basic attitude of the church Prophet himself.

During her visit Lauren was undoubtedly exposed to almost every aspect of my religion up close. But in our free time we didn't talk much about it - after all she was there to have fun.

However, our vacation was about to become short-lived. Kathy, who had recently learned that she was pregnant for the fourth time, approached me once again for help. "I need to go meet with the doctor in Casas Grandes," she told me as Lauren sat listening. "He may be willing to deliver my baby without doing a C-section. I can catch a ride over with Joel and be back in a week." She looked at me hopefully.

"Can the kids stay here for the week with you guys so I can spend some time with Joel and get it all taken care of?"

Casas Grandes was an average sized city close to Colonia LeBaron where an elderly Mormon doctor practiced in his own clinic. Dr. Hatch had delivered many children for our church members, and knew how important a natural childbirth was to Kathy, for he understood her belief that bringing children in the world was one of the most noble things a woman could do. Kathy would never stop having children as long as she could become pregnant, and her body could not survive the numerous cesarean sections she would require. Having her next baby delivered without surgery, the old fashioned way, would make the following births possible, yet no doctor she approached in the U.S. would consider it because of the scar tissue that had formed on her uterus from the two previous surgeries. The possibility of a ruptured uterus made the natural delivery of this baby dangerous. Yet Dr. Hatch felt that it could be done. He was Kathy's last hope.

I knew that my sister would continue having babies no matter what the risk, for she had told me more than once of her church-sanctioned belief that "to die in childbirth is the most honorable way for a woman to go." I agreed to watch her children.

This time I wasn't alone. I was pleasantly surprised when Lauren once again rose to the occasion throwing herself into cleaning, cooking, and helping me with the children. Thank heavens we now had a bed in each bedroom.

On the second night following Kathy's departure, the three children had just fallen asleep when there was a tap at the door. Lauren and I looked at each other in surprise before I cautiously opened it a crack and peeked out into the darkness. My sister Judy, who was in the early months of her fifth pregnancy, stood on the porch holding a flashlight and looking uncomfortable. "Is everything okay?" I asked worriedly as I ushered her inside. "What's going on?"

Judy sighed. "I'm having pains and spotting," she answered, looking tired. "I'm afraid I'm having a miscarriage." She paused and took a few deep breaths before continuing. "Paul just came down from San Diego. He told me Mom and Dad are there. They just bought a mobile home at a park in Imperial Beach." This came as only a slight surprise to me. I knew that our parents had been talking about moving closer to the colony since Dad was nearing the age of retirement. I guessed that this would be the first step towards leaving Sacramento.

"I need to be near medical care," Judy continued, speaking in a weary monotone, "and if I can just stay down and get rested, I may not miscarry. Paul wants to take me to San Diego tonight if you'll watch the other kids." She looked embarrassed. I looked helplessly at Lauren, leaning against the kitchen counter, who shrugged her shoulders as if to say: *How can we say no?*

Before leaving, Judy decided to take her oldest five-year-old daughter along, but the number of children Lauren and I would be tending had just doubled from three to six. Since Judy's and Kathy's kids were about the same ages, ranging from one to four, it would be like having three sets of twins.

Amazingly, things started out fairly well. Helpful young people from the colony came and went from our house to visit and check on us throughout the day, and soon Lauren and I had organized the children and ourselves into simple routines. Wake up, dress and feed the children, bring in water to heat for cleaning up the kids and washing dishes, clean the house. Then it was time to make lunch, watch the kids outside before starting dinner and hauling water to heat for dishes and bedtime baths, which were given in a large metal washtub in the living room. And there were diapers - always diapers, to be changed. Looking back, I wonder if perhaps we were simply too busy to notice how tired we were, and too tired to complain.

A couple of days after Judy left, Lauren and I worked at the side of the house near the clotheslines preparing to do the laundry while the children played in the yard. It was a warm, sunny day and Kathy's thirteen-month-old son Luke toddled about with his curly redheaded cousin Tony of the same age, inspecting the ice plants in the yard. Sometimes they stopped to splash in the clean buckets of water we had pumped to be used for the laundry.

While Lauren stood sorting clothes on the cemented area where the washer stood, I bent over a large diaper bucket, filled with cold well water, to rinse out wet and soiled diapers. As I worked, I held my breath and tried not to gag at the sight of the increasingly darkening and dirty water I was putting my hands into.

It was with a great sigh of relief that I emptied the last bucket of filthy water onto the ground, well away from where we worked, and walked back to begin pulling the cord on the pull start wringer washer. The motor sputtered but nothing happened. As Lauren busied herself pouring a second bucketful of water into the washer, I wound the cord once again around and around the starter and pulled hard. Still nothing.

Suddenly, catching a movement out of the corner of my eye, I turned to see Mark watching us. How long had he been there? "Here, why don't you let me try," he said walking forward to reach for the cord in my hand. But to our dismay Mark couldn't start the washer either.

I stood looking helplessly at the piles of dirty clothing that surrounded us. "Are we going to have to wash all this stuff by hand?" I asked miserably, struggling with a surge of despair.

"I hope not," Mark muttered after checking to see that the washer wasn't out of gas. "Let me go get my dad - he's good at fixing this kind of thing. I'll be right back."

Mark soon reappeared, coming around the side of the house with his father who carried a box of tools in his hand. Bud Chynoweth was smiling. "Let's take a look at what we've got here," he said, getting right to work as Mark hovered over him watching and asking questions. Already feeling reassured by their presence, I clapped my hands in delight when a few minutes later the motor roared to life.

Lauren and I thanked Mark and Bud profusely over the noisy sound of the washer as they packed up their tools and cheerfully waved goodbye. Thankfully, we would still have enough daylight to dry the clothes on the lines, and the diapers would be ready to fold before bedtime.

That evening we washed our tired dust-caked feet and legs in the washtub. It was just after dark that we fell wearily into bed - but that night, little Tony didn't sleep well. Never crying hard, he fussed and stirred in his bed, only taking small drinks from his bottle. Finally, after walking the floors and patting him on the back late into the night, I brought Tony into the bed that Lauren and I shared, where I laid him across my chest on his stomach. His breathing sounded a little wheezy and he felt a bit warm - was he getting a cold? By morning the baby and I had only dozed fitfully.

It was in the early afternoon that Donna and Laura showed up at our house the next day to say hello, and a little later Mark arrived. Lauren was patiently tending to the needs of the other children while I cared for Tony who refused to eat and was drinking very little water. I had resorted to fixing a bottle of water flavored with a little Karo syrup that Tony sucked tentatively, when Irene also knocked on the door.

"I'm just on my way to the clinic in San Quintin to see the dentist," she told us hurriedly, "but I wanted to check and see how things are going here first." I had never heard of a clinic in the small town of San Quintin which laid less than an hour south from where we were, but I knew that Tony needed to see a doctor.

"Will you take him for me?" I asked Irene hopefully. She agreed without hesitation and I ran for a small blanket to cover him.

It was a only few hours later as my friends and I talked and worked in the kitchen preparing lunch for ourselves and the children, that we heard a car stop out front. Mark put down the guitar he was strumming as I looked through the kitchen window before running eagerly out to meet Irene. As she got out of the vehicle holding Tony's little blanket, I looked anxiously around for the baby. Something was wrong. Irene shook her head sadly as she walked toward me. "The baby has pneumonia," she told me gravely. "They don't know if he's going to make it."

"What?" I cried in stunned disbelief. It was then that another large unfamiliar car approached, and came to a stop nearby. Irene looked uneasy. "That's Dan Jordan," she said as the driver threw open the passenger door and waved her over. " He's following Ervil now," she told me quickly. " I need to go find out what he's up to." Irene walked briskly to Dan's car and got in before they slowly drove away, leaving me standing alone clutching the empty blanket.

It was in a dreamlike state that I slowly walked towards Mark's pickup parked in front of our house and sat down on the rear bumper. I don't know how long I sat there, overcome by a numbing sense of unreality, before I looked up to see my friends gathered round me with concerned looks on their faces. Could I tell them? It seemed that by speaking I would turn this bad dream into reality.

"Kim? What's wrong?" demanded Lauren. "Where's Tony?" The spell was broken. I stood and turned away from them so that they couldn't see the sudden tears that filled my eyes and spilled down my cheeks.

"He stayed there," I answered without looking back. "He may not live," my voice was thick with emotion as I struggled to maintain control.

It seemed that I could hear my friends' voices talking to each other from somewhere in the distance, and then Mark was at my side, escorting me to the open passenger door of his pickup. As I slid inside, Lauren placed my purse on my lap. I looked at them questioningly. "I'll take you there," Mark said simply.

"Don't worry about the kids," Lauren called as Mark started the engine, "I'll take care of things here." I nodded gratefully.

We made two stops before leaving the colony. The first was at Mark's house where he conferred with his parents. As I sat waiting in the pickup, his little sister Rena stepped out of the kitchen door where she stopped to wave at me with a sad smile.

The next stop was to pick up a young Mexican man I had seen from time to time but never officially met. Perhaps knowing that I was not confident with my Spanish-speaking skills, he smiled and nodded sympathetically as he climbed up onto the pickup seat next to me. I had nothing to say during the seemingly endless trip to San Quintin as I stared at the road ahead, determined not to break down in front of the young men who sat on either side of me.

Mark, who drove mostly in silence, tried awkwardly to comfort me. "You know that this wasn't your fault," he reassured me at one point. "You were taking good care of the kids. Excellent care -you really were." I nodded dumbly. Then as if to prepare me for the worst, he added gently, "I've heard that when a baby dies, its spirit returns directly to God." Now uncontrolled tears coursed briefly down my cheeks and I clumsily brushed the loose fitting sleeve of my tee shirt across my face.

After arriving at the small clinic, we were approached just inside the entrance by a dark haired, brown eyed woman who had a surprisingly American look about her. Mark stepped forward and politely inquired about Tony using his flawless Spanish. The lady took a step backwards. "Don't you speak English?" she asked looking thoroughly confused.

Mark's cheeks reddened. "Sorry - I didn't know you did," he replied. "We're here to see the baby who was just brought in." The lady, who we gathered was a nurse, smiled before turning to lead the three of us down a short hallway.

"This clinic is actually the ministry of a Christian organization from the United States," she explained briefly before turning into the open door of a small clean room where we followed her to the foot of a narrow twin bed. And there, in a small portable crib, lay Tony who opened his eyes at the sound of our voices and stretched his arms up reaching for me. "You can pick him up," the woman said gently. I gladly drew him into my arms. "How well he does depends a lot on if he will take nourishment," she continued.

"Can I stay here to help take care of him?" I asked, speaking for the first time.

"That would be wonderful," she answered with an understanding smile. "I'll leave you all alone for awhile."

Mark quietly closed the door behind her, then he and the other young man stood on either side of me in front of the baby who I held cradled in my arms. From his pocket Mark produced a small bottle of oil and I realized that they were going to anoint Tony before saying a prayer. "What's his whole name?" Mark asked as he clumsily tipped the bottle, pouring what seemed to be a large amount of oil into the palm of his cupped hand. He seemed self-conscious and I realized he had probably never done this before.

As I continued to cradle Tony, Mark put his hands on the baby, placing the hand that held the oil over Tony's head, wetting his thick red hair; the other he placed on Tony's chest. Our companion reached to gently take hold of Tony's small feet as we all bowed our heads.

"Anthony Phillip," Mark solemnly prayed. "By the priesthood vested in us, we call upon the Holy Spirit to attend you. We ask your Father in Heaven that His will for you be fulfilled in all things." As Mark spoke, Tony stared trustingly into my face - his large, deep blue eyes starkly contrasting frighteningly pale skin. "Father," Mark continued, "we humbly ask in the name of your son, Jesus Christ, that you will bless this child and restore his health that he might complete his mission here on earth."

As my head bowed lower, unchecked tears began to fall like rain, dropping onto Tony's shirt and running down Mark's hand, still placed over Tony's heart. Mark paused to take a deep breath before continuing. "But if it is your will that he return to you, we ask you to comfort Anthony's family at this time, and give them the strength to honor your wisdom in all things. Amen."

There was a brief silence. I raised my head and thanked the two young men before placing Tony back in the crib and starting quickly from the room. Mark was alarmed.

"Kim! Are you okay? Where're you going?" he called as I marched down the hallway.

"I have to blow my nose..." I called back before turning into the doorway of a small room that held a sink, a toilet and - thankfully- a roll of toilet paper.

When I returned I found Mark sitting in the only chair in the room, alone with the baby. I looked around questioningly through puffy red eyes. "I sent him home," Mark said calmly, "I'm staying here - I don't want to leave you alone."

I closed my eyes and nodded. "Thanks."

For the rest of the evening only small talk passed between us as I cared for Tony, giving him medicine and coaxing him to drink from the bottles provided by the clinic staff. I felt comforted that he didn't appear to be suffering but rested quietly in his crib for the most part. Sometimes tiring of sitting, Mark would take a stroll up and down the hallway before returning to sit in the uncomfortable slightly-padded office chair. Our stomachs rumbled with hunger, but food was the last thing on my mind.

Later that night the nurse brought Mark a pillow which he placed against the wall behind his chair. In the dim light from the hall I watched him lean back, cross his arms, and stretch out his legs, as I laid my head on a pillow at the foot of the small bed to be closer to Tony. Although my body was completely exhausted, I had not been able to sleep when, a few hours later, I opened my eyes to see Mark standing over me. "I have an idea," he was saying in a tired voice, "scoot over."

I raised up to see him putting his pillow at the other end of the bed and the next thing I knew, his feet were occupying the space just under my face. Mark grinned sleepily as I stared pointedly at a hole in the toe of his sock. "Don't worry, they're clean," he assured me.

Just before sunrise the next morning, I awoke and looked around. Without rising, I carefully peeked over the side of the crib, and was relieved by the sight of the steady rise and fall of Tony's chest. Then I looked at Mark sleeping peacefully on his side with his feet against my arm, and pondered our situation.

I was only sixteen years old, and here I was in Mexico, tending to a gravely ill baby at a strange clinic sponsored by the Christian people of "Babylon." I felt warmed by their kindness, their willingness to help- and was reminded of my grandparents.

I remembered the heartfelt blessing Mark had asked over my little nephew only yesterday, and knew that something had changed in our young lives. It seemed we had both grown a little older. I looked again at my nineteen-year-old friend whose head lay at my feet. If it hadn't been for him rising to the occasion, I would have been here alone.

Sliding quietly off of the bed, I padded in my socks down the quiet corridor to the restroom where I rinsed my puffy face in cold water and tore off a coarse brown paper towel to dry my skin, gently removing a smudge of brown mascara. Still looking in the small mirror, I used fingers to untangle and smooth my straight shoulder length red hair. I noticed dark circles under my eyes.

Walking softly, I returned to the room to find Tony still sleeping, but Mark had put on his shoes and stood staring at the bed. Rubbing a hand over his unshaven chin, he slowly shook his head. "Geez, I can't believe we slept on that little bed," he murmured, then turned to look at me with a hint of a smile. "Let's sneak outside and get some fresh air before Tony wakes up," he whispered, walking quietly towards the door.

Outside the entrance of the tidy clinic the sun had just risen. We stretched and took welcome breaths of cool fresh air in the tree-lined parking lot before turning to stride briskly down the graveled drive. "You know what?" I asked absently, "I'm hungry - are you?"

"Man, I'm starving," Mark confessed. " Don't you have any candy or gum - anything in your purse?"

"Uh- uh," I shook my head apologetically. After a moment of walking in silence we stopped and turned to walk back towards the clinic. As we approached the front door we stopped to listen to what sounded like tires against gravel on the road behind us.

"I wonder who's coming," Mark said, craning his neck towards the drive. Just then, a familiar blue Pontiac rolled into the parking lot. "Isn't that your parents' car?"

Before he had finished asking the question, I was running - first into the arms of my mother, then I was hugging my father, as Judy and Paul climbed stiffly out of the back seat. I took one look at their faces and spoke quickly. " He's alive. Come and see him - we need to try to get him to eat. Did Irene call you from town?" I talked breathlessly as Mark stood quietly, holding the door open for my family before I led the way to Tony's room.

Now it was Judy who tearfully cradled her son as Paul and my parents talked quietly to a doctor who had just come to check on the child. Mark and I stood outside the crowded room in the hallway where Mom and Dad soon joined us. "They don't have what Tony needs here," Mom was talking hurriedly. "The doctor thinks our best chance is to get him to San Diego right away. But first we are going to get you two some breakfast in town while they take care of things here. They'll need to settle with the clinic and get Tony ready for the trip."

Sitting in the tiny Mexican restaurant, Mark and I looked at each other in relief. It felt as though quite a burden had been lifted from our young shoulders. We lit up when the spicy plates of food arrived, and dug in with relish. "These are the best huevos rancheros I've ever tasted," Mark said between mouthfuls, "no kidding..."

Things now went into fast motion. Mark drove himself home while my parents sped us back to the colony to find that Lauren had kept the house and the children in perfect order. Still, she welcomed us with relief. Mom thanked her for all she had done, then told me to help her get Judy's two other little boys ready for the trip to San Diego.

"Who knows how long Judy will have to be up there?" Mom said firmly as she and Dad headed for the front door with the children. "Her pains have stopped, and the kids should be with their parents."

"I think you and Lauren have done enough already," Dad added as he hugged me goodbye.

A few days later Kathy returned to Los Molinos with news from San Diego. "Tony's going to be fine," she assured us. " They got him to the hospital in time, but Mom said his fingernails were turning blue. They put him on oxygen in the emergency room and admitted him right away." The other good news was that Dr. Hatch had agreed to deliver Kathy's next baby. Her trip had been a success.

~~~

For the last week of her stay, Lauren and I found ourselves free spirits once again. "Let's make a bunch of burritos and go to the beach!"one of us declared, and word was passed along to all of our friends.

It turned out to be a perfectly unforgettable time. We body surfed, relaxed in the sun, and played tag - before running yet again to plunge headfirst into salty cold waves that seemed to purge us of our cares before buoying us up to be delivered safely onto the sandy smooth - pebbled shore.

And on that special day Mark agreed to let Lauren drive the dune buggy his brother Duane had built. She had been wanting to try this for some time and at last Mark seemed convinced that she was fully capable. Still, "You sure you can handle it?" he asked one last time after giving her some final pointers.

"Sure, sure," Lauren was grinning with confident anticipation, her big blue eyes sparkling in the sun. A few moments later we all broke into noisy laughter as the dune buggy's tires spun wildly before lurching forward, throwing one of her passengers into the soft sand.

Summer was coming to an end, and in a few days Lauren would be returning home to Sacramento. Before she left we decided to invite Mark over for dinner to show our appreciation for all the help he had given us.

As the three of us talked and laughed over heaping platefuls of spaghetti, my little dog Lady became a pest, yapping at the table begging for our food then running to bark at something outside the screen door. Finally Mark, who had never owned an inside dog, had heard enough. He turned in his chair to confront the noisy creature. "Shuut uup!" he yelled in mock anger before turning composedly back to the table.

Mildly surprised by the outburst, I stopped eating and, with my fork poised in midair, looked him directly in the eye without a trace of a smile. "No need to be harsh," I said levelly.

I knew that my timing was perfect when, after a priceless look of confusion, Mark burst into a fit of laughter. Shaking his head, he gave me a long sideways look. "No need to be harsh..." he repeated still smiling.

Thirteen

Return to Babylon

S teven Silver was gone and my sister Carolyn was pregnant and alone with four children. For days, tears had flowed from the bottom of her broken heart, until she could cry no more, and now the time had come for her to act. Feeling that she had no other choice, she made the decision to move to San Diego to find help for herself and her children from the government of the United States.

Carolyn didn't tell me why Steven had abandoned his four wives and their children, I only knew that he had met with Joel before disappearing. Joel had given him money and he had left. No one knew where he had gone, but it seemed that the whole church grieved at the loss of this talented smiling man who always walked with an enthusiastic spring in his step.

I secretly wondered if the pressure of being a father to so many children had become too much for my brother-in-law. Also I was aware of the rumor that two of the women he was married to had chosen him, and that he was not personally attracted to them. Had he cracked under the stress and unhappiness of the pretense in his life? Then came the whisperings that Steven had been struggling with homosexual tendencies.

During this distressing time Carolyn chose not to acknowledge these rumors nor did she discuss any problems that existed between herself and Steven or any of her sister-wives. But from my point of view there was no question that Steven had cared for my sister, for I had seen him being openly affectionate with her and responding enthusiastically to her unmatched sense of humor and articulate conversation.

As I searched my mind for any possible reason - any little thing that might have discouraged Steven and contributed to his reasons for leaving, I remembered a sisterly conversation that took place with Carolyn one day concerning two of my good friends.

"Ervil had a talk with Steven about Tina," she had told me dryly. "He tried to bargain for Steven's help in influencing her to marry him. In exchange Ervil said he would use his authority to put pressure on Lillie to marry Steve."

She paused, taking in my look of astonishment, and nodded wisely. "Ervil is interested in Tina because her ancestor, Parley P. Pratt, was a close associate of Joseph Smith," she explained, "and we all know that

Lillie is being pursued by quite a few men. But Steven wasn't interested, it goes against his principles to operate that way." I could see that my sister was proud to be married to a man who had been strong enough to oppose one of Ervil's schemes.

Even though I was already aware of Ervil's gluttonous appetite for women, hearing firsthand that he was actually looking at the bloodlines of young girls of the church and trying to barter for them like cattle, brought home the incredible arrogance of the man. Luckily, my friend Tina was already involved with Joel Junior, the oldest son of our prophet and his first wife, Magdalena. I expected to hear news of their engagement any day.

Now I wondered if Ervil's behavior had been a bigger disappointment than I realized to Steven who, as an idealistic man by nature, had come into the Church of the Firstborn full of enthusiasm following his mission to France for the Mormon church. I knew that Bill Tucker, the handsome former Mormon intellect I used to babysit for, had already sent shockwaves through the church by moving with his families out of Colonia LeBaron. After claiming that he felt threatened by Ervil, Bill had cut all ties with the church, and I had heard rumors that he had even abandoned his belief in God.

"Will you come and take care of the kids when I go to the hospital to have the baby?" Carolyn now asked me as she loaded her car with a few meager belongings from the one bedroom trailer.

"Of course I will," I assured her, "just send word when it's time."

"We'll see you in the spring then," she said, trying to sound cheerful. "Oh, here," she added fumbling with her key chain then turning to me with an outstretched hand, "I wanted to leave you with a key to my trailer. You can scare away the mice by listening to some of my records that are still in there." Then she and the children were driving away, leaving behind a trail of dust as they headed for San Diego to search for a place to live.

As I watched them leave, I was troubled. Things were not as I thought they should be in lives of people who were supposed to be saints. Rosalinda, Judy's sister-wife, had recently left Paul for good, and Judy had left him once only to return. They had good reason to complain. Their husband, a talented artist and architect who was working in San Diego, was spending too much money on nice cars and clothes for himself while his families did without. And he was showing very little interest in his growing number of children. Then, he had jolted the entire church by having an affair with a Mexican woman he had met in Tijuana, before taking her as his fourth wife. This had resulted in his removal from his position as one of the twelve apostles of the church.

Meanwhile my sister Kathy was not only learning how to deal with angry sister-wives, but she was also learning what she could and could not expect from her husband and that there were certain lines she should not cross with him.

One day she relayed to me an unusual conversation she had with Joel after becoming curious about his legendary visit with prophets of old on the mountain in Utah. Kathy had pressed him for details about the fascinating event. When Joel became irritated by her questions, Kathy naively pressed on. "Did you really see the Lord?" she had asked with almost child-like curiosity. There was no response. "Well, did you?" Kathy repeated stubbornly. "Did you ever see the Lord?"

Joel was suddenly overcome with anger. He struck out at Kathy knocking her backwards. "Don't ever question me like that again," he warned before walking away.

Later Kathy would excuse Joel's anger and blame herself for the outburst. Maybe she had sounded mocking or doubtful.

I could also see that Kathy had become unconsciously involved in the constant competition to win her husband's approval that is so common in polygamous marriages. She tried to demand very little from her husband and kept her complaints to herself in an effort to win his love and attention. Unfortunately, her meekness usually backfired, for it was the "squeaking wheels" who were most likely to get the grease. Still, Kathy was reluctant to nag or to displease her husband in any way.

Women of the church were expected to share their husbands willingly, and those deeply committed to the principle of plural marriage were expected to actively court new wives for their husbands. Except for a few unexpected comments that confirmed my suspicion that Joel was interested in me, this was not something my shy sister would do, even though like the others, she was convinced that the more wives and children a man possessed, the greater would be his inheritance in eternity.

Within a few years of his marriage to Kathy, Joel would court, marry, and move into Los Molinos two other pretty young women of the church. Of course, his new relationships with the attractive, soft-spoken Claudine, and lovely and confident Priscilla would only serve to make my sister even more subdued and insecure. Still, Kathy religiously continued her efforts to be a good wife.

Her efforts did not go entirely unnoticed, for in a conversation with my mother, Grandmother LeBaron once spoke admiringly of her. " Kathy is a queen," she had said smiling benevolently at Mom. "Hers is one house where Joel knows he can go to find peace and quiet." Unfortunately, Joel sometimes gave into the pressure to go to certain of his other wives' houses to keep things peaceful and quiet.

I believe that most of Joel's wives often felt displaced when, in his attempts to be Christlike, he put other people not only before himself, but before the needs of his families. Although the women would complain and cry, they seemed to embrace the idea that allowing their own welfare to be sacrificed was a necessary part of suffering for their religion.

Church doctrine states that the practice of birth control denies life to awaiting spirits in the "pre-existence." This is why it is still common for a girl in the church to marry young and have as many children as possible until she is past the age of childbearing, resulting in as many as eighteen or nineteen births in some cases.

This was proving to be a tremendous responsibility for my sisters and for the other women in the church. Time with a woman's husband was always scarce since the men had to divide their time and attention between church business, personal business, and numerous wives and children. Women who could not afford to hire outside help had to face daily hardships and care for growing large families alone.

I suppose that I shouldn't have been surprised when shortly after Carolyn's departure, Kathy decided to join the growing numbers of women of the church who were discovering a convenient source of money and medical care available in the United States. Yes, Babylon would provide something Zion could not: "Welfare."

Along with Kathy, Judy soon left behind her trailer in Los Molinos to be used for summer visits, and took government-subsidized apartments in the same complex as Carolyn in San Ysidro. In my following visits with them, I was amazed by the number of women I recognized from the church who were now their neighbors and also on Welfare. The place was almost like a third church colony.

I'm sure that to the heavily-burdened, poverty stricken women of the colonies this all seemed to be an answer from God to alleviate some of their suffering. Besides, they reasoned, didn't people who sacrificed to serve God deserve the help of this rich, ungodly nation?

The only man that I knew of that took exception to this way of thinking was Joel's youngest brother, Verlan. He flatly refused to let his families participate in such dishonest activities. But his noble intentions did not enable Verlan to support his immense family on his own. He now depended heavily on his older boys who worked in construction in the San Diego area, to help support their father's families.

This arrangement occasionally brought my friends Rhea, Laura, and Donna into the area to keep house and cook for their brothers in the mobile home they had purchased. I can remember vividly, helping them hand scrub buckets full of work clothes caked with white taping mud before putting them through the washers at the local laundromat. I found this to be a pleasant change from the soiled diapers we had so often rinsed by hand in Mexico.

Well before the birth of her fourth child, Kathy had half-truthfully identified herself to the Department of Welfare as an American citizen who was married to a poor resident of Mexico unable to support his family. Of course, Joel was never named as the father of her children.

To Kathy, the simple two-bedroom apartment she was awarded almost seemed like a palace. She had never appreciated hot and cold running water this much. Lights at the flip of a switch, an inside toilet that flushed, along with the warmth of a thermostatically controlled heater were luxuries beyond her wildest dreams. Not to mention the coin operated washing machines and dryers located just at the bottom of her stairs. She reasoned that to have this comfort for herself and her three small children, while pregnant with another child to be raised for the church, must really be a blessing from a kind and understanding God.

Soon Kathy became a yard sale pro, waking up early on weekends to hunt for bargains with which to furnish the apartment and decently clothe herself and her kids. Thanks to their mother's untiring treasure hunts, the children had toys scattered everywhere! But even with a higher standard of living, I knew that my sister wasn't happy.

Like my friends, I had been traveling back and forth from the colony to either stay with my parents at their mobile home, or with my sisters and their children at the apartments. Once I was at Kathy's apartment during one of her long awaited nights with Joel, where I slept on one of Kathy's new yard sale bunk beds in the children's room. In the middle of the night, I awoke to the disturbing sound of Kathy's sobs. I shivered with sadness at the unmistakable sound of heart-wrenching pain I heard in her voice as she talked to her husband behind the closed door.

A few days later the unhappy incident was forgotten as I strolled across the playground that separated Carolyn's apartment from Kathy's, when I heard a familiar voice calling my name. I stopped and turned to see Mark Chynoweth walking fast to catch up. "Hey! Where did you come from?" I called out, pleasantly surprised.

"My sister Lorna and her kids live right over there in that apartment," he said pointing to a second story window facing the playground. Apparently, some of Ervil's wives were in on the Welfare action too. "And my mom just got an apartment over near old San Diego,"he continued. "But what're you doing here?" he asked. "I thought you came up to visit your parents."

"I'm helping Carolyn," I explained as he fell in step beside me. "She lives right over here. She has a new baby girl named Leslie." Mark smiled. "You know who BB King is?" I asked, changing the subject as we approached her door. "Carolyn just bought one of his albums."

Mark scowled at my naive question. "What do you mean - do I know who BB King is?" he grumbled playfully. " Of course I know who BB King is. Geez, he's almost a legend."

Ever the gentleman, Mark held the door open as we entered my sister's modest living room where the sound of Mr. King's guitar could already be heard loud and clear over the speakers of her cherished second hand stereo.

My friends and I were now in a seemingly different world. There were new horizons for us to explore in the form of movies, restaurants, parks, and new beaches. Sunday meetings were held at a building on the property of Joel Jr. and Tina who had finally married and settled in the area, and there were weekly fireside meetings where the youth would gather at different homes each week to be taught by a man or woman of the church followed by discussion and refreshments.

During one of his stays in the good old U.S.A., Mark somehow managed to invest in a top-of-the-line electric piano complete with amplifiers that could almost take the place of an entire band. One day he invited me over to his mother's apartment to take a look at it. As we drove along in the by-now very familiar pick up, he suddenly reached under the seat and tossed a package onto my lap.

Out of the bag, I pulled a box and opened it. Inside was a sturdy professional looking microphone. I wasn't sure how to react to this unusual present but Mark was clearly pleased. "I chose it for you," he told me, trying not to sound proud. "It's specially designed for a female voice. Now, when we're both in the area, you can come over and sing in style."

"Wow, thanks..." I said smiling uncertainly. I didn't tell him that I was experiencing some of the same apprehension I felt when he first asked me to sing with him in Los Molinos. What did Mark have up his sleeve?

It was a ways to their apartment, and as we drove along the unfamiliar streets, Mark nodded towards what would become a familiar landmark to me. I gaped in mock horror at the business - an ordinary brick building, bearing the peculiar name of "Goodbody's Mortuary."

Before long Mark had me sitting comfortably in a chair beside him inside the small apartment, singing into my new mike. Once in awhile, as the hand holding my microphone gradually dropped from my mouth, he would skip a few notes on his piano to reach over and push my hand closer to my face, giving me that stern look I had seen so often.

I didn't know why we needed all this fancy equipment, but I sure liked the way the new Carly Simon and Roberta Flack songs we were learning sounded. As we sang, I turned to see Mark's sister Rena, who was now a teenager, smiling her approval. Looking tan and pretty, she waved and smiled as she flounced through the room on her way to the nearby public swimming pool.

After that, I found myself feeling pretty independent as I flitted back and forth from Los Molinos to Southern California with my friends. In those days, I tried not to give it much thought, but the truth was my own life seemed to be on one track, while my sisters' were on another. I was having the time of my life as the three of them suffered with everything from abandonment to neglect, burying their pride to deal with condescending welfare workers and food stamp lines. They faced paying bills, sick kids, and feelings of rejection and loneliness as they struggled daily with the many decisions of raising large families - almost alone.

It was during my visits with Kathy and her children that I became aware that Joel was unhappy with Kathy's relationship with her little boy. Lynn was not quite three years old, and although he was a very bright and talkative little boy, he was also very nervous. Joel felt that Kathy was much too lenient and expected too little from her toddler. Therefore he demonstrated a method of discipline to be used when Lynn cried or was uncooperative. Joel simply scooped the startled child up by one leg, and hung him upside-down in midair as he spanked him.

Although I never did see my sister use that method of punishment, she did put more effort into using strict discipline. Audrey and Lynn would be sent to find a hanger, a belt, or a hairbrush to be used for their spankings. They would return with heartbreaking looks of fear and dread in their eyes, meekly waiting to receive their punishment.

Sometimes sensing the pity that I felt for the children, she would explain that she was only doing what was best for them. "You can't be so soft-hearted when you're raising children," she admonished me. "Wait until you get your own kids - then you'll see how important it is to make 'em mind."

Although Kathy tried to be kind to her children for the most part, both Audrey and Lynn developed nervous habits - constantly rocking in the rocking chair or bouncing their heads against the back of the couch or chair where they sat. Even while traveling in the car, we would hear the constant thump, thump, thump of their bouncing.

As my parents and I watched all this, we began to realize that Audrey's and Luke's disabilities would prove to be terrible hardships for them - for they were being raised in a church where children were expected to understand and instantly obey the parent or person in charge. We were seeing that, sadly, there would be little patience or understanding for children with special needs such as my niece and nephew.

Observing the upbringing of my sisters' children as well as some of the other families we had close contact with, it became apparent that even without punishment life could be very unkind for many children of the church. Being born close together under stressful circumstances often meant that a child's basic emotional and physical needs were overlooked.

While their busy and preoccupied fathers were usually more like visitors coming and going in their lives, I noticed that some of the unhappy, love-starved women took out their frustrations on their kids who in turn took out their anger upon one another. Yet the men would be treated to the best that their families had to offer during their rare and coveted visits.

I wondered: Was this why so many of the otherwise good-natured men, like my brother-in-law Paul, seemed to be growing steadily more self-centered and egotistical as they became less aware and considerate of the hardships and suffering their women and children faced each day? In my developing teenaged wisdom, I had a sneaking suspicion that it was so.

In an interesting twist, Mom had found a scripture in the Book of Mormon that specifically condemned and forbade the plurality of wives, and she brought it often to the attention of my sisters and anyone else who would listen. Then she took to using the very same scripture in the Bible that Joel had shared with her to justify plural marriage. "You see, it says plainly that a man must be able to support his families," she pointed out. "Most of these men who are living plural marriage aren't even supporting themselves!"she complained bitterly.

Besides my dad, I could tell that nobody else paid much attention to her arguments. They were unable to refute her points, but after all she was merely a woman and certainly not a member of the priesthood which immediately disqualified her from teaching scripture.

Both of my parents were learning that to argue or debate would get them nowhere, for the people of the church honestly believed that their children were growing up in a Godly and blessed environment. They felt that their offspring would learn to be strong and unselfish in this atmosphere of strict discipline, hard work, unquestioning obedience, and in many cases, bleak poverty. Although young people's activities were very much encouraged for those who had already been thus trained, a happy or carefree childhood seemed to be both unnecessary and unimportant to many of these heavily-burdened, care worn travelers on their weary path to Heaven.

Fourteen

Kathy's Dangerous Delivery

O n May 17 of 1972, Mom and Dad set out from San Diego for Colonia LeBaron with Kathy, who was due to have her baby at any time. I had just turned seventeen and was by now extremely experienced in caring for younger children. In reality, I had spent more of my teenage years with my sisters and their families than at home with my parents.

Once again I agreed to baby-sit Kathy's three children, this time in her apartment, while she went to Mexico on the dangerous mission of giving birth to her fourth child.

When Kathy and our parents arrived at Colonia LeBaron they were welcomed and provided with food and shelter at the home of Joel's mother, Grandmother LeBaron, who was regarded by many church members as a saint.

Although I would later hear rumors that she had been cruel to some of her own children, Grandmother LeBaron now showered over a hundred grandchildren with motherly attention, while treating her sons' many wives with kindness and respect. She was an equally hospitable hostess to any other church member who found occasion to come to her home - and they often did.

Grandmother resided in one of the nicest homes of the colony-- a large four bedroom constructed of bricks, that had been given to her by a church member who had moved away from the area. Although it too had an outhouse in the back yard and no running water, the large living room had a lovely built-in fireplace near which sat an upright piano that Grandmother used to provide lessons for the colony children.

When Kathy and our parents arrived at her home after their long trip, they were greeted not only by Grandmother LeBaron but by Joel, who was lying in bed after having a tooth pulled. Mom was amused to also see petite and feisty Linda, the colony nurse and midwife, who had just had many of her own teeth pulled, patiently attending to Joel who lay groaning pitifully.

The next day Mom decided not to beat around the bush, "Joel, we don't expect to take Kathy to the clinic in Casas without you coming along," she informed him. "This is a dangerous delivery and you should be there with us."

"I wouldn't have it any other way Mother Wariner," Joel promised with his familiar comforting smile.

Two days later Kathy felt the familiar sensation of labor pains beginning. Preferring to wait out most of her labor in the comfort of Grandmother LeBaron's home, she spent the rest of that morning and afternoon alternately pacing the floors and resting. Eventually she complained miserably to Mom of an almost unbearable pain in her back that came and went with each contraction.

By seven o'clock that evening, Kathy decided it was time to begin the hour long ride to Casas Grandes. Joel was summoned from the house of one of his other wives, and the four of them left in Dad's car for the clinic.

Dad was clearly nervous and in a hurry. "Brother Wariner, I would slow down," Joel, who had driven these roads many times, reminded him. " You never know when you might come upon a cow or horse in the middle of this highway." Embarrassed, Dad obligingly let up on the gas pedal.

At the clinic, my parents sat in the small waiting room while Joel escorted Kathy into the delivery room and stayed with her there.

Several hours passed while Mom and Dad waited anxiously. Sometimes growing restless, they would tiptoe up to the delivery room door and listen. Kathy's back pains had become almost unbearable, but true to her nature, she bore them meekly and quietly. Once Mom peeked in to see her standing in front of Joel as he sat on a table gently massaging her back. She was crying softly as she rested her head on his shoulder.

It was nearing ten p.m. when our tense parents jumped to their feet at the welcome sound of a baby crying. Soon Dr. Hatch emerged from the delivery room wiping beads of perspiration from his brow and shaking his weary gray head. "I was expecting any minute to see that baby floating in blood," he said, heaving a big sigh of relief. "But we did it!" he announced happily. "You have a new granddaughter."

Mom wept openly as she hugged Kathy and examined the beautiful baby girl. She was not wrinkled or red as many newborns are, but fair with smooth skin, blue eyes, and a head full of auburn hair. "Have you decided what to name her?" Dad wondered, smiling like the proud and loving grandfather he so naturally was.

Kathy appeared blissful, basking in the attention of her husband and parents while enjoying her lovely newborn. "I want to give her Mom's middle name," she announced proudly. "We're going to call her Ruth."

Joel smiled and nodded in agreement, obviously pleased with his new daughter's name. "I've always wanted a daughter named Ruth," he mused good-naturedly.

Fifteen

Calm Before the Storm

et's see your dance," sister Bateman said turning to her daughter
Malinda and myself. The party at their house in Los Molinos was
slowing down and now the large group of people gathered there
joined in the clamor for my friends and I to perform the modern dance
we had been practicing all year.

I objected. I objected strenuously, but it was no good. The excited
group of adults and young people in attendance wouldn't take no for an
answer. Before I knew what was happening I was standing at the center,
in front of my friends to signal the start of our dance. Someone put on
the Credence Clearwater Revival record and we began, moving in
unison, keeping the beat with neat footwork. Next to me, I could see my
friend Deanna smiling enthusiastically as she smartly kicked her feet
before executing a smooth turn in her favorite part of the dance.

This had been fun to do in our own little private group, but as always
I was uncomfortable being the center of attention. And I wondered if the
people of the colony would think all this was inappropriate for us church
girls.

I shouldn't have worried. Our dance ended to the sound of
enthusiastic cheers and vigorous applause as we slapped each other on
the backs before collapsing into chairs. People were still smiling and
congratulating us when the party ended a little later. As usual, Mark
offered me a ride home.

When we got to my gate, I wasn't surprised when he turned off the
engine to talk for awhile. "You were brave," he said, turning towards me
and leaning against the pick up door. "I heard you were a good dancer,
and you really are."

I smiled in the darkness. I could tell by his voice that he was proud
of me, and that made me happy. Mark was always trying to convince me
that I should have more self confidence. *"Sit up straight - be proud of
who you are and what you can do."* Tonight I had broken a barrier by
performing in front of a large group of people - including him.

I was thoughtful. "You know, I can't help being embarrassed
sometimes," I reflected out loud, "and I don't think I'll ever like getting a
lot of attention." I paused to consider my next statement. "Don't get me
wrong or anything," I finally blurted, " but I'm still glad I'm me."

Unable to see his features in the darkness, I waited for his response. When it came, his voice was tender with emotion, "I'm glad you're you too."

I caught my breath. Mark had been my friend for several years now and I had never heard this tone in his voice. I wondered if he was speaking to me with the affection of a brother.

"You know how sometimes when you're with a certain person, you feel awkward and don't know what to say?" he asked quietly. "It happens with someone you like a whole lot," he tried to explain. "That's how I feel around you sometimes."

"No kidding?" came my weak response. I couldn't figure him out - he probably talked to me more than he talked to anyone. Not only that, but *he* was supposed to be the confident one. Everything seemed unexpectedly turned around and unfamiliar.

I didn't know if Mark expected me to delve deeper into this subject, but I was finding myself on shaky ground. I cared for him in a way that was almost impossible to explain, but I couldn't imagine being in his arms or even holding his hand. There was a comforting security I experienced from our friendship alone. I innocently believed that as friends we would never hurt each other, and unlike the relationship he had once shared with Lillie - ours would last forever. Yet now there was this unexplained flutter in the place where my heart should be.

After a few moments of silence, Mark gently changed the subject. I think he knew me well enough to understand that I was uncomfortable and uncertain about how to react to what he had just said.

As I crawled into bed that night, I thought back to one day in particular of the last conference meeting in Los Molinos. At the time there were new families visiting the colony, some staying at the Chynoweth house and a cute new girl my own age stayed with me. All of us colonial teens had been eager to entertain the newcomers.

For the entire weekend Mark had been busy being his popular self - wise cracking with everyone, and flirting with the girls while I remained in the background visiting quietly with the stragglers. After church, as we all sat eating tacos, almost filling up the little restaurant in town, it suddenly occurred to me that Mark was like a total stranger, so distant and caught up was he. That afternoon, I made a conscious decision to accept the unpleasant fact that we weren't as close as I thought we were. In fact, I wasn't even sure that I knew him at all.

But that night before my visitor from Utah and I got ready for bed, I recognized the familiar hum of the Chynoweth dune buggy approaching our house followed by loud knocking on the front door. I opened it to see Mark standing alone in our yard which was glowing with an ethereal light. "Hi," he said with a smile, "Come on let's go. You guys get a jacket, it's kinda cold out here."

I was confused. "But where are we going?" I asked. "It's getting late and you don't have headlights."

"Check out the moon!" he laughed. "It's really neat out here. It's bright enough that we can go drive along the beach. What are you waiting for?" he admonished. "I've got a spotlight in the buggy if we need it."

My new friend, named Lynn, and I grabbed our coats and ran out to the dune buggy where Mark sat waiting. As I stood back to allow her to climb into the middle where a cushion had been placed to allow three people to sit up front, Mark politely asked her to scoot over to the passenger side. "Why don't you ride in the middle?" he asked me matter-of-factly.

I stood staring at him suspiciously. Was he planning a practical joke? "Will you just get in?" he demanded with an exasperated smile. "Please?" I shrugged my shoulders, warily squeezed in, and we were off.

It was almost like being on another planet as we raced past eerie shadows cast by tall weeds and bushes that were bathed in a pale cold light. The earthen roads before us glowed like an illuminated moonscape, giving our adventure a dreamlike quality.

As we neared a tall dune, Mark picked up speed, gathering momentum, and the dune buggy roared like a giant hornet as we tackled the steep climb to the top. Then over and down we went in an exhilarating ride towards the ocean. Cold damp air rushed against our faces as we flew along the edge of the water.

After awhile Mark called over the roar of the engine, "I don't want us to get stuck in the tide - let's head back up!"

Speeding upwards again, we were suddenly straddling a sharply angled sandy plateau at the top of the dune. Lynn and I jumped out to give the buggy a push before jumping back in for the thrilling ride downhill followed by a slower ride back to the colony.

Mark parked us near his house facing the moon where the three of us talked and relaxed, looking up into the sky. Later, hearing our laughter, my little dog Lady showed up to join our merry little company on the darkening road as Mark walked us home.

Now, as I lay in bed remembering that day, I was certain of one thing: if our relationship became a romantic one I would be jealous of his attention. When there were new and attractive young girls around to flirt with Mark, and he flirted back - I would feel the need to compete.

After all, we expected to be polygamists and it was not unheard of for a man to court several women at the same time in our church. Knowing this, I would even be tempted to compete with my friends living in the colony. And if I no longer felt free to be myself, it would threaten the very thing Mark liked about me. It would be the end of a perfectly good friendship.

~~~

For some reason I never told Mark about my occasional dates with some of the men of the church, and he never discussed the girls I knew he had gone out with in Utah when visiting his older brother who lived there. The truth was that I rarely discussed my dates with any of my friends because they were sometimes with one of their fathers. Besides, I didn't consider myself seriously involved with anyone and was only trying to do my duty by politely considering offers of courtship.

By now I had been out to the movies several times with Verlan in San Diego, and for a few walks along the beach. One of my best friends, Mark's old flame Lillie, had decided to settle down and marry Verlan the year before. She seemed happy to accompany me on my first date with her husband. As for myself, I thought nothing of it - this was what plural wives were supposed to do, and Lillie had always been a fine friend. If, as we were taught, my husband's other wives would be like sisters to me throughout eternity, Lillie would surely have been one of my first choices.

Verlan was smiling as he settled down between the two of us to watch the new release. Somewhere in the middle of the movie, he reached over to take my hand which he placed on top of Lillie's before cupping them both within his own. Because I honestly didn't know him very well, I found this rather awkward, but not wanting to be rude, I left my sweaty palm on top of poor Lillie's for the duration.

Verlan was attentive and funny on our private dates that followed. With an engaging smile that lit up his intense blue eyes, I found him impossible to dislike. But I was a young girl so much more interested in my friends and youthful activities that memories of my early dates with him are vague. I only knew that when he was around, he would ask to spend time with me and I didn't find it unpleasant. Thankfully he was always a gentleman.

Another man I dated briefly was Keith Bateman. He was probably in his late thirties, not unattractive, and had an extraordinary personality. The man was full of wit and life. But he was also the father of my friends Malinda and her older sister Debbie, one of Ervil's youngest wives. To complicate matters even more, Keith's only wife, Ruth, had become like a substitute mother to me during my stays in Los Molinos.

One night Keith and Ruth invited me out for dinner when we were all in San Diego. As we sat talking over our Chinese food I felt extremely out of place. I didn't know how to relate to these two kind people with whom I had always been perfectly comfortable before. Here I was - a tongue-tied teenager trying to fit into their adult world as a prospective plural wife, and from my perspective, it wasn't working. I would've been better off having hamburgers with their kids. I only hoped that there would be no hurt feelings as I silently decided that this second date would be our last.

Secretly, I imagined that Ruth would be relieved not to have to share her husband with me. That was until I learned that she had angrily confronted Irene believing she had influenced me to end the short courtship because of Verlan.

During this time I was friends with many young men closer to my own age, and although a few had shown some interest in me, none had ever followed through after making me aware of their attraction. Perhaps my habit of neither encouraging nor discouraging their attention made some of them uneasy about approaching me a second time. It seemed that Verlan alone was not put off by my aloofness, for he became my most persistent suitor.

I really didn't mean to be indifferent, it's just that I was more of a laid-back observer of life at that time. Like an overgrown kid, I was always watching and waiting - wondering what would happen next. It wasn't what I expected.

Sixteen

Ervil and the Chynoweths

O ne day I learned that Ervil and Dan Jordan were in the colony and, conveniently for them, most of the other men were gone.

I knew that following his removal from office Ervil had at first seemed repentant in the face of Joel's unexpected strength, but over time it had become apparent to those around him that his meek attitude was only temporary. Ervil's humility had turned to outrage, and now fueled by self-righteous indignation, he was out to repair his wounded pride.

After doing all that he could to influence the residents of Colonia LeBaron, he had come forth to expand his efforts, finally reaching us in the colony of Los Molinos. It was now his intention to prove beyond a shadow of a doubt that his own office in the church had been seriously underestimated and was in reality even more powerful than Joel's. To my horror, I learned that he was not only labeling Joel a fallen prophet, but was calling upon the church to reorganize under new leadership: his own.

Dan, a former French missionary, was one of Ervil's first and most loyal supporters. I was dismayed to learn that they were both staying at the home of Ervil's in-laws, the Chynoweth family. A day or so after their arrival, all colony residents were invited to a meeting right there in the large living room, where I had so often sung together with Mark and our other friends.

Standing at the front of the room next to a chalkboard and holding a piece of chalk was our teacher, Dan Jordan. On the board I saw diagrams of various priesthood positions with their purposes labeled, placed in order of importance, which Dan proceeded to explain. It seemed to me that the meeting was designed to be a beginner's crash course on the gospel according to Ervil - although he himself was nowhere to be seen.

Dan was a confident man who was non-threatening and quite witty as he led us through the chalkboard maze. In a way it all made perfect sense the way he explained it, but then again - I wondered who was making up the rules? As the meeting broke up I realized that I was leaving there not really understanding any more than when I came. I only knew that Ervil believed he held a priesthood position remarkably close to God, and we should take him very seriously.

A few days later Mark was at my door, excited and wanting to share something with me. "Get me some plates," he demanded, "I want to show you something." I handed him four or five plates out of the cupboard which he proceeded to spread over our table, placing them in positions that looked very much like those I had seen on Dan's chalkboard. Then, using words that sounded more like Ervil's than his own, he began trying to sell me on the ideas into which he had obviously been buying.

I knew that over the last few days, Ervil and Dan had been holed up, tirelessly inundating the Chynoweth family with their doctrine, and now I had the impression that Mark had been to an intensive pep rally. The plates were to make Ervil's ideas visual and tangible - they were the same sales aids that had just been used on Mark.

"Do you get it?" he finally asked after finishing his spiel.

"Kind of," I replied not wanting to make him feel stupid. "But I still don't know that it proves Ervil right," I added quickly. Mark seemed a little disappointed - but at least I had been willing to listen.

"I know - it's confusing," he admitted. "Just be patient and you'll understand."

In the months that followed, it became clear that Mark considered himself my teacher. Now in the evenings when he would give me a ride home from one of the homes of our friends, we would sit in his pickup where he would always end up trying to explain to me all that he was beginning to believe. I would listen patiently and struggle to understand. It all sounded so pressing and important, but it was all so complicated. I would promise to think about what he said, and then I'd walk into the house with my mind reeling in confusion.

One night I decided to put up an argument using logic that I *did* understand. "Mark, Ervil is just such an arrogant person - I can't look up to him," I explained. "He stole men's wives. And do you know what? He actually talked about his and Rosemary's sex life in front of my mother." There. That should prove to anyone that Ervil was no respectable man of God without even using a chalkboard.

This remark did succeed in distracting Mark from whatever scriptural point he had been about to make. My religious instructor was suddenly all ears. "What did he say?" he asked with interest.

"It's embarrassing, Mark!" I responded indignantly. "You expect me to tell you?"

"Oh, come on," he begged. " It's not like you're saying it... you're just *repeating* it. Please?"

I sat quietly, trying to get up the nerve to tell him. Mark leaned forward expectantly.

"Well, he said... um... anyways he told my mom that..." I stuttered to a stop.

"Just tell me!" Mark urged impatiently. But it was useless.

"I can't."

"Why not?" he demanded. "Man, you've got me all curious and now you won't tell me?"

I shook my head, "I just can't make myself. Sorry. I can't do it." My innocent inhibitions had tied my tongue. And besides, it wasn't my place to go around revealing personal things about Rosemary. Still isn't.

He sighed and sat back in the seat. "Okay," he said resignedly. "Look - I know that Ervil doesn't have a lot of tact. In fact he can be a downright jerk sometimes. But that doesn't mean that God can't use a crude vessel for His own purposes. I'm telling you, the guy knows what he's talking about."

The situation seemed hopeless. Mark and I had become very close, yet I could see him slipping away as if under some strange spell he did not really understand himself.

Now some of Ervil's family members began coming into the colony to stay at the Chynoweth home, including his firstborn son who was a few years younger than myself. We had always known him as Morrel, the middle name he shared with his father, but now we were told by Mark's mom, Thelma, to call him by his more dignified first name - Arthur or Arturo.

Macho was not the word for Arthur, and I was aware that the slightly built, friendly fellow had been something of a disappointment to the egotistical Ervil. I wondered if, now that he was becoming a rather timid young man, he was being groomed to better fit his position. I hoped they wouldn't change him too much - I liked Arthur. And he liked me.

One night as I stood in the Chynoweth kitchen talking briefly to Mark about something, Arthur suddenly appeared wearing baggy flannel pajamas and smiling. I looked at him in surprise - I hadn't even realized he was in town. Thelma pulled me aside. "When Arthur recognized your voice in here, he perked up and jumped right out of bed to come and see you," she whispered with a grin. "He thinks a lot of you." I walked over and gave him a friendly hug hello.

Besides Arthur, two of Ervil's older daughters were also making occasional visits to Mark's house. One was a pleasant and friendly young girl named Elsa, the other was the tall and beautiful Lillian. These girls had been raised in Colonia LeBaron, but quickly fit right into our Los Molinos circle of young people.

Not surprisingly, both of the girls developed crushes on Mark, and even though he tried not to show it, he was obviously interested in Lillian. How could he help it? Not only was she flawlessly olive-skinned with long dark hair and lashes, but she was the daughter of Ervil - making her like a princess in her father's kingdom.

As I got to know the two girls, not once did we discuss their father, and maybe because we were both the same age, Lillian and I soon became friends. Occasionally, she would even spend the night at my house. Because of my close friendship with Mark, she and Elsa would in turn talk to me in private about him, sometimes asking for advice.

While I was busy making friends with his family, Ervil was in the process of organizing his own church which he called the Church of the Lamb of God. I'm sure he was bitterly disappointed when his own brothers, and most of the other high-ranking church officials, chose to remain faithful to Joel's teachings.

However, along with Dan Jordan and the Chynoweth family, several other Mexican and American families were impressed by Ervil's claims. Around this time Mark began making mysterious trips to Utah where I learned his older brother Victor and Victor's wife Nancy were also being converted to Ervil's teachings.

It was during one of his absences that, out of the blue, an unexpected confrontation took place between Ervil's followers and us Church of the Firstborners. One typical Sunday as we were in the middle of a sermon, the church door was abruptly thrown open, and in marched a group of people led by Thelma Chynoweth. As we watched with our mouths hanging open, she paced to the front of the room and ignoring our speaker smiled fiercely and began leading the insurgents in a hymn.

I looked around. Wasn't anyone going to do anything? Everyone looked too shocked to move. Finally feeling violated, hurt, and angry, Joel's followers began exiting the church. I looked straight in front of me as I headed down the aisle to the open door, refusing to meet the gaze of the intruders, some of whom I had always considered friends.

It wasn't until years later that I learned why no one from our church had confronted them. Ervil and Dan had not entered the church with the others, but stood mysteriously out in the parking area. Unbeknown to us young people, they were carrying guns. Our elders were afraid we were about to be attacked as we sat unarmed and defenseless in our own church. Along with many others of the church, I was at this time terribly ignorant of the violent ideas already being taught to Ervil's inner circle.

As usual Mark came to see me after his return. After casually engaging me in some small talk about a concert he had attended in Utah, he decided to bring up the encounter.

"I wanted to talk to you about what happened at the church while I was gone," he began before continuing to explain that Ervil's followers were only trying to establish themselves as the rightful owners of God's meeting house. "Don't you see that when the people of a church are in apostasy they lose certain rights?" he asked me firmly.

I had the sudden urge to participate in this conversation on much simpler terms. "No, uh- uh," I contradicted angrily. "Those people were adults - they could have waited for their turn." Slumping down in the kitchen chair I stared at him accusingly before adding, "I thought you guys were our friends." I was not about to let Mark think he was persuading me to see it his way with his high sounding words. I had been there, I had seen it, and it was wrong.

" It was wrong," I said out loud. For a moment I thought Mark looked a little ashamed.

"Did you cry?" he asked gently.

"No," I scoffed dramatically.

"Someone told me you cried," he insisted calmly. What the... was someone spying on me? I was embarrassed.

"Just a few tears fell out," I said stubbornly. "I wasn't sobbing or anything."

~~~

It wasn't long after these events took place that most of Mark's family left their house in the colony and moved to the apartment in San Diego. But in spite of our differences, we never lost touch. When I was at my parents' mobile home in Imperial Beach, he would call regularly, usually to invite me over to sing, and sometimes he even took groups of us to the drive-in where we would sit in the back of his pickup with the speaker hanging over the edge of the bed.

One night we backed into a spot to watch a movie called "The Graduate." As usual, some of us became uncomfortable with no place to rest our backs. Mark's brother, Duane, turned to me. "Want to sit back to back?" he asked.

"Sure," I answered. I felt comfortable with Duane who was actually closer to my own age than Mark. Duane was an easy going guy with a funny personality. Soon the others picked up on our idea and paired off to do the same. I saw my friend Laura leaning with her back against Mark's, as Rhea leaned back against Donna.

Since it was late after the movie, Mark decided to stop by the Chynoweth apartment, which was fairly close to the drive-in, to drop off Duane before giving the rest of us rides home. But when we got there and after everyone had visited the Chynoweth bathroom, Mark had a bright idea. He went into the kitchen to talk with Thelma and then reappeared

"Why don't you guys all just sleep over here tonight?" he asked. "Mom has a bunch of extra blankets and you can just bed down in the living room."

A slumber party! Cool. Not only were we all willing, but we were looking forward to hanging out with Mark and Duane til late. We would talk, listen to music, and of course laugh at Duane's funny stories - it would be fun.

But when I called my mom she didn't see it that way. When I told her our idea she responded with a firm and resounding "No!"

I couldn't believe my ears. I was used to going around making decisions for myself by this time - and even when I was at home I was rarely told no. I thought she just needed a little extra persuasion. "Come on, Mom," I begged as the others listened. "Mark's mother is here, and it's a long ways back to that part of town for Mark to drive us this late."

I had never heard my mother so adamant. "You can't do it," she said firmly. "Just come home."

I was embarrassed but Mark seemed to understand. "Your mom's worried about you being with me," he explained somberly as we loaded back into the pickup. "Every time I pick you up, she thinks of this guy named Ervil who she doesn't like. She's afraid." Mark didn't sound at all angry. He spoke as if he was sorry about troubling my mother. He was more understanding than I was about her feelings.

Mom *was* very concerned, but because we were in the religiously neutral area of San Diego, I was beginning to relax once again around the Chynoweth family, even though at some point Mark would try to convince me of Ervil's teachings every time we were alone. It was almost driving me crazy.

Finally I decided to get to the bottom of it all. I arranged to have Mark and my friend Deanna's father go over their religious differences at the mobile home of my parents. At the appointed time my parents joined us as we sat around the kitchen table while the two men brought out scriptures, and a friendly but lively debate ensued.

Brother Tracey was an unpretentious, intelligent man and I respected his opinion. I thought hearing their discussion would clarify for me the differences in doctrine between Joel and Ervil. I was wrong. It all went right over my head.

Nothing said seemed to apply to real life, and I couldn't see how it should affect how I lived my own. Yet to others it apparently made sense enough to argue about. I wondered if I was stupid, but took comfort in the fact that my parents didn't seem to get the point of it all either.

"Are you beginning to understand now?" Mark asked hopefully when we were alone. I think he was feeling rather pleased with himself although there had been no clear winner of the debate.

"I think I understand it a little better," I lied. Even though everything inside me rebelled at the thought of following Ervil, Mark was my friend - I wanted to give him another chance. And if he was wrong, maybe someone with more understanding than my own would be able to break the spell that held him.

"Will you talk to Joel in front of me?" I asked him now.

"You want me to talk to Joel?" he sounded surprised - maybe a little nervous.

"I can arrange it through Kathy the next time he's in town."

Mark was thoughtful. "Okay. You make the arrangements and I'll do it," he resolved.

Joel was friendly and seemed relaxed on the day that he joined us in my parents' kitchen. Mark was respectful yet serious as we sat at the table with my parents. I am ashamed to say that I don't remember most of what was said that day. But open books of scriptures were spread once again across the table, and the discussion revolved heavily around "the Melchizedek priesthood" which Joel was supposed to hold, and "the Aaronic priesthood" which Ervil claimed Joel had never had the authority to take away from him.

I was amazed by the number of scriptures they were able to produce regarding these two priesthood offices, and the different angles they managed to examine them from. How was I ever to understand it all? The only part that I vividly remember of that discussion was when Mark presented Joel with a scripture that seemed to prove that a person holding the office of the Patriarch, or the Aaronic priesthood, had the right to appoint his own successor.

Mark firmly challenged Joel with this fact. He was playing his trump card. "Ervil should have been allowed to appoint his own successor," he said defiantly as he shoved the open book containing the scripture towards Joel. "You can't deny it - it says it clearly right here."

"I don't deny it," Joel admitted. "It says it right there."

The implication was clear - Ervil had been deprived of this important right when Joel removed him from office and this had been a grave mistake on his part. Understandably, Mark was confused by Joel's present calmness - he should have been upset to be proved wrong here in front of witnesses.

Mark leaned forward, looking irritated. "But Ervil didn't choose a successor," he pointed out, trying again for the desired result.

"No, he didn't," agreed Joel.

"Well, why didn't he?" Mark's voice was now raised in exasperation.

Joel sat up straight in the kitchen chair and shrugged innocently. "I don't know. Why didn't he?"

I struggled to keep a straight face. Joel looked so unruffled as Mark sat glowering. Mentally, I chalked the only point of the debate up to Joel who had turned the failure to appoint a successor into Ervil's mistake - not his own.

~~~

Although I never told my parents or anyone else of the pressure I felt coming from Mark, my mother seemed to now realize that he, along with his family, was almost completely under the influence of Ervil's powerful and intriguing personality.

One day she told me about a dream she'd had. "You were holding this giant lizard, Kim," she said, "and even though it was kind of pretty, I knew it was dangerous. I tried to tell you so, but you just kept on handling it like it was nothing. And then," Mom's voice trembled, "right before my eyes it turned around and bit you! I knew it was deadly and I was afraid it wouldn't let you go." She shivered at the memory.

I was impressed by that dream. But I was still too naive to completely understand the deeper meaning that my mom surely recognized. Nor did I understand her concern. As I saw it, Mark would never do anything to hurt me, and just because we believed differently it shouldn't interfere with our friendship. But Mom was wary of Ervil in a way that I had never seen. "That man is crazy," she warned me emphatically.

Getting together to sing with Mark seemed like a legitimate activity. In fact, she and Dad and some of my sisters had even come to listen to us, so Mom continued to allow it while limiting the amount of time she would let me spend with him otherwise.

She made an exception one night when Mark invited me out to dinner with Thelma along to chaperone. Mark had told me it was a nice place, but that evening, as we entered the high class restaurant, I was totally unprepared.

As we were led by the maitre d' past an elegant busy lounge where a man sat crooning into a microphone as he played a piano, I looked self consciously down at my casual tan slacks and brown polyester blouse. Then I looked at Thelma, a beautiful woman who looked especially nice tonight dressed in classy clothes and jewelry, with her hair pulled up and topped by a crown of curls.

We entered a formal dining room adorned in varying shades of blue with white, and were seated at a table with decoratively folded cloth napkins laying near rows of glistening silverware and long-stemmed glasses.

I took a deep breath. I didn't want to ask Mark in front of Thelma, but what was I supposed to do with all of those forks? Then, when the menu came, I wanted to go somewhere and hide. I didn't understand what foods were offered and the prices were exorbitant.

Mark seemed to read my mind. "Don't worry, we're paying," he assured me. Feeling a little guilty, I took a wild guess and ordered one of the lesser priced dishes.

As we waited for our food Mark broke the uncomfortable silence by asking me if I'd noticed the lounge with the live music which we had passed. I nodded. "Would you like to sing in there?" My heart beat faster.

"I don't know," I tried to sound casual, "why do you ask?"

"Because I already talked to the owner. I played a song for him - told him about my own professional experience, and it sounds like he'll give us a job." I stared at him.

"Of course he wants to hear us - said we'll have to do our more mellow songs," Mark smiled. "But he likes the idea of a female vocalist who can sing like Karen Carpenter." He paused to let his words sink in. "Think you can do it?"

I rubbed my sweaty palms together under the table. " I guess I can try."

Good Lord! How was I going to get out of this one? It didn't occur to me to just say no. If I did, not only would I be letting Mark down but as he would surely point out, I would be giving into my fear.

Now our practices took on a more serious tone as we chose and polished our songs. Even though I tried to hide it, I wasn't happy. I was so tired of wrestling with religious questions that I didn't understand, and now struggling to feel confident about singing at a fancy restaurant. Not only was my sense of style nonexistent - I didn't even own a nice enough outfit to perform in.

My life had been changing too fast. My good friends Tina and Lillie were now married women with growing families and responsibilities, and just recently another best buddy had married one of Alma's older sons. I had been honored to serve as Deanna's bridesmaid, but our little lighthearted family of friends would never be the same. Although I could still turn to Rhea, Laura, and Donna who were also unfettered and single, I was no longer able to deny that my friendship with Mark was now precariously unstable.

Then there was the sad news from Sacramento that my aging Grandma Flowers had fallen and broken her hip. After recovering for awhile at a nursing home, she was now at home with Grandpa again, but not yet able to walk.

One evening in the middle of practicing, Mark sensed my sadness. He stopped playing the piano and spun around on the bench to look at me. "What's the matter?" he asked quietly, leaning forward with his hands on his knees.

"I don't know," I mumbled uncertainly, "something's bothering me." I felt like a wilted flower sitting there with my shoulders drooping. "I have a headache," I added softly.

Mark's reaction was thoughtful. Rising to walk behind me, he massaged my shoulders for a few seconds. "Why don't you just lay down on the couch to relax for awhile," he suggested kindly.

In the small living room of the apartment, it only took a few steps for me to reach the sofa where I kicked off my sandals, then curled up on my side. Resting my head on my arm I closed my eyes.

That was when I heard soft music coming from Mark's piano. It was a song I had never heard him play before, but I recognized it. Once again I felt a strange flutter in my heart. Mark was singing the words to a popular song by Herb Albert called "This Guy's in Love With You." He paused before finishing the words to the last verse: *Say you're in love with this guy - if not I'll just... die.* Here he abruptly ended the song. It was the most romantic moment of my young life. I opened my eyes and briefly returned his smile before closing them tightly again.

After a few moments of complete silence, I looked up to see Mark standing over me still smiling as he offered me his hand to pull me to my feet. "I don't want to practice anymore," he said quietly. "Let's stop and get a soda or something before I take you home."

Going to sleep that night proved to be impossible as a multitude of feelings and thoughts invaded my being. As I tossed in my bed, I tried to imagine being with Mark's relatives and Ervil's followers - away from my own family and friends. Impossible.

Then I thought of the darkly intimidating man named Ervil, Mark's new spiritual leader. I knew that never in a million years would I be able to follow him. It was inconceivable.

Finally I remembered my friend Lillian, now living in San Diego who I wondered if Mark might already be dating. I certainly didn't want to be competing for Mark's affection throughout eternity with Ervil's gorgeous daughter. I knew that Mark was drawn to my personality, but there was a certain worldly fact with which I had already become well-acquainted in my young life: female beauty almost always reigned supreme.

Sadly I faced the truth. No matter which angle I examined it from, I didn't belong in Mark's new world. If I didn't want my heart to be broken, I must keep it to myself. I realized I had been kidding both Mark and myself - trying to put off the inevitable division that would come between us if I were to be honest.

A few days later the phone rang. "Can you come over to sing for some friends?" Mark asked. I was standing in my parents' small living room, clutching the receiver to my ear - wondering what I should say. "It'll be good practice for us," he continued cheerfully. "There are some new people here from Utah I want you to meet." Hearing the welcome sound of his voice, I knew that I wasn't ready to turn him down.

"Okay... if you insist," I said begrudgingly.

"I insist." I could hear the smile in his voice. "If it's okay with your parents, I'll be there to pick you up in about twenty minutes."

At his apartment Mark introduced me to a middle aged man named Lloyd Sullivan, his polite blond-headed son Don, who was about Mark's age, and Don's sweet new bride. These were apparently new followers of Ervil. Amazingly, I found them to be very friendly and immediately felt at ease as we chatted. Mark sat me down in front of them with my mike and after we sang a few of our best songs they, along with Mark's family who had joined us, all clapped politely.

"You two sound great together," Don addressed me with a smile. Then he turned to Mark. "You were right Mark, she really does sound like an angel." I looked at Mark in surprise, who looked even more astonished than me. He never gave me such compliments - and now, looking a little red in the face, he abruptly changed the subject.

I lingered there with them that afternoon and it was evening when Mark drove me home. Nobody was there, so we stayed in the pickup to talk. Although the subject of religion soon came up, it was different this time. He didn't preach but seemed more serious as he talked to me about making a choice between the teachings of Ervil and Joel. Mark was completely convinced that his brother-in-law had been chosen to accomplish an important mission that would bring about God's kingdom on Earth. He wanted me to join him in his beliefs.

I sighed deeply before responding. "Mark, I will never understand all the things that you want me to." I shook my head hopelessly. "You know I've tried. And you've done everything you can to teach me." I hesitated before continuing quietly, "I don't think there's anything more that you can say."

Mark nodded slowly. "I know you've tried," he agreed sympathetically, "and you've been under a lot of pressure. There has to be another way." We sat in silence as the evening grew darker. He seemed to be deep in thought. "Something has to happen to help you see," he said finally, turning towards me. "I think I know what it is, but I can't tell you." He sounded like he wanted to share something important. "I don't know when, but I promise that one day - maybe soon - something will happen to make it perfectly clear which brother is telling the truth."

I looked at him curiously, wondering what this mystery could be. Did Mark expect Ervil to start performing miracles?

Seventeen

The Sign

It was a mild August morning in Los Molinos. Kathy, who had been spending some of the summer in her little trailer there, was hurrying about as she prepared to take her four children on a trip to Colonia LeBaron to attend the conference that would be held there on the following weekend.

"You kids be good and help Mommy," she cheerfully told three-year-old Lynn and Audrey who would be turning five soon. "We want to be ready when Daddy comes to get us. We get to go visit Grandmother LeBaron!" Ruth, who had just turned three months old, slept peacefully in the old porta crib. She was a happy and peaceful baby. In fact, now that their mother had access to a variety of healthier foods, the whole family seemed to be thriving. Aside from rarely seeing her husband, things were going relatively well in the life of my sister.

It was the day after Kathy's twenty-fourth birthday and she was in unusually high spirits because on this rare occasion she and her family would be traveling with Joel. Joining them on the trip would be one of Joel's other wives, Jeanine, and Ivan - Jeanine's fourteen-year-old son from a previous marriage.

By midmorning the group had finished their preparations, piled into Joel's well-used pickup now bearing a camper shell, and were driving down the dusty colony road leading to the main highway. As they bumped along, Joel informed his wives that he needed to stop in the town of Ensenada before continuing north to San Diego.

"I need to check on the Buick I left to be fixed at Benjamin Zarate's house," he explained to Kathy and Jeanine, "maybe it'll be fixed by now." Although Benjamin Zarate and his sons were reputed to be followers of Ervil, Joel still tried to be on good terms with them and it seemed that in return Benjamin also regarded Joel as an old friend.

It was early afternoon when the hot and tired party arrived at Ensenada, but Joel chose not to go directly to the Zarate home located on Espinosa Street. Instead he went to the home of my friend Lillian's mother, Delfina LeBaron. Although Delfina was Ervil's first wife and bore him nine children, including his first son Arthur, Ervil had by now lost interest in the poor woman, practically abandoning her in his zeal to organize his new church. Realizing her desperate situation, Joel had been helping Delfina regularly, and after leaving her with a small amount of money on this particular day, they gave some of her children a ride to the local marketplace before heading over to the Zarate residence.

There they were greeted at the now almost vacant house by two young Mexican men, Andres Zarate and Gamaliel Rios. Both were early converts to Ervil's church, but today they were as courteous and friendly to Joel and his family as they had always been.

"I'm sorry, my parents have already moved from this house," Andres told Joel in Spanish, "and they have taken the keys to your car with them. I think I know where they are," he added hastily. "I can ride with your wives and the children to get them while you two stay here and talk scripture." Then leaving Joel, Gamaliel, and young Ivan behind, Kathy, Jeanine, and the children climbed wearily back into the pickup with Andres, anxious to retrieve the keys and be on their way.

After they left, Joel and Gamaliel stood outside talking for a bit, then disappeared into the house to finish the conversation. Perhaps not interested in hearing more of the religious banter, Ivan climbed into the very dusty unrepaired 1966 Buick to sit and wait.

Only about twenty minutes passed, but it seemed to the extremely bored young man that he had been waiting in the car for an eternity when he noticed a short, dark haired man approaching the house on foot. The man walked quickly without looking towards the car where Ivan sat.

As he neared and entered the house, Ivan suddenly recognized him as Dan Jordan, Ervil's most prominent and outspoken follower. Within a matter of minutes, the silence of the hot and boring afternoon was pierced by the sounds of excited shouting.

Completely shaken from his daydreams, Ivan sat listening - electrified by the sounds of scuffling and vigorous fighting coming from within the house. He heard the crash of a window breaking, then to his horror there came the thunderous clap of a gunshot which was quickly followed by another. Ivan shrank down in the seat in terror when he saw Dan Jordan emerging from the house and walking straight towards the car where he sat. But the layer of dust covering the windshield, proved to be his salvation. Dan passed the car without seeing him, and walked rapidly down the street followed by Gamaliel who had climbed out of a side window of the house.

For a moment Ivan sat stupefied, then sensing by the stillness that the danger was past, he numbly made his way into the house - terrified of what he might find. As he entered the living room, he stopped suddenly, his heart hammering against his chest. On the tile floor he saw his stepfather laying motionless on his back near an overturned broken chair. He was surrounded by a pool of blood.

~~~

It was a pleasant late afternoon in the peaceful mobile home park in Imperial Beach where my parents now lived. The sprinklers were running in the small grassy yard outside, while Lauren and I bustled about in the compact kitchen. "Do you have any more Parmesan cheese?" Lauren asked as she stirred the creamy sauce in the pan. She was making dinner for a young man of the church named Kimball.

Since her first visit to the colony, Lauren had become a regular visitor over the years, and during this summer she had joined us in the San Diego area to keep me company while my parents took a trip to Texas to visit with my father's older brother. They would be staying with Uncle Milburn and his wife for over a week.

Kimball, who already had a Mexican wife in Colonia LeBaron, had been attracted to Lauren since their first meeting in Los Molinos a year ago, and Lauren had recently been regarding him with growing interest. He was Jeanine's younger brother, a handsome and good-natured man with striking blue eyes and dark hair.

Wondering why I hadn't heard from Mark in over a week, I had spent the day with Lauren and Kimball at a carnival in Tijuana before returning to help fix the stroganoff dish Lauren had decided to make for dinner. Now as I searched the refrigerator for more Parmesan, the phone rang. Closing the fridge door, I ran into the living room to answer it.

"Kim, can I talk to Mom?" Kathy's voice said, sounding far away.

"Mom and Dad aren't here," I told her cheerfully, "they've gone to Texas."

To my surprise, she began to cry. "Texas! What are they doing in Texas?" she sobbed desperately. I gripped the receiver in alarm.

"Kathy, what's wrong?" I asked her firmly.

"They killed Joel."

I suddenly felt unsteady on my feet - surely I had not heard right. I shook my head to clear it. "Kathy, who did? What are you saying?"

"Dan Jordan shot him," she continued as she wept, "while Andres took me and Jeanine on a wild goose chase." She paused to regain her composure. "He led us around Ensenada for hours looking for some ol' keys," she said bitterly, "then he just disappeared! When we got back to the house where we left Joel, the police were there and they told us our husband had been shot to death." There was a long pause as Kathy cried silently. "We didn't believe it. Jeanine made them take us to him," she said quietly, her voice stunned with sorrow. Then she began to cry again. "We went to the morgue. He's dead."

I put my hand against the wall to brace myself. After taking several deep breaths I asked helplessly, "Where are you? What should we do?"

"I'm still in Ensenada. Me and Jeanine are here at the police station with all these kids." The pain and desperation in her voice was heartbreaking. "We don't know what to do."

Kimball and Lauren had come into the living room and stood grimly waiting for me to tell them whatever bad news I was obviously receiving. I looked at their worried faces. "Kimball's here," I told my sister, " he'll come."

Trembling, I turned to hand him the phone. "Joel's been murdered in Ensenada," I said in a hollow voice. "Kathy and Jeanine need your help." I only had time to take in his stunned expression before collapsing in tearless shock into the welcome arms of Lauren.

After Kimball left, we took a moment to recover before calling Judy and then other church members. As the news spread, word of Joel's death rocked the church to its foundation. Members reacted with profound sorrow and disbelief, for Joel's followers had trusted steadfastly in his prophecy that he would live to usher in the "millennium" – the one thousand years of peace spoken of in the Bible.

I was overcome with the bitter realization that this was the thing that Mark had foretold. Joel's brutal murder was supposed to be the Sign - the proof I needed that he was the brother who had not been telling the truth. Mark's calm demeanor when he had hinted about this horrible event was almost more than I could bear to remember.

Joel's body was flown to Casas Grandes and then transported to Colonia LeBaron. Lauren and I somehow managed to catch a ride with some of Tina's family members to attend our prophet's funeral which would be held in place of the conference over which he was to preside.

Although hurried, it had been a long tiring trip, and it was evening when we reached the colony the next day. At the entrance we were stopped by a group of men carrying guns to make sure that no one from Ervil's group was in our vehicle, for by now it was well known that some of Ervil's followers had also been seeking Verlan at the time of Joel's murder. They were planning to try to kill him too, for he was now holding the office of Patriarch of the church - Ervil's coveted old position, but Verlan had unknowingly evaded them. For now, I continued to avoid the obvious question that tried to surface in my mind: *Would Mark have been one of the assassins?* The thought was too much for me to endure under the already nightmarish circumstances.

As we entered the colony and drove slowly down the road, we saw that the main street was lined with people. Along with the extended members of Joel's families - a large number of his friends, followers, and Mexican admirers stood in reverent tearful silence in the gathering twilight.

Our vehicle slowly made its way to the home of Joel's first wife, Magdalena, for it was here that his coffin had been placed. As we stepped out of the vehicle into the yard, I saw that my sister Kathy was already there standing off to the side of the small crowd that had gathered. She looked so alone. It felt like my heart was breaking as I approached with arms open to comfort and embrace her. But to my astonishment, she pushed me away. "No," she said, sounding angry, "he should be here. Joel should be here." Feeling hurt and confused I turned to pick up Audrey who stood wailing nearby in fear and exhaustion.

Suddenly Kathy was at my side. "Come inside and you can see him," she said quietly. I handed Audrey to Lauren, and as we entered Magdalena's dimly lit home, Joel's oldest daughter came forward and fell into my arms. Nora was my age, and although she spoke English only a little better than I spoke Spanish, we had somehow managed to become acquainted. My friend had not been able to eat a bite of food in the days since her father's murder, and now I held the weak and anguished girl in my arms as we both wept.

Then I approached the open coffin. I stood staring in silence at the still figure behind a sort of plastic window placed over the upper half of Joel's body. Although I knew that he had been beaten and shot in the head, there were no clearly visible wounds, and it looked as if he were sleeping, oh so deeply. His familiar rough hands rested peacefully on his stomach. I couldn't believe he was dead - I even imagined that I saw him move. I blinked my eyes hard. Would he rise up out of the coffin?

The sound of Kathy's voice broke my trance-like reverie. "You see him?" she was asking each of her children as she lifted and held them one by one over the coffin. "That's Daddy," she told them. "Try to remember your daddy."

This was the eve of Joel's funeral. Church members continued to gather, gazing woefully at his mortally wounded body as his wives and older children looked on in distress. For the last time, they lovingly observed his work-stained hands as they tried to comprehend that he would no longer work beside them.

Our beloved prophet had become a martyr. The man of good will in whom we had placed our faith, hopes, and dreams for the future was gone.

Eighteen

The Church With No Prophet

Kathy rarely returned to Los Molinos after Joel's death. Neither did I. However, it was there that I attended the celebration of my friend's new marriage to Kimball.

"Who goes first?" Lauren asked nervously as we stood uncertainly in the darkness outside the crowded lamp lit church of Los Molinos. She and Kimball had already quietly taken their vows at a small service the week before in Colonia LeBaron. In all of the confusion following Joel's death, and to my disappointment I hadn't even been in the area. But tonight I was included in the wedding party as they went through some of the motions of a large festive wedding without an actual ceremony.

"I think the bridesmaid is supposed to go before the bride," I whispered as the door was held open for us. I shrugged and, wearing one of my best homemade long dresses, walked in just ahead of Lauren. To my embarrassment, at that moment Kimball's sister began to play the first notes of "Here Comes the Bride" on the old church piano. I blushed at the sound of a few amused chuckles and was relieved when Kimball's brother Goodwin, stepped forward to escort me to the front of the room. Then the crowd grew quiet as the real bride entered, smiling and glowing radiantly in her lovely wedding dress. When Kimball stepped forward to claim his new wife there was a joyful applause.

It was only a few months after Joel's funeral. During this time of grieving and sorrow their budding relationship had burst rapidly into full bloom. Shortly before their marriage Lauren made arrangements to take her fiancé to visit her parents' home in Sacramento. Her family was actually delighted that she had found such a charming, clean cut, and handsome fellow to call her own. They knew nothing of Kimball's other wife now waiting alone in Colonia LeBaron.

Following the unrehearsed wedding party I attended with them in Baja, the couple departed for a short honeymoon in Ensenanda. Kimball then settled his idealistic new bride in a small trailer parked in National City where several other church members were living at the time.

One of the people she befriended there was Keith Bateman's daughter Debbie who had succeeded in the dangerous mission of escaping with her two children from her husband Ervil's violent cult. During this time of upheaval and change, I rarely saw Lauren, for I had chosen to spend much of my time with my widowed sister and her children.

Somehow, Kathy had been awarded a dwelling on a small piece of property in Colonia LeBaron after Joel's death. It was a forlorn little building with unpainted brown adobe walls inside and out, except where the gray plaster hadn't fallen off. Inside was a single wall which separated the bedroom from another larger room which served as both a living room and kitchen. The single cozy bedroom was packed tightly with Kathy's full sized bed and a set of children's bunk beds separated by a dresser.

If it weren't for the green weeds and grasses strewn about the yard, the house would have blended in perfectly with the brown earth that surrounded it. Although water had to be hauled in from a neighboring well, a familiar looking old gray wooden outhouse stood off to the side, humbly offering its service.

This was no vacation home, but it was bigger than the camping-sized trailer where Kathy had lived in Los Molinos. And it was hers. It was here that my grieving sister decided to live for part of each year without giving up her apartment and the desperately needed welfare benefits in California.

I was staying with her in the tiny house about six months after Joel's murder, when a hand-written letter was delivered to me by another church member arriving from San Diego. I examined the plain white envelope curiously. The letter, which had been originally sent to my parent's address in Imperial Beach, had no return address. When I opened it my heart skipped a beat. It was from Mark.

The two page letter written on lined binder paper began with the words: "Dear Kim, It's been so long since I've seen you, I've almost forgotten what you sing like!" I read eagerly through the rest of the letter before slowly putting it down in disappointment. I couldn't fathom why Mark's letter contained only small talk and trivia with no mention of Joel's murder or anything else that had transpired since I had seen him. Looking at it again, I noticed that some of it was written in handwriting while other sentences were printed. It also had many words crossed out and rewritten -as though he was distracted or unsettled when he wrote. However, he did provide me with a PO Box address to respond to. I wanted to cry.

As I took out a sheet of paper and a pen and walked into the semi-privacy of Kathy's bedroom to begin my own letter, I found myself trembling with emotion. I tried to steady my hand as all of the confusion, anger and pain I had been experiencing since Joel's murder poured onto the rapidly filling page.

"Did you really believe that a man murdered in cold blood would prove something to me, Mark?" I asked indignantly. As I tried not to wet the paper with tears, I told him how badly church members missed Joel, and how I wished that he himself had been with us to share our grief. I ended by saying, " I want you to tell me that everything will be okay, that things can somehow be the same - but my heart is aching because I know that they never will be. This has been so hard - don't you understand the suffering of your friends?" I asked imploringly.

Months passed as I awaited Mark's response, hoping that my letter would awaken feelings of guilt. "Please, God," I prayed fervently, "let him admit that Joel's murder was wrong." My letter went unanswered.

What I didn't know was that before his brother's murder, Ervil had successfully brainwashed Mark and his family into believing that Joel was the bloodthirsty one. Amazingly he had managed to convince his entire congregation, named the Church of the Lamb of God, that our leaders were all dangerous criminals needing to be destroyed before they attacked Ervil's more godly church. In my friend's deluded mind, Joel's murder was not only fulfilling the will of God - it was an act of self defense.

Since Colonia LeBaron was now being closely guarded by the men living in the colony, many other church members were spending more time there like Kathy and myself. Perhaps that was why my parents decided to buy a nice little house in the area, having sold their old one in that colony long ago.

The house they decided on this time was a cute little two bedroom place with a well in the basement, and was just down the road from Kathy's house. It had tile floors, painted walls, a tidy little bathroom and kitchen. And, like most real estate in the colony, it was bargain priced.

Mom and Dad packed up their single wide mobile home in Imperial Beach, California and had it moved to a pleasant little trailer park in Deming, New Mexico. This would be their main residence for the following year. Even though they were now closer to Colonia LeBaron, their visits were rare, so except for when I was in the colony the cute little house stood empty.

Slowly, Kathy adjusted to her new life without Joel. I'm sure she missed him terribly but since she had never truly had a mate to support her or help with the care of the children, in some ways her life was the same - but without the competition and jealousies she had come to accept as normal. At times, I actually sensed a peace within my sister that I hadn't seen during her marriage. She seemed more relaxed in her everyday life which benefited her children, for she also began to have more patience with them. As a result I saw no more fear in their eyes, and their compulsive behavior was replaced with a more calm exploration of their childhood.

On the other hand, I knew that Kathy was lonely and sad. I became very aware of this the next August when I traveled with her to California to take care of some Welfare business. After all of her affairs were in order there, we prepared for the long trip back to Colonia LeBaron. Early that morning, as we loaded the little yellow cigar- shaped Datsun wagon my parents had helped to provide for Kathy, it suddenly dawned on me that this stressful and busy day was her birthday. She hadn't said a word about it and apparently expected no one else to either.

"Hey!" I called out to her as we settled the three older children in the back seat of the car. "Happy twenty-fifth Birthday, Old Lady!"

Kathy stood up and straightened her blouse. "Oh - thanks," she replied half- heartedly with an embarrassed little smile. Then she got into the driver's seat as I climbed in next to her holding one-year-old Ruth in my lap, and we were off - heading east to New Mexico where we would stop to check in with my parents in Deming before heading to the nearby border and crossing into Mexico.

On this eternally boring trip, I studied my sister as she drove steadily on in the miserable August heat with no air conditioning, stopping only for gas and to let the children out to use the toilets at an occasional rest stop. For lunch we stood around the car in the parking lot of a strange grocery store and made sandwiches using plastic utensils we had purchased with the bologna and marked-down bread.

There was no doubt about it, Kathy's responsibilities were many and her joys were few. It grieved me to realize that this birthday, almost exactly a year since her husband's traumatic murder, was no different than any other day of her life.

By the time we got to the mobile home in Deming, not only were we tired and sweaty, but the children were extremely cranky. This welcome stop would only be a brief one, for Kathy wanted to travel the rest of the way to the colony in the coolness of night while the kids slept.

Mom and Dad were happy to see us but, because they didn't know we were coming, they had no food for our late dinner. "Leo, why don't you and Kim go over to the little market and pick up some potato salad and chicken while I help Kathy with the kids?" she asked. I was happy to comply - for I had a plan.

When we got to the family-owned market, I made a bee line to the greeting card rack while Dad rounded up the food. It didn't take me long to find exactly what I wanted. The second card I picked up had a Happy Birthday greeting complimented by a peaceful scene, and on the inside I can still remember what it said: *Don't look back, in joy or sorrow, just live for today, go bless tomorrow.* It was perfect.

When we got back to the mobile home, I disappeared into my small bedroom carrying an empty brown grocery bag while the others ate. There I opened my hope chest, and after moving aside a box of silverware Verlan had given me at a surprise birthday party thrown for me by my friends in Los Molinos, pulled out a soft and beautiful maroon-colored afghan trimmed in pink. This had been the first big project I had tackled after learning to crochet. I folded it carefully before placing it inside the paper sack, and laid the card complete with my handwritten message on top. Then I carried it casually past the family still eating in the kitchen, and quickly stuffed it into the back of the Datsun alongside a box of pots and pans Kathy was hauling from the San Diego apartment to use in her little kitchen in the colony.

It was almost midnight when we finally turned off of the deserted Mexican highway into the sleeping colony where not a lamp or streetlight glowed. Kathy let me off with my suitcase at the house my parents had purchased before continuing down the road to her own. After groping around on a darkened shelf, I finally found the matches to light a lamp then dipped cold water from the cloth- covered bucket into a large flat bowl to carry into the bathroom to wash my face. Everything else could wait til tomorrow. I wanted nothing more than to climb into my bed - which I quickly did.

I was just beginning to doze when I heard a familiar voice coming from somewhere outside. "Kim?" it called softly. "Are you asleep?" It was Kathy. Afraid that something was wrong, I jumped quickly out of bed and ran into the yard.

"Where are you, Kathy?" I called, squinting into the darkness. And then I saw her, holding a flashlight and standing next to my bedroom window.

"You didn't have to do that," she said beginning to cry. I hurried to where she was and put my arms around her, then stood quietly as she sobbed on my shoulder. " That's the nice blanket that you worked so hard on," she reminded me through her tears.

Now it was my turn to cry. "I can make another one," I finally managed to tell her. " And I wanted you to have this one... for your birthday."

Nineteen

Erv

It was just as Ervil intended. We Church of the Firstborners now found ourselves in the same confusing predicament as the followers of Joseph Smith at the time of his assassination. Before his death, Joseph had appointed no one with the authority to take his place. Neither had Joel. In fact, this had been part of Joel's challenge to the Mormon Church. He pointed out that none of the Mormon leaders claiming to succeed Joseph Smith in his office had been properly ordained over the years, because Mr. Smith himself had not chosen his successor by a direct "laying on of hands."

And now, along with Joel, our own prophet's authority had suddenly disappeared from the earth, with no one to rightfully claim it. It was with a confused sense of urgency that although now a hunted man, my long time suitor, Verlan M. LeBaron, was elected by our remaining church officials to function as our new leader.

Since none of our priesthood authorities felt safe after Joel's murder, they had been moving about almost invisibly from one hiding place to another. Verlan was especially cautious, for it had become well known that Ervil wanted him dead above all others. The two brothers had become engaged in a deadly game of cat-and-mouse, with Verlan always managing to stay just out of reach of Ervil's hit- men. Still, at their secret meetings our leaders successfully worked out a plan enabling them to raise a substantial reward which they offered for information leading to the arrest of seven of Ervil's men, including Gamaliel Rios, Andres Zarate, Dan Jordan, Ervil himself, and my friend Mark Chynoweth.

Thus for awhile our men weren't the only ones being hunted. Not only was Dan Jordan wanted by the Mexican law for Joel's murder, but Ervil was also being sought as the intellectual author of the events that took place on that dreadful day.

It was in a surprise move after several months of hiding out, that Ervil decided to take matters into his own hands. With the confidence of a man who believes that the Lord is on his side, he came forward, presented himself at the police headquarters in Ensenada, and demanded that the charges against him be dropped for lack of evidence. I imagine Ervil was surprised and extremely displeased when instead he was not only arrested, but put into prison.

Our hopes ran high when a year later he finally went to trial for masterminding the murder of his own brother. Witness after witness came forward to testify of hearing Ervil's threats in person, and Grandmother LeBaron even wrote a letter to the governor of Baja asking that her dangerous son not be set free to cause more harm. There was great joy and relief when word finally reached the body of our church that Ervil had been found guilty and sentenced to twelve years in prison.

But on the very next day, Ervil walked away free! Our joy turned to horror and heartbreak when we learned that almost overnight his sentence had mysteriously been overturned in a higher Mexican court. There was no doubt in our minds that this action was not the divine intervention that Ervil claimed it to be, but the direct result of a large sum of money that we knew had been raised by the sale of land by some of Ervil's followers to be used to bribe certain Mexican authorities. Our people became more guarded and tense than ever.

Surprisingly, it was into this climate of fear and confusion that a new member from Dallas, Texas was converted to the now barely-functioning Church of the Firstborn. Somehow a wealthy business man named Erv had listened to some of our more persuasive leaders and apparently he liked what he heard.

The first time I became aware of the new gentleman in our midst was when a small group of girls were invited out to Casas Grandes to dine with him. The group consisted only of Verlan's available older daughters - Rhea, Laura and Donna, who were in Colonia LeBaron at the time. It was apparent to me that the beautiful girls were being paraded for the married, middle-aged man's inspection. Somehow my rather uncomfortable friends managed to get me invited along for the outing.

As I climbed into the back seat of a new Lincoln Continental, I was introduced to a dark-haired man in the driver's seat, dressed immaculately in an expensive suit and tie who turned to greet me with a polite Texas drawl. As we headed out to the main road leading to the highway, I could see that he wore a large diamond ring mounted in gold. Then when he laid his arm casually across the back of the front seat, I noticed a clear coating of nail polish on his well-manicured, rather pink hand. This was not the type of man who appealed to me. I was grateful to be a tag-along in the company of my very attractive friends.

After almost an hour of sporadic chit chat along the way, Donna, who was the passenger in front, guided Erv through the streets of Casas Grandes to the largest restaurant in town. It would have been considered a very middle classed establishment in the United States - but it was clean, the food was delicious, and to the residents of our colony, was the first choice for eating out.

"You girls choose anything you like," Erv told us jovially, after we were seated at a large family-style dinner table with our menus. "The sky is the limit."

My stomach growled as my eyes scanned the menu and stopped at the description of the restaurant's special T-bone steak. Meat was a rare treat for us colony girls and I ordered it without hesitating.

I was beginning to enjoy myself. Because I felt unthreatened by the situation and the conversation was presently stiff and uncomfortable for my friends who felt they had been put on the spot, I made the conscious decision to loosen up and help it along. I can't remember what we talked about, but I was happy to answer any questions about our religion and put in my two-cents worth about any topic that Erv brought up.

When our waitress returned at the end of our meal, Erv looked around at us. "Did you girls get everything you wanted?" he asked benevolently. "Remember what I said - tonight the sky is the limit."

Well.... we knew they really did have the best homemade yogurt anyone had ever tasted. It came in little glass bowls - plain, white, and creamy. Some of the girls sprinkled sugar on theirs, but I liked mine with only salt and pepper. I savored each bite, for besides the large rounds of Mennonite cheese that Kathy sometimes bought, dairy products were also a rarity in my diet.

It was dark as I climbed with a full stomach into the pleasant-smelling leather-lined back seat of Erv's car for the return trip to the colony. "Thanks for inviting me along," I whispered to Rhea. I looked at her beautiful Bridget Bardot face and hoped he wouldn't pick her, because I was certain he wasn't her type either.

The next day found me enjoying myself at the home of Grandmother LeBaron where I had spent the night with Rhea and Donna. It was mid-morning and we were finishing chores, when through the front window we noticed a certain Lincoln Continental driving up to stop in front of the house. Erv stepped out and smoothed his jacket before approaching the front door.

"Hello," he said smiling politely at everyone present after stepping inside. Then he looked at me. "Could I have a word with you for a moment?" he asked, motioning with his hand to the front yard as though he were inviting me into his parlor. Apprehensively, I followed him outside. He turned to face me. "I would like to invite you as my guest to a lovely dinner party in my honor planned for this afternoon in the Widmar home," he drawled confidently. "May I pick you up at two?"

I looked around uncomfortably. "Are you just inviting me?" I asked, hoping I had misunderstood. "Er...not the others?" I added trying not to sound fearful.

"Well...no," he laughed awkwardly, "I don't think Judith and Sigfreid would appreciate it if I brought more than one guest. You will join me won't you?"

I could hardly breathe. It was bad enough that Erv was inviting me to be his only guest, but the thought of eating with him in the Widmar home at a special dinner party froze my insides.

Sigfreid and his first wife Judith were German converts to the church. Although I didn't really know them I had heard that Sigfreid, who had a high- paying job as a commercial artist in El Paso, could be rather temperamental. Many regarded him and Judith with their classy German accents as the aristocrats of the colony. I had been friendly with their two oldest daughters, but neither Sigfreid nor his wife had ever looked my way to say hello or even smile. I'm sure that to them I was nothing more than an unremarkable, nondescript colony teenager.

The word for what I was experiencing was terror with a capital T. Yet I couldn't tell Erv no - I just couldn't. Not after the nice dinner he had paid for last night. And I felt obligated to be gracious to our new church member who thought he was honoring me with this invitation.

"Okay," I finally said, offering him what I'm afraid was a sickly smile. Then I eyed his designer suit and shirt and tried not to sound forlorn, " But I don't have anything really nice to wear, so I hope I don't have to dress fancy."

"Don't worry about that," he reassured me kindly, "just wear what you would wear to church."

At two o'clock I had donned my long, homemade plum-colored dress made of cotton, and stood wringing my hands as I watched for Erv at the front door of my sister's house. I felt a little like a lamb going to the slaughter. Somehow I had to get through this. I told myself that I would go there, be polite, and eat my dinner. That's all I really had to do. And then it would be over. Yes, that was the key to my emotional survival - remembering that it would soon be just another day in the past.

Sitting in her little wooden rocker Kathy watched me sympathetically. "Don't worry, Kim," she said, trying to sound cheerful, "You are just as good as anybody else. Your dress is nice, and you look real pretty. Just go and have fun."

I sighed deeply and turned to give her a look of utter despair. There was a brief silence before she continued shyly, "Joel thought you were pretty." She paused again. " He wanted to court you himself, but he felt bad about not having anything to offer you. He knew how much you would suffer being married to him." As I gazed at my sister who now sat staring at the floor, my despair was momentarily forgotten. I was still silently absorbing Kathy's unexpected words when Erv's fancy car pulled to a stop in a cloud of dust alongside her humble abode.

The dinner at the Widmar home was remarkably like my experience eating out at the fancy restaurant with Mark and Thelma Chynoweth, except that here I had no friends at all. I sat next to Erv and stared stupidly at my plate that held sauce-covered duckling and other unfamiliar foods. I glanced out of the corner of my eye to see others cutting the meat off of the duck bones with fork and knife, then proceeded to chase mine around my plate trying to copy them. I only hoped I wouldn't dump the whole thing in my lap.

Then I sat like a deaf mute as the others talked and laughed after dinner. No one was rude to me, but neither were they particularly friendly. As I had foreseen, I was miserably out of place. I politely thanked Judith when it was time to go an hour or so later, and as we walked outside I had an almost uncontrollable urge to run to Grandmother LeBaron's house, which was nearby, and fall into the arms of my friends and tell them that it was over - I had made it through the dreaded ordeal and I was free! I realized this was not quite true, when I saw Erv standing by the car with the door opened for me.

"Let's find a nice shady spot where we can talk for awhile," he told me as we drove slowly down the dirt road. Finally seeing a spot he liked near Maudie's store, he pulled over to the edge of the road and parked.

After a few minutes of small talk, he turned in his seat to look directly at me. I tensed up, knowing that the time had come for him to get to the point. "Kim," he said speaking in a slow, easy drawl, "I would like to get to know you better. I see that you are a very nice young lady, and I think I could make you happy one day." Here he stopped to pull out his wallet. He fumbled with its contents, then handed me a picture. "This is my wife."

I looked at the professionally-taken photograph of a matronly middle-aged woman with elegantly coiffed hair wearing a stylish blouse and expensive jewelry. She looked both wealthy and confident.

"We would like you to consider being a part of our family," Erv said earnestly as I sat gazing at the picture. I glanced up at his face to see if he was being serious, for I was almost certain that the woman in this photo had no idea that her Mormon husband was entertaining thoughts of marrying a young lady from a polygamist church in Mexico.

His face betrayed no sign of insincerity as he sat waiting for my response. I shifted uncomfortably in my seat then handed the picture back to him. "I'm flattered," I told him politely, "and I think that you are a nice person yourself." Then, trying to sound calm while speaking over the beating of my heart, I added, "But the truth is - I'm actually dating Verlan right now."

This was true. Verlan had continued to show an interest in me over the years, almost always managing to find me whenever we were in the same town. I was in no way committed to him, but our tall church leader with the masculine hands and expressive blue eyes seemed at the moment more appealing than ever.

Disappointment showed in Erv's round brown eyes. "Would you be willing to just give me a chance?" he asked hopefully. "I would enjoy taking you into Casas tomorrow to watch a movie with me."

"I'm sorry," I said looking down at the seat between us. "I just don't think that would be the right thing for me to do." I clasped my hands tightly together on my lap, feeling awkward and guilty about rejecting Erv. "I'm sorry," I repeated miserably.

Then I looked directly up at him. "You know that there are lots of other available girls in the colony," I reminded him optimistically. "You've met some of my pretty friends."

"Yes, I know," he nodded.

I hesitated for an instant, took a deep breath, then blurted out the question I was dying to ask. "Why did you choose me?"

I thought I saw a twinkle in his eye, as though he understood my confusion. "It was your conversation," he told me with a smile. "You're an interesting girl. I like the way you talk."

I took his words as a compliment. "Thanks," I said, genuinely returning his smile. Then cautiously I added, "I hope you understand. No hard feelings?"

"Oh no," he assured me as he started up the car, "no hard feelings at all."

~~~

I didn't expect to hear from Erv again, and a few months later Rhea, Donna and I made the decision to take jobs in El Paso. Temporarily, we were staying in El Paso at the house of one of Ervil's daughters named Alicia.

Alicia was a few years older than her sister Lillian and had miraculously managed to land herself in a monogamous marriage outside of both her father's church and the Church of the Firstborn. Now the mother of her first child, she graciously allowed us to stay a few days at her home while we applied for work at a business that would be opening soon under the supervision of Brother Jensen, a prominent member of our church.

The three of us had never held jobs before, and Brother Jensen had suggested that we move to El Paso and apply for positions at what was soon to be a glove factory. Using his influence, he would see to it that we were hired.

On the day of our interviews, Alicia loaned us nice clothing and make-up and helped us fix our hair. Then she pulled out a pair of heels that she thought would go well with my outfit. I laughed and shook my head. "These shoes will make me stand six feet tall," I said dryly. "Thanks anyway."

Alicia looked amused. "I'm just as tall as you," she reminded me, "and I always wear them." Reluctantly I tried them on and walked around the room, pausing in front of a long mirror. They really did look very stylish. I decided that for the first time in my life, I would wear a pair of heels in public.

We shouldn't have worried too much about our appearance. The interview took place in a large factory room, empty except for a desk where the lady sat who interviewed us. It had all been prearranged - we walked away with a job. When the factory opened we would be learning to operate machinery to make sterile disposable gloves to be used in hospitals and clinics.

That evening as we celebrated over dinner at Alicia's, I was surprised when the phone rang and that the call was for me. "Hello Kim, this is Erv," a friendly voice with a Texas accent drawled. "How are you?"

"Oh fine, just fine," I answered uneasily. I silently wondered how he had found me at Alicia's. Then I remembered that he was good friends with Brother Jensen.

"Listen, I have a business favor to ask of you girls," he continued cheerfully. "I have a van that I need to have transported to California. You do have your licenses don't you?"

"Yes," I answered truthfully. The summer before, the three of us had taken an evening driving class in San Diego with Chad, one of Verlan's sons. By now Rhea and I had succeeded in passing the required tests and received our drivers licenses.

"Well, I would like to fly you three girls here to Dallas in exchange for you driving the van to California. You could use it all you want there in El Paso and take your time getting it to San Diego," he continued. "I'll put you up in a nice hotel for the night when you get here, and have one of my employees show you around Dallas the next day before you leave."

I stood quietly holding the phone as Alicia, Rhea and Donna listened to my side of the conversation. "You want to fly us to Dallas?" I finally asked in disbelief. My friends' eyes widened with interest.

"That's right," replied Erv, "and don't worry - no strings attached." He had read my mind.

"Can I call you back after I talk to the others?" I asked.

"How about if I call you back instead?" he countered. " I'll give you twenty or thirty minutes to discuss it, okay?"

My friends were eager to take Erv up on his enticing offer. I had to agree that this would be an exciting adventure for us as we waited for our jobs to begin. Alicia, who was growing tired of having company, enthusiastically encouraged us to go for it. When Erv called back, I told him the answer was yes.

But as the evening wore on, I was uneasy. I wondered if Erv's generous offer really was without an ulterior motive. I didn't want to disappoint my friends but I knew that I had to deal with this nagging doubt before the final arrangements were made. I gathered up my courage and dialed the number he had given me.

"There's something I need to ask you," I began nervously before getting to the point. "Does all of this have anything to do with your interest in me?"

Erv seemed taken aback, but after a short pause responded. "I already told you, Kim, there are no strings attached," he stated firmly. "If that's the way you want it, that's the way it will be."

I didn't hesitate to reply, "That's the way I want it."

It was a short flight that took us to Dallas the next day where we were met at the airport by Erv himself who drove us to an elegant hotel where he led us into an elevator. " I hope you three will like the room I chose for you," he said in the uncomfortable silence as the elevator lifted us quietly to one of the upper floors.

As he unlocked and pushed open the door, we entered a luxuriously comfortable suite with a plush king-sized bed near a large window. I walked over, and looking out of it, took in the pleasant sights of the busy shops and businesses on the street below. There was nothing not to like about this place. The three of us had never had it so good.

To my surprise Erv didn't stay for long. I suspected that the busy man still had work to do before going home to his wife. "If you need something to eat," he told us before leaving, "just go down to the restaurant on the first floor. Kim, you just sign for whatever you all order and put down your room number." Then he paused at the door to hand me the keys and say good night. "I'm sending someone to pick you girls up in the morning," he told us congenially. "I'll see you tomorrow at dinner. Have a wonderful time!" he called over the sound of our voices thanking him as he closed the door behind him.

For some reason instead of being happy and carefree on our little adventure, I found myself feeling grumpy and tense for the rest of the evening. I even got irritated at Donna for joking around. Seeing that I was not amused by her humor, Donna turned up the drama, and I slumped into a chair and glared at her wordlessly. Rhea, who had been watching in quiet amusement, burst into laughter at Donna's silly antics.

The next day was better. That morning Erv's personal aide arrived to escort us around the extended Dallas area. "Good morning, ladies," said a dark- haired young man with a big smile when we opened our suite door. "Is everybody ready for breakfast?" Brett was an attractive fellow who didn't seem to mind at all being paid to show three young women around his city. In fact I noticed that as the day wore on, he seemed rather taken with Verlan and Irene's oldest daughter. Donna looked especially cute that day with her long hair down and wearing her new bell bottom jeans and red knit blouse.

We crossed a long toll bridge after lunch on the way to the Six Flags Amusement Park where we spent the rest of the day taking in the sights and sounds and going on exciting rides. Before we knew it, the evening had sneaked up on us and we hurried to a classy restaurant at the top of a tall building where we waited for our host to join us for dinner.

When Erv finally approached us in the dimly-lit, informally comfortable room, we each shook his hand politely. "How was your day?" he asked smoothly as he took the cushioned empty seat at the other side of the round table. "Did Brett take good care of you all?" We assured him that we'd had a great time.

"Thank you for everything," I chimed in with the others. Then, trying not to repeat my previous blunder of being too talkative and friendly, I sat quietly listening to my friends chatting as we enjoyed our first steak and lobster dinner.

Donna and Brett kept things lively, laughing and joking. There was no doubt about it - they were definitely hitting it off.

As we left the restaurant relaxed and well fed, Erv casually pulled me aside as the others walked on. "I just want to wish you a safe trip back and give you some money for gas and expenses," he said, speaking in a low voice and pulling out his wallet. Then he looked at me hopefully. "I also wondered if you might reconsider getting to know me better."

I felt a stab of guilt. "Did I mislead you by coming?"

Erv shook his head firmly. "No strings attached," he reminded me. Then he shrugged and gave me a smile before adding, "But I did hope you would change your mind. Come on," he drawled amiably, as he offered me his arm "let's catch up with the others before they get away."

Twenty

Separations and Reunions

auren's marriage to Kimball did not survive. It didn't take long for my friend to realize that she had made a terrible mistake. Long periods of loneliness, combined with the unexpected pain of sharing her husband with another woman, had rudely awakened her to the fact that plural marriage was not for her. From start to finish, their marriage lasted seven months.

I heard this unexpected news sometime after I began working at my new job at the glove factory. Rhea, who had experienced enough independence for awhile, bailed out on our working-girl plan after the long and exhausting trip from Dallas to San Diego. So after delivering Erv's van as promised, Donna and I caught a ride back to Texas without her. In El Paso we found a two bedroom apartment and began to settle in. It was here that Lauren came to visit us before her return to Sacramento.

"Where will you stay when you go back?" I asked her with a heavy heart. "What will you do?" My concern for my friend was genuine. I could see the pain of her failed marriage etched plainly into her lovely features. And I felt responsible. Although Lauren did not seem bitter and had no harsh words for the man she was leaving, I knew that she was suffering. She cared for him but she couldn't stay.

"I'll live with my parents," came her simple reply. "They said it was okay after I explained to them about plural marriage." She gave me a rueful smile. "My dad wasn't too happy when he heard that my husband had another wife." I experienced a fresh wave of guilt mingled with embarrassment. After a few moments of silence, she added, "I may go back to college and get a degree."

I was sad for her to leave, but I should have known that my resilient friend would bounce back. Within a few years her tentative plan became a reality. Lauren would eventually earn an advanced degree in administration. But first, she would marry a former sweetheart and start a traditional American family

In contrast to the new journey Lauren was beginning, Donna and I found ourselves lonely and bored after Lauren's departure from El Paso. Not only did we not have anyone else close enough to visit, we found that we rarely had enough money to spend on anything except bills. Although we did manage to save up enough cash to take the bus to

Colonia LeBaron to visit a few times, the long slow trips down and back made our visits miserably short. It was hard for us to live so far away from our families and friends. Since we had no television to watch, in our free time we took to reading used paper-back novels out loud to each another.

One day the monotony of our routine was temporarily broken when Verlan, who was in town, came to visit us in our second floor apartment.

He looked around with his characteristically boyish smile, pretending to be pleased with what he saw. It wasn't really much to brag about. My parents had supplied us with an old sofa, a table and two chairs, and Donna and I each slept on mattresses on the floors of our separate bedrooms. In our parking spot at the bottom of the stairs sat a 1958 Chevy pickup Dad had loaned me to drive back and forth to work.

Verlan, who was busy as usual, stayed for only a few minutes. But it was almost the weekend, so he pulled me aside to ask me out to a movie for the following night. Since I had been bored silly, I fairly jumped at the idea. It was only after agreeing to go, that I wondered if Donna felt uncomfortable about me going out with her father. It was a subject neither one of us chose to discuss.

But the next day I wasn't feeling well. By the time Verlan telephoned that evening with instructions for me to pick him up at one of Sigfried Widmar's homes, I was beginning to feel worse. "Let's go anyway," Verlan urged. "We can go to the drive-in. Come and get me and I'll do the rest," he promised.

Later as we sat in the uncomfortable old pick up watching the movie, I began to shiver with chills and struggled to stay alert. Unexpectedly, Verlan scooted from behind the over-sized steering wheel and gently pulled me to him. At first I was tense as he cradled my head against his chest - I had never been this close to him. But feeling comforted by the beating of his heart, I began to relax. I almost felt like a little girl again, leaning against my father.

Gently he used his chin in a not-so-fatherly fashion to massage the back of my neck. This ended suddenly when I excused myself and made an abrupt exit. I didn't tell him I had diarrhea, but he may have guessed as he watched me tripping along unsteadily, making a beeline for the restroom. Thankfully, after the first feature we left.

As I walked into my apartment that night, besides feeling ill I was bothered by a nagging sense of guilt. I had abandoned my good friend Donna who was now soundly asleep, leaving her lonely and bored while I had been off cozying up with her father. And I knew she rarely saw her dad. For the majority of the polygamist men of our church, spending quality time with any one of their children was not a priority. In fact, it was almost impossible. By now I had lost count of how many children Verlan actually had.

I reminded myself that this was all about living a higher law and imagined that Donna was used to it by now. My short-sighted young mind didn't recognize the fact that it could one day be my own daughter staying at home alone while my husband dated one of her good friends. Too sick and tired to give the matter more thought, I fell into a restless slumber.

I was feeling much better when a few days later I was awakened by the flat chiming of our cheap doorbell. Groggily I made my way through the living room and squinted to look through the little peep hole on our door. There on the landing I saw a young Hispanic man wearing some sort of uniform and holding what looked like a letter. When I opened the door he smiled and held the white envelope out to me. It was a special delivery letter and it was addressed to me.

Puzzled and concerned, I used my teeth to tear it open quickly to discover that it was a note from Verlan. In it he apologized for waking me but explained that he was thinking fondly of me that morning and wanted me to know it. He added that he needed to leave the area that day, but wanted to thank me for our time together and hoped to see me again soon.

But I wouldn't see Verlan in El Paso again. A few months after my date with her father, both Donna and I decided we'd had enough of our lonely lives there. Donna was first to give notice at the glove factory and, after staying a few months longer with a new roommate from the colony named Debbie, I soon followed suit. We both thanked Brother Jensen for our jobs, and while Debbie returned to Colonia LeBaron, I eagerly packed up my possessions and moved back to California. I knew that Mom and Dad had already rented a modest two bedroom apartment in Chula Vista.

~~~

"Carolyn's gone back to Steve," Mom told me as I sat eating the fried eggs and toast she prepared for me in the unfamiliar but tidy little kitchen on my first morning back. "He sent for her and the kids to live with him in Mexico City."

I stopped eating, flabbergasted at this news. "Is he back in the church?" I asked incredulously. "What about his other wives?"

"No, no...he doesn't want to live plural marriage anymore, but he still believes in Joel," Mom tried to explain as she sipped on a cup of coffee. Mormon or not, this was one habit she had never given up. "He's got a high-paying executive position at some big optical company down there. They claim he's a genius! The owners are thinking of making

121

him a partner. I guess he doesn't feel comfortable in the church colonies anymore."

"I suppose he wouldn't," I remarked, thinking of the wives and children he had left behind. "But why did he send for Carolyn?" I asked, pondering this strange new development in my sister's life.

Mom shrugged. "You tell me," she said with a sad smile. "Why does anybody do the things they do?" Then she added, "Carolyn contacted him first - but he claims he felt inspired about it."

I felt bad for Steven's other families, but I was happy for my sister who had been so lost and lonely without him. And now my little niece, Leslie, would finally get to meet her daddy.

As for me, I was glad to be far away from the glove factory and the lonely little second story apartment in El Paso. Soon I would have to look for a new job but for now I would use the money from my last paycheck and relax with my parents. I also wanted to spend some time with my sister Judy who, with her family of five children, still had the apartment in San Ysidro.

I was especially happy to be reunited with two of my close friends. Verlan's daughters Rhea and Laura were in the area and they introduced me to a new girl our age. Laurie was a cousin of theirs who had practically been raised in Nicaragua. The tall, blond, athletically-built girl was very easygoing and we quickly became friends.

One morning the two of us had nothing to do and we decided to defeat what would have been an otherwise boring day. Together we came up with the idea of catching a ride across the border to Tijuana where we would board a bus going to Ensenada. There we intended to spend the day attending the festivities celebrating Cinco de Mayo - the official Mexican day of independence - then catch a bus back later that evening.

Our plan was unfolding perfectly, and after a relaxing and picturesque two- hour ride alongside the ocean, two hungry and energetic seventeen-year-old girls emerged from a bus in downtown Ensenada ready to go exploring. As we walked along the busy streets, passing crowded tourist shops and sidewalk vendors, the first thing to catch our interest was a busy little indoor taco café.

"Should we try it?" I asked Laurie uncertainly as we eyed the long line of people placing orders at the counter. "It looks pretty busy."

Laurie was undaunted. "Come on, let's go for it," she replied heading for the door. "That means the food is probably really good."

We were about to enter when I heard an unfamiliar voice calling my name. I turned to see a young man leaning out of the driver's window of a small brightly- colored car. "Kim! Over here!" He was actually holding up traffic as he waved frantically in our direction. I waved back uncertainly, still not recognizing this person who so obviously knew me.

Suddenly, the car swung into a newly available parking spot near the café and we watched as a tall, lean, brown haired teenager unfolded himself from the driver's seat and emerged, smiling broadly.

"Oh my goodness!" I cried in disbelief as he drew closer, "Is that you Arthur?"

Ervil's oldest son came forward with long strides to warmly enfold me in his arms. "You've grown up," I said, feeling rather dazed.

"You didn't recognize me, did you?" he laughed. "Well I recognized you - I'd know you anywhere." In the meantime Arthur's passenger, a young Mexican fellow, had joined us and Arthur promptly introduced us to his friend.

"Do you know Laurie?" I asked uncertainly "She's your cousin." We all laughed.

"Sure I do," said Arthur, turning to give her a hug too. "But it's been a long time," he added with an apologetic smile. "You guys going in here to eat?" he asked pointing to the restaurant's glass front door. We nodded. "Can we join you?" And without waiting for a reply he led the way to the counter where he not only ordered, but paid for our food.

As we sat crowded together in wooden chairs at a small table in the middle of the bustling taco shop, I took a bite of my grilled steak taco covered with fresh salsa and savored it. "Mmmm, this is great," I managed to say through my almost-full mouth. Then forgetting my manners completely, I quickly devoured the first half of my taco before pausing to ask, "Can you believe that we ran into each other in this busy city?"

Arthur shook his head before replying, "No - and you'll never guess who lives not too far away from here." I could tell by the gleam in his eyes that he could hardly wait to inform me.

I chuckled. "How 'bout we save time, and you just tell me?"

Arthur sat back in his chair and studied my face. "Mark and Lillian."

Determined not to show surprise, I casually raised my eyebrows. "I heard they got married," I said in a calm voice although my heart was racing crazily.

Arthur nodded. "Lillian had a baby boy about a week ago," he continued. "Want to come over to their house for a little while to see them and say hi?"

I shook my head a little too vigorously. "Oh, no," I answered quickly, "I don't think we'd better."

Arthur was not about to give up easily. "Please," he begged, ignoring my protests, "let me take you to them. I know they'll want to see you and I'll bring you right back into town whenever you say."

I looked helplessly at Laurie who shrugged. She had no knowledge of my history with Mark, and Lillian was another cousin she hadn't seen in ages. "Let's just go," she said simply.

My stomach was in knots as we squeezed into the tiny back seat of Arthur's compact car. I was far too preoccupied with my own thoughts to notice the roads we were taking. I only knew that we were soon walking up a steep set of stairs to a cute little house sitting upon a hill in a pleasant middle-class neighborhood.

Arthur tapped on the front door and then led us inside. Lillian, who sat in a rocking chair nursing a blanket-wrapped infant, looked up in surprise. Her mouth actually dropped open as her brown eyes registered recognition. "I found them downtown," Arthur announced proudly.

I walked over and leaned down to hug her where she sat, followed by Laurie. Lillian's long dark hair was tied back and, even without a trace of make up, Mark's seventeen-year-old wife looked simply beautiful as she smiled up at me.

"Who do we have here?" I asked quietly as I knelt down beside her.

The new mother gently unlatched the sleeping baby from her breast and turned him slightly towards me. "This is Brandon," she said, her eyes glowing with pride. "He's a week old today."

I gazed at the ruddy, little round face, and smiled as I examined the tiny fist clutching his mother's finger. "He's darling, Lillian," I told her honestly.

"Thanks," she said with a satisfied grin. "He should be healthy. We made sure that I ate really good foods and did all the right things while I was pregnant."

Here Arthur interrupted "Where's Mark?" he asked.

"He's playing with his band in Mexicali," she said looking at me. "He won't be home until early morning. How long will you and Laurie be in town?"

"Just 'til early this evening," I responded, trying not to look relieved.

"We're catching the last bus back to Tijuana, after we hang out downtown for awhile," Laurie added.

After sitting down in the small living room to visit for awhile longer, our two escorts appeared anxious to leave. Arthur stood up and stretched. "You girls ready to go downtown?"

"Why don't you come back and spend the night?" Lillian asked as we hugged her and headed towards the front door.

"Thanks, Lillian, but we really need to get back tonight," I told her. Then just before the screen door slammed shut behind me, I called out, "Say hi to Mark for me!"

Back in the heart of Ensenada, we got out of Arthur's car and waved good- bye. I tried not to think about it, but somehow I couldn't shake the feeling that I would never see the friendly young man again. Laurie and I turned and went on our way.

We spent hours walking around visiting the small shops and outdoor stands laden with handmade jewelry, ornate sombreros, and colorful pictures painted on black velvet. We enjoyed talking with the vendors, sometimes listening as they haggled with their *turista* customers. Of course they were all impressed with my tall blond friend who could speak Spanish like a native.

Then we headed for a pleasant restaurant that specialized in seafood where we sat at a comfortable table and counted out our money before ordering. We needed to save enough to pay for our tickets on the bus that would be leaving in the next two hours.

"I was actually a little afraid to go to Mark and Lillian's house," I confessed to Laurie as we sat eating our fish and fries a little while later. "I just didn't know what to expect, since Ervil had Joel killed."

"Maybe they don't believe like that anymore," Laurie replied thoughtfully. "It's been over a year." Then she shrugged. "Lillian seemed pretty normal to me."

After dinner we strolled leisurely towards the bus station. Laurie checked her watch. "We've still got almost another hour before the bus leaves," she remarked casually. As we passed one of the busy nightclubs, we could hear the pulsating rhythm of a live band. The sound drew us like a magnet and we stepped inside to watch the dancers move about the floor.

I was enjoying the music and wishing someone would ask me to dance, when I felt a tap on my shoulder. I turned to see that it was only my friend trying to get my attention. "It's time to go!" she shouted above the almost deafening noise and turned to lead the way, weaving through the steadily growing crowd.

Since the station was almost a mile away, we headed down the quiet streets at a fast pace. "Are we going to make it?" I asked Laurie as we panted along.

"Oh yeah," she responded confidently after checking her watch again, "with time to spare." But when we arrived at the small building, the lights were out and the doors were locked.

"Look there's a sign by the door," I said, fighting a growing feeling of panic. "Maybe they took a dinner break?" I asked hopefully.

Laurie shook her head in disbelief before translating what she had just read. "It says that because of the holiday the station closed early and there will be no buses departing from here tonight." She turned to look at me in alarm. "What're we going to do?"

I shook my head incredulously. Since arriving in Ensenada, we had not seen any of the hoped-for festivities celebrating the Cinco de Mayo holiday, yet now they had canceled the buses!

"Even if we use our bus money we won't have enough to get a room somewhere," I whimpered, beginning to feel terrified.

But Laurie had an idea. "We'll have to go back to Lillian's," she said without batting an eye.

"Laurie, it's too far!" I almost shouted. "We don't even know where it is!"

Ignoring my outburst she continued calmly. "We can find a cab. I think I can find their house again, I was watching the street names on the way there." She paused and shrugged her shoulders. "What else can we do?"

"But I don't want to sleep at Mark's place!" I cried in dismay before trying to explain. "What if Ervil or Dan Jordan shows up? And if we pay for a cab we won't have enough money to take the bus home tomorrow." Then I added pleadingly, "It would be awkward, Laurie."

My friend gave me an icy stare before getting to the point. "So. You just wanna sleep on the streets tonight?"

It was now completely dark. I glanced around at the deserted sidewalks and shuddered. The two of us turned and slowly headed back downtown to look for a cab.

I felt like I was dreaming as I followed Laurie back up the dark steps to Mark's quiet house. Lillian, who was ready for bed, seemed happy to see us. "Don't worry, you didn't wake me up," she assured us as we apologized and explained our dilemma. She led us to a room and opened the door. "Rena's already in bed in here," she said, pointing to a double bed in the dimly lit room. "Just tell her to scoot over." Then before closing the door, she added, "Don't be afraid if you hear noises when Mark gets home. He has to unload his equipment."

I spent an almost sleepless night fully clothed, wedged in between Laurie and Mark's younger sister. I couldn't believe that I was here, spending the night in the home of Ervil's daughter and son-in-law. I was haunted by the thought of seeing my ex-best friend again. It had been almost two years.

Just after dawn I was awake again, worrying about our predicament. *How the devil did I get into this mess?* I asked myself. No longer feeling like the mature young woman of yesterday out on an exciting adventure, I scolded myself for being nothing more than a stupid teenager stranded in Ensenada.

It seemed that I had just managed to doze when I was awakened by a tap on the bedroom door. It was still early morning. I froze in anticipation as I watched the door open slowly towards us. And then Mark was there, standing near the side of the bed looking down at me with his hands on his hips and an oh-so-familiar smile. He was shaking his handsome head as if to say, "Well, well, well. Look what the cat brought in."

I smiled back self-consciously, and slowly scooted up in bed. "Would you believe we're traveling missionaries?" I asked foolishly. Mark still hadn't spoken a word when Lillian pushed in from behind him.

"He didn't believe me last night when I told him you were here," Lillian laughed. "I had to keep repeating myself to convince him."

Mark smiled and shook his head again. "I still can't believe it," he said as he crossed his arms. "So I hear you ran into some trouble last night," he continued with a look of amusement. I decided that now was the time to spill my guts.

"Oh, Mark," I groaned, "we were supposed to go home yesterday but we couldn't catch the bus back because of the holiday, and then we went and used most of our bus money to pay a taxi to bring us here, and...." I dropped my eyes in embarrassment, "and I feel really stupid."

My old friend chuckled good-naturedly. "So you're a poor, penniless traveling missionary?" he chided as Rena crawled out of the crowded bed and put on a robe over her modest night dress. I watched her as she looked for her shoes under the bed. No longer a child, she had grown into a very attractive young lady with long golden-brown hair, a flawless complexion, and wide-set eyes. I secretly wondered how soon she would be married off to Ervil or Dan Jordan.

"Will you come help me make breakfast for everyone while the baby's still asleep?" Lillian asked her.

"Where's the bathroom?" Laurie inquired as she stood up and stretched before following them out of the room. Mark sat down on the foot of the bed, and for a few minutes we were alone.

"I got your letter," he said quietly. Then his tone became defensive. "I figured there was no use in writing back," he said with a shrug of his shoulders. "Geez..." Now he was frowning at me, and like a child who had been treated unfairly, I could see anger in his eyes.

I stared back at him without expression and nodded politely. This was not the time or place to get myself into a religious argument. Besides, the fact that he seemed annoyed by a letter expressing my shock about Joel's murder, told me everything I needed to know. The chasm between us was without doubt too wide for us to breach with conversation.

I was relieved when Laurie re-entered the room and plopped down on the other side of the bed to engage Mark in a more carefree line of small talk. "So what kind of music does your band play?" I heard her ask as still barefoot I headed out to look for the bathroom.

Later we all sat talking around the small living room where we had just finished eating the fried potatoes and eggs that Lillian and Rena had fixed for us. "What're you doing with yourself nowadays?" Mark asked looking at me as Lillian went to check on the baby.

I told him about my recent experiences at the glove factory. "I need to look for a new job soon," I added. "What I'd really like to do is write for children. Maybe I'll find a class to take."

Mark looked surprised. "You've changed," he said, and he seemed to be studying me. "You never used to think about doing things like that." I tried not to shrink from his thoughtful gaze.

"Look at you!" I retorted, eager to change the subject. "You're a daddy now." Mark smiled and looked a little embarrassed himself as he turned to look at Lillian who now sat in the rocker nursing their son. Then the conversation turned to little Brandon and some of the details of his mother's pregnancy and childbirth. Lillian and Mark were both excited and proud to share this new part of their lives. Soon the morning had passed and I began to get antsy - we still didn't know how we were to get home, and I was reluctant to ask Mark for further help.

The next thing I knew, he stood up and walked casually to the familiar old electric piano that took up a good portion of the living room. I shifted nervously as he turned it on and began playing different parts of popular new songs. I recognized several tunes written by Elton John. Then Mark got up and casually came towards me carrying a familiar looking microphone. I took it and examined it uncertainly as he sat back down at the piano without saying a word.

The song he began to play was one we had never sung before. I looked at him in confusion, just as Rena squeezed in next to me in the oversized chair. In her hand she held the printed lyrics to the melody he was playing. "Do you recognize it?" she asked before quietly beginning to sing the words herself.

> *White bird in a golden cage,*
> *on a winter's day,*
> *in the rain.*

I nodded and slowly raised the microphone to my lips. As usual Mark had chosen a song I couldn't resist trying to sing. It seemed that I was transfixed and time was standing still as Mark joined me, singing into his own microphone for the rest of the song. All our differences were forgotten as our voices rose in a crescendo:

> *The sunsets come, the sunsets go*
> *The clouds pile high, the air moves slow*
> *And the young birds eyes do always know*
> *She must fly - she must fly - she must fly!*

For a moment everything was quiet after the song ended. I suddenly realized that this was the first time Lillian and Laurie had ever heard us sing together. Mark smiled over the top of the piano as I gave my head a vigorous shake and handed the microphone to Rena.

"Well, on that note," Mark said, rising from his seat, "we'd better get you girls to the station before you miss another bus home! I think this is about the time one will be leaving for Tijuana."

He was right. At the bus station he bought our tickets and refused to take what was left of our own money. The busy surroundings seemed surreal as he walked us out to our bus to say goodbye, and I suddenly felt shy. "Mark, I don't know what to say," I told him uneasily before we boarded. "Can I send you the money to pay you back when I get home?"

Mark shook his head, then pulled my right hand up to shake it firmly. "This is on me," he told us with a warm smile. "Maybe someday you can pay me back if I ever need help."

It was with a strange mixture of sadness and relief that I thanked my old friend and said goodbye before climbing up the steps of the bus that would carry me home. Mark waited on the sidewalk to give us one final wave goodbye as we rolled out onto the busy street.

"Nice guy," Laurie remarked as she adjusted her long legs and leaned back in the seat to rest.

As we neared the highway and the mighty ocean came into clear view, I leaned back in my own chair and considered the unexpected experiences of the last two days. I found myself wondering: Did all of this happen by chance? Or, like the unseen powers moving the endless waves, had some strange fate shaped the last few days of my life, leading me to briefly reunite with my old friends? It's a question I ask myself still.

Twenty-One

Courtship Polygamous Style

I don't remember Verlan actually proposing to me. But I began to notice after our drive-in date in El Paso that the subject was coming up indirectly. When we would walk along the beach or sit talking in his pickup he would suddenly ask me a question like: "If we were to have a son together one day, what would you want to name him?" I didn't have an answer.

Maybe Verlan was questioning how deeply my feelings ran for him. I really had grown to enjoy his company, and I felt comfortable when he put his arm around me or held my hand, but I knew that I wasn't in love. I think he did too. During our time together he never pressed me to give my heart to him or commit myself to marriage, and for that I was grateful.

But things were about to become complicated. One day after returning from visiting with Kathy who was back in the area, my mother sat me down at the kitchen table to talk. "Your father and I had a visitor while you were gone," she told me nonchalantly. Although she was obviously pleased, she was trying not to show it.

"Really?" I asked. I could see that she was eager to tell me. "Who was it?"

"Verlan's son Chad was here," she responded almost too casually. "He is such a nice boy. Your dad and I really enjoyed talking to him." Here her expression became more serious, and she paused before continuing. "He asked for permission to court you."

I was taken aback. I had always enjoyed being around Verlan's and Lucy's oldest son, and had spent plenty of time with him lately along with my friends Rhea, Laura, and Donna who were his half-sisters. It was just last summer that we had taken our Driver's Training course together at the high school. The problem was that, even though he was probably only a few months younger than me, I had always related to him as my friends' younger brother.

I thought back to my recent outings with his sisters. Chad had often been there - friendly and thoughtful with a ready smile. We had fun together, and I liked that he was willing to laugh at my silly jokes. He had even paid my way to a movie when I was broke. The truth was he had become an unusually special young man. But now I was confused. "Does he know that his dad has been courting me for years?" I asked my mother.

Mom was expecting this question. "We talked to him about it," she said. "He thinks that life will be too hard for you if you marry his dad." I was touched that Chad wanted to protect me, although at this point I didn't really understand as well as he did all the difficulties I would face as a plural wife in such a large family. His mother was Verlan's third wife and Chad had experienced firsthand the stress, poverty, and rugged living conditions Lucy had endured with her many children.

Mom was moved by Chad's concern for me too. "He wants you to have a good life, and be happy," she continued. "Why don't you give him a chance?"

"I don't know, Mom," I said with a sigh. "I need some time to think." But the more I thought about it the more I became aware of the awkwardness of it all. If I were to consider Chad as a suitor, I would have to break off my relationship with his father. I certainly couldn't be courted by a father and his son at the same time, could I? I tried to imagine myself explaining to Verlan that I had decided to date his son instead of him. Would he become angry at Chad? What if it caused a rift between them? Thinking about it made me dizzy. It didn't take long for me to face the fact that my situation was more than awkward - it was bizarre.

I can't remember what Chad and I said to each other when he approached me looking handsome and clean-shaved a few days later. I knew that he was nervous as we talked alone in his car. I was numb with confusion. How could I tell him that being close to him in a romantic way, after being held in his father's arms, was something that I couldn't deal with emotionally? The truth was that I wasn't sure that I would ever marry either Chad or Verlan, and I couldn't bear to come between them.

But on that day I was tongue tied - I didn't know how to put into words all the thoughts and feelings that were troubling me. Did I tell Chad I cared for him like a brother? I'm not sure. At the time I only knew that I didn't want to hurt him. Ironically, what I do remember vividly about that day was the acute inner pain I experienced for doing just that. I told him my answer was no. It's a memory that haunts me to this day.

During this time of my life, I was being invaded by growing feelings of intense uneasiness and confusion. Unexpectedly, Verlan's daughters, Rhea and Donna, moved into the Los Angeles area where they were provided with jobs by a visiting English teacher they had met at a public school near Los Molinos. The friendly woman had even given them a place to stay, thus opening the door outside the church environment they were born and raised in. My friends had suddenly stepped out of my life into a new world.

Verlan's daughter Laura was now the only unmarried friend living close enough for me to socialize with, and even she was often in Los Molinos at the home of her mother, Charlotte. A sense of loneliness added to my depression.

In the midst of my discouragement, I was approached by the mother of my friend Lillie. Jeanine, a friendly lady with pretty blue eyes and thick brown hair always pulled back, had been Joel's second wife. I was told that she had converted with her family from a different FLDS polygamist group where she had been the very young bride of a much older man. At the time of her marriage to Joel she already had four children. One of them was Lillie, and the youngest was Ivan, the boy who remained with Joel at the house where his stepfather was murdered.

Following Joel's death, Jeanine had taken a special interest in me. Perhaps sensing my growing loss of direction, she tried to encourage me to find my own special calling in our church. One idea she discussed with me was to consider becoming a sort of colony nurse in Colonia LeBaron. She went out of her way to arrange for me to have a few special sessions with Linda, the midwife who, in spite of having a large family of her own, also fulfilled the duties of a practical nurse in the growing colony. Linda taught me how to give shots to oranges and let me look through her many medical books but that was about as far as my medical education went.

Now back in San Diego Jeanine sought me out again. One evening in late summer after inviting me out to a popular movie about a polygamist named Dr. Zhivago, she lingered to talk in her car outside my parents' apartment before dropping me off.

It was here that she took upon herself the unusual task of proposing to me. "Have you ever considered marrying Joel?" she asked, seemingly out of nowhere.

The unexpected words hung between us in the cool night air as I struggled to comprehend their meaning. I turned to look at her. The dim light from a nearby street lamp revealed a genuine smile on her gentle features. "You still can, you know," she added softly, "if you want to be in our family."

"But...how?" I asked, feeling a tinge of morbid fascination. "Joel's dead," I reminded her foolishly.

"You can be sealed to him in this life," she explained. "Then you and all of your earthly children would belong to him in eternity." Jeanine clasped her hands together and studied me with a loving smile as she let her words sink in. I knew that in Mormon doctrine two people could be married not only for time, but sealed to one another for all of eternity - but I had never considered that it was possible to marry a dead man.

"But what about the person I marry on earth?" I asked in confusion.

Jeanine shrugged her slender shoulders. "He would have to agree to raise a family for Joel," she said simply. I realized that this might not be a problem since my future husband would likely already have numerous wives and children to claim as his own in the hereafter.

I looked away from her and shook my muddled head. Like a little girl, Jeanine giggled at my bewilderment. "Why don't you just think about it?" she urged gently. "And if you decide that you would like to be a part of Joel's family - a part of *our* family - it can still be done."

After a moment, she changed the subject. "Kim, why don't you consider asking Brother Wakeham for a patriarchal blessing while he's in town?" I stared at her as a second wave of confusion washed over me. "It's a special blessing conferred by a man of the priesthood," she continued. "I had one when I was a young woman going through a trying time and it helped me to keep my faith."

"How does it work?" I asked with growing interest. Jeanine must have sensed the truth that I was trying to hide from myself. The fact was that my faith in our church was being severely challenged since the death of our prophet.

"Well," she explained solemnly, "in my case, a man in the priesthood of our old church laid his hands on my head and told me special things about myself and prophesied things that God wanted to reveal to me. It was really inspiring." Here she paused to observe my thoughtful expression. " Why don't you go talk to Bruce Wakeham?" she repeated. "He's staying in a room at one of the apartments in San Ysidro."

A few days later I wasn't surprised to find Brother Wakeham, who had three wives, living like a bachelor in a second story bedroom at the apartment of one of Jeanine's sisters. By now I thought it was normal to encounter a polygamist man of the church traveling and moving about separately from his wives and families, and I didn't question it at all.

I had seen this prominent church leader many times and had heard him speak at conferences. I knew that he and his beautiful first wife, Juna, were from the group of former French missionaries who had converted from the Mormon church, but I had never spoken directly to Brother Wakeham. Understandably, I was a little self conscious as I sat in an old upright chair and explained to him the reason for my visit. He was seated in an office chair at a desk placed near a double bed, the only piece of furniture that reminded me we were in a bedroom.

I soon relaxed as the friendly dark haired man, who looked to be in his late thirties, leaned back in his chair and listened to my request for the special blessing, focusing on me with intelligent dark-lashed eyes. After asking a few questions about myself, he told me to return in a week. "I would like to give the matter some thought and prayer," he told me kindly. His smile was warm and easy.

When I returned the following week, Brother Wakeham had more questions for me and I answered them politely, hoping that our conversation would end with an inspiring blessing that very day. But seeming to have temporarily forgotten my request, he suddenly took the conversation in a whole new direction. "Is there anyone you are interested in right now?" he asked rather casually.

Although I felt a surge of embarrassment, I straightened in my chair and answered boldly. "I've been dating Verlan for some time."

Mr. Wakeham didn't seem surprised. "Are you considering marrying him?" he asked as he absently reached over and fingered a pencil on his desk.

I hesitated before nodding, then answered, "Yes."

My spiritual consultant sighed and gave me a sad smile. "Verlan is in a position of great danger from Ervil's followers right now," he said quietly. "Are you aware of that?" All I could do was nod my head again. "You run a high risk of becoming a very young widow if you marry him," he added solemnly. "You could even be harmed yourself."

Brother Wakeham leaned back in his chair and studied me before continuing. "Verlan is constantly on the move to avoid Ervil's death threats," he reminded me. "His wives and children never know when they'll see him again." I gulped and stared at him. My anticipated blessing had somehow turned into a lecture on some very good reasons not to marry Verlan LeBaron.

Then he got right to the point. "I don't mean to embarrass you, but I believe the Lord wants you to be a part of my family." Taking in the look of surprise that must have been on my face, his voice softened. "I've already spoken to some of my wives about you," he said gently, "and after praying about it we agreed that I should get to know you better."

"I don't know what to say, Brother Wakeham..." I began shakily, but he interrupted me.

"Call me Bruce," he said breaking into a handsome smile.

"Bruce," I repeated lamely and felt myself blushing. Bruce chuckled.

"Will you go out to dinner with me sometime next week?" he asked.

I cleared my throat and nodded my head helplessly. "Okay," I croaked awkwardly. From that point on, all discussion of my patriarchal blessing somehow vanished into thin air.

My courtship with Bruce turned out to be a short one. Unlike Verlan, he was not willing to wait indefinitely for an answer, and as with Verlan who for the time being was nowhere to be found, I was not inclined to commit myself to him.

On our fourth date Bruce gifted me with a lovely small silver and turquoise necklace of an unusual design he had purchased in New Mexico. I felt uncomfortable accepting it, but at the time I didn't understand why. I thought it would be rude to simply say, "No thank you."

On our fifth date, after draping his jacket over my shoulders, he put his arm around me as we walked along a deserted beach. But when he pressed me for my feelings about marrying him on our next outing, I was honest. The truth was that I liked talking to him - enjoyed his company - but I wasn't ready to say yes to marriage. He didn't call on me anymore after that.

Later I learned that Bruce Wakeham treated his wives differently than most of the other men of the church. For one thing, they were allowed to participate in the decision of who would join their family. He also agreed that he would not kiss anyone to whom he was not engaged, which was somewhat of a comfort to his women as they stayed home raising large families. In practice, Bruce was not a frivolous courter of women. He wouldn't waste his time or his families' money courting someone who was not genuinely interested in him. I respected Bruce for that. But I didn't love him.

Thoughts of courtship and marriage to the living and the dead were pushed to the back of my mind when my sister Carolyn reappeared on the scene from Mexico City with her husband and five children. However, adding to my dismay, was the surprising fact that they would not be in town for long.

"I can't believe that you just got back, and you're leaving again," I complained as we hugged each other good-bye one autumn day on the sidewalk outside of Judy's place. All of our family had gathered there for a farewell lunch.

"I know," Carolyn responded with a slow understanding smile. Her long red hair which had never been cut short, was pulled gracefully into a bun on the back of her head. "But this is something we feel is important to do," she explained as she pulled away to straighten the black jacket of her modern pantsuit, "and it's something Joel wanted us to do also."

It seemed to me like a scene from a far-fetched dream. Incredibly, my sister and brother-in-law were taking their children and heading half way around the world to a little country I had often heard about in the news. Their destination was Israel, and they weren't going as typical American tourists, but as a Jewish family migrating to the promised land. Steven was a man who knew how to make things happen, and somehow he had won the assistance and financial aid of the Israeli government. Upon their arrival in the Jewish homeland they would be assimilated into a communal styled settlement called a "kibbutz."

My brother-in-law, whose last name was Silver, believed that out of shame his father had not only rejected but denied his own Jewish identity. Now Steven was about to reclaim it for himself and his family.

Later it was explained to me that before his death, Joel had encouraged Steven to learn more about the daily operations and government on an Israeli kibbutz. Both of my brothers-in-law wondered if the principles lived there could be used as a blueprint for what used to be called the "United Order" in the days of Joseph Smith. Such an ideal society once envisioned by the Mormon church founder, where folks shared the work and wealth of the community, might be put to use by the struggling people of our own colonies.

But now as they prepared to leave, I only knew that my father was taking my sister's family to the airport, and none of us was sure when we would meet again. "We'll send lots of pictures and postcards," Carolyn promised us as she squeezed into the front passenger seat of the car. "Good luck on your job search, Kim!" she called before pulling the door firmly closed.

It wasn't long before the postcards started arriving as the family toured Israel before settling on their kibbutz. And before summer, I had found a job.

I was to be a nanny for the two-year-old granddaughter of a wealthy widow named June. Coincidentally, the family was Jewish. Leila was a beautiful and intelligent child whose mother was a divorced international model who traveled extensively - in fact I didn't meet her for at least six months after I began taking care of her daughter.

Leila's grandmother lived in a penthouse on the upper floor of a high security building in an exclusive area of San Diego. To my delight I would be sharing a smaller, cute one bedroom apartment next door with little Leila.

After working at a glove factory, this was a young girl's dream job. I was expected to clean up both apartments and do the laundry, but aside from those duties my main responsibility was to care for Leila and keep her entertained. The two of us loved to snuggle in the big chair near the balcony of our apartment where I would read to her out of her favorite over-sized picture books. And if we needed exercise and fresh air, we had only to walk across the street to the serenity of lovely Balboa Park to feed the birds and chase the bubbles we blew.

June was a kind and easygoing woman who appreciated having a younger energetic person around to play with her granddaughter. She enjoyed making our dinner and introduced me to such delicacies as boiled tongue-- which I cut into tiny pieces and tried to swallow without chewing - and liver cooked rare. "Why are you using all of that ketchup?" she admonished me on one of those evenings. "You're ruining the flavor of the liver!"

I thought Leila looked like a child version of Snow White. Sometimes strangers even stopped me on the street to comment on the beauty of the raven- haired child whose copper brown eyes and dark lashes contrasted vividly against lily-white skin.

On weekends I would leave Leila with her grandmother and return to my parents' apartment, visit with any friends who happened to be in town, and on Sundays I would go to church. Sometimes on an evening during the week, I would get away to a fireside youth meeting. And I would see Verlan when he was in town. I really had nothing to complain about, but inside I was becoming restless. It seemed that something was missing from my life.

One day while I was watching Sesame Street on the television with Leila, I got an unusual phone call from Kathy who was staying at her apartment in San Ysidro. "I just got some interesting news," she said with an hint of excitement in her voice. " I thought you should know about it."

"What did ya hear?" I asked with keen interest. Kathy was not the type to indulge in idle gossip. I knew that this news would be worth listening to.

" I just heard that Verlan got married to Helen in Colonia LeBaron," she told me. There was a moment of silence as Kathy let the information sink in. I didn't know what to say - I felt as though I had just been given a mild shock.

Helen, one of my favorite people in Colonia LeBaron, was a long-time widow and the mother of one of my best friends named Debbie who had been my roommate in El Paso. They had a pleasant home in the colony with dairy goats and a cow to provide the large family with milk. Helen always welcomed me to sleep over with her hardworking daughter, and shared the tasty food of her homey kitchen.

Already a grandmother, my friend's mom was the kind of person who always seemed to be doing something useful with her time. Even when chatting with company in her living room, or while watching a group of us young people play board games at her table, she usually had some sort of sewing project on her lap to keep her hands busy.

No, I had nothing at all against Helen. It was just that, after years of courting me, Verlan had given no hint of his intentions to marry her. It made me feel so... unimportant. "This is not the way for a polygamist to make the women in his life feel special," I told Kathy gloomily.

At this Kathy let out a half-hearted laugh. "You'd better get used to it," she cautioned, "he probably didn't even tell all of his wives!" I found out later that most of Verlan's wives were as surprised as I was. Their husband had gone and taken a new wife pretty much without warning anyone.

After saying goodbye to Kathy, I hung up the phone and shook myself. Who was I to complain? Although Verlan had been very patient in our courtship, I had never committed myself to him in any way.

But at the next fireside meeting I heard something else that troubled me. It was there that I met up with my good friend Deanna who now had a little boy of her own, named Samuel after his father. Sammy, as we called her husband, was one of Alma's older boys.

I didn't get to see much of Deanna these days and we eagerly sought each other out after the meeting. I was beginning to feel like my old self again as we talked and laughed, indulging ourselves in the cookies, cupcakes, and punch being served in the kitchen of the home where the meeting was held.

At some point everyone else wandered back into the living room and we found ourselves alone. It was then that Deanna suddenly became serious. "Did you know that the women of the church are supposed to be like possessions to their husbands?" she asked me unexpectedly. The question was an honest one - as if she thought it was something we had neglected talking about in our younger days.

"What do you mean?" I responded in surprise as I dipped myself a glass of punch from the punch bowl.

"You might as well get used to it," she continued, sounding very matter-of-fact as she leaned against the wall. "Wives are sort of like valuable cattle to them."

"Oh come on, Deanna," I said with a laugh. I assumed that she was joking... but she refused to smile.

"No, Kim - it's true," she insisted. Although her voice was calm she sounded a little stunned by her own discovery. Taking in my look of disbelief she became frustrated. "I'm serious!" she exclaimed. " A married woman doesn't get to make decisions about much of anything. Even little things. It's like we rank just above our husbands' livestock." Then she added in bewilderment, "Why do you think God did that to us?"

The next time I saw Verlan, he didn't mention hearing anything about my dating Bruce, and I didn't say a word about his marriage to Helen. But I did have a few questions for him. "Is it true, that in our church a woman is almost like an animal under her husband's authority?" I demanded.

Instead of being defensive, Verlan looked amused. "Who told you a thing like that?" he asked, trying to suppress a smile.

"My friend did," I responded curtly. "Is it true? Because if it is, I want to know."

Verlan, who was leaning against the inside door of his pickup, sat up straight. His face was serious, and earnest blue eyes looked directly into mine. "A woman wasn't meant to be treated like an animal by her husband or anyone else," he replied emphatically.

"Do you think we're not much more than valuable livestock once you marry us?" I pressed on bluntly. I wanted to know flat out if our church leader saw things the way that Deanna's husband did.

If Verlan was feeling the urge to smile at this unexpected question, he kept it firmly in check. "I absolutely don't think that way," he replied without hesitating.

Feeling my indignation ebbing under his innocent gaze, I let out a sigh. Verlan seemed so sincere. How could I doubt him? But after he dropped me off at Kathy's apartment, I was left with a puzzling emptiness inside. After all this time, I really didn't feel that I knew Verlan very well, and I was even more confused about how I felt about him.

Such feelings didn't really disturb me for long because, as usual, Verlan was soon gone again.

Twenty-Two

Superstition

O ne day not long after my last date with Verlan, I stopped by
Judy's apartment. It was the last day of my weekend off from
caring for little Leila, and that evening I found my sister busily
fixing dinner for her brood of five children. Although her belly
was already swollen with a new family member waiting to be born, she
moved about the small kitchen with expert efficiency. I pulled up a chair
and watched as she tossed patties made of cooked macaroni into a hot
frying pan to brown. This was Judy's own low-budget original recipe
which her family loved to eat with her special homemade sauce.

She paused behind the counter just long enough to tell me some
surprising news. "Mark Chynoweth called for you yesterday." She gave
me a look of concern as she reached for the spatula before returning to
the stove. "He said his name was Mike." She shook her head and rolled
her eyes. "I didn't tell him that I recognized his voice. I just took down
the number he told me to have you call."

My sister left the pan of sizzling patties to rummage quickly through
a pile of miscellaneous papers on the counter near the phone. She
examined the back of an old envelope before tossing it in my direction.
Picking it up, I saw an unfamiliar phone number she had written there in
her neat script. "You'd better be careful," she admonished me firmly. I
nodded in agreement.

After I left Judy's a few hours later, I drove along the relatively quiet
San Diego freeway, heading north for the apartment I shared with Leila.
As I whizzed past a slow-moving car, I found myself smiling as I
remembered how Mark used to tease me about having "lead toe nails"
when I would speed around on the dirt roads of Los Molinos in my
parents' car.

Pulling into the underground parking lot of our apartment building, I
resolved to sleep on the decision of whether to return his phone call. But
I was only kidding myself. The truth was that by morning, I was dying
of curiosity - I couldn't wait to hear what my old friend had to say.

I went through my morning routine with Leila, and a few hours later
after dialing the number Judy had given me, Mark was surprised when he
answered the phone to hear me asking for him by name. "How did you
know it was me?" he asked sounding mystified.

"It's not like Judy doesn't know you, Mark," I reminded him dryly.
"She recognized your voice." There was a pause.

"Why didn't she just say so?" Mark was clearly embarrassed.

I tried to suppress a laugh. "Maybe she was under the impression you didn't want her to know who was calling?"

Mark chuckled. "I thought I was being smooth," he confessed sulkily. For a moment I felt at ease. It was good to laugh with him again - almost like old times.

"Listen," Mark said, bringing me back to reality with his serious tone, "I was wondering if we could get together somewhere. I have some important things I want to talk to you about." He waited quietly as I considered his request.

It had been over two years since Joel's murder, and no other acts of violence had taken place. Was it possible that Mark and Lillian had decided to leave Ervil's church? For some reason I still trusted Mark. Perhaps because of our uneventful stay at his house in Ensenada, I decided that there would be no real risk in meeting with him again.

"I'm a nanny now, Mark," I told him cheerfully. "I can't get away until next weekend." I hesitated before asking. "If it's okay with my boss, would you like to talk at my place?"

The next evening, Mark rang the buzzer to my apartment. I pushed the button that would allow him into the elevator and then waited for him in the hall with Leila by my side. He emerged from the open elevator doors looking impressed. "Nice place," he said with a familiar grin.

"Come on in," I told him with a heartfelt smile. No matter what the upcoming subject was to be, we were both happy to see each other, and it was in a relaxed mood that I plopped down on the couch with Leila, while Mark took the comfy chair opposite us after looking around the room.

There was a tap at the door and Leila's grandmother, who had been expecting his arrival, came in to say hello. "This is my old friend, Mark," I said, introducing her. June didn't stay long but before she left Mark had her smiling and at ease with his friendly conversation. How I wanted to believe that my charming companion had changed back into the person I once knew.

For the next half hour or so we engaged in small talk - about his little boy who was growing fast, and about my job with Leila. Of course one of the topics of discussion was music. "Have you heard Stevie Wonder's new album?" he asked enthusiastically. "It has 'Living for the City' on it." Mark shook his head with a look of awe on his face before adding, "I swear - the guy is a genius."

When it was Leila's bedtime, we visited a little longer until she was sleeping soundly. Then I had an idea. "You wanna take a look at the view from the roof?" I asked suddenly.

Mark stood up and stretched before answering. "Sure," he said with a relaxed smile. I rang up June and asked her to listen for Leila over the intercom before leading Mark up a flight of private stairs located in the hallway. The locked door we exited opened out onto the expansive roof of the tall building near the entry of a modern exercise room.

As we emerged from the tiny stairway, the night was dark but the sky was clear and stars were shining as we stood leaning on the rail side by side, shivering in the crisp air of early December. Gazing out over the rooftops of buildings and houses, we took in the endless landscape of the glittering lights of San Diego. To our right they sparkled like diamonds someone had generously scattered across the dark water of the distant bay.

"Wow," Mark breathed almost reverently. I nodded in silent agreement. Our eyes met and we both smiled. He seemed so at ease - so much like his old self. Once again I found it hard to believe so much had changed in our lives. After a few minutes of thoughtful silence a cold breeze urged us back into the warmth of the building.

The first indication that the comfortably illusive spell that had settled over us was about to be broken, was when Mark pulled out a small briefcase he had left sitting beside his chair back in the apartment. "What is Steven Silver doing now- a-days?" he asked absently, as he pulled out a Bible and a trilogy of Mormon scriptures along with several small pamphlets that I couldn't identify.

"He and Carolyn are coming back from Israel soon," I told him enthusiastically. "They've been living on a kibbutz and learned all about it."

"Kibbutz?" Mark looked puzzled. For a moment, I hoped that this topic of conversation would take the place of whatever Mark was obviously gearing up for.

"Yeah, it's a real interesting way of life where the people share all of the property and the money they earn from a common business."

"Isn't that communism?" he asked with interest.

"Steven says it's different because the communities are small and all the members get to vote on everything - even money issues. Each kibbutz sort of governs itself."

Mark nodded thoughtfully. "Steven always was a smart guy," he remarked. "I liked him." He frowned and shook his head before adding, "But somehow he's gotten off on the wrong track."

Then, as in the past, Mark began to teach me. His tone was different than it used to be - his words sounding more urgent and serious than ever. I listened and shrank inwardly as he spoke. There was no doubt that the teachings of Ervil were still at the center of his beliefs. In the mind of my old friend, the towering dark man who had succeeded in having his own brother murdered, was still a powerful prophet of God - a prophet who had shown himself to be feared, and now intended to leave no doubt in the minds of the rest of the world, that he meant to be obeyed. Mark believed that a new world was coming.

His voice softened as he spoke of his little boy again. "I look around and see all of the corruption in the world today, and I think to myself..." he paused and shook his head sadly, "I don't want this for my son." He continued on this gentler note - trying to convey to me what the earth would be like once all governments were subject to the laws of God. Here I found myself nodding in agreement. How truly wonderful it would be to watch each child grow up in a perfect and blessed society. But the peaceful image in my mind quickly faded as Mark continued, explaining that it was Ervil who would be responsible for revealing these laws. He would also see to it that the laws were enforced.

Now Mark thumbed expertly through the pages of the books he had brought, reading scriptures Ervil had obviously hand-picked - verses that seemed to imply that the use of force would be employed by God's fearless people to establish His Kingdom.

Mark began reading about a man named Ananias from the book of Acts in the Bible. *"'Ananias, how was it that Satan so possessed your mind that you lied to the Holy Spirit, and kept back part of the price of the land?...You have lied not to men but to God.' When Ananais heard these words he dropped dead."*

Mark chuckled wisely. "Don't you see that this was written to shield the apostles from the authorities at that time?" he asked. He scanned ahead, then read out loud again, *"Then Peter said (to the wife of Ananais) 'Why did you both conspire to put the Spirit of the Lord to the test? Hark! There at the door are the footsteps of those who buried your husband; and they will carry you away.'"* Mark shook his head gravely. "Isn't it obvious what really happened? Ananais and his wife were both executed by the disciples of Jesus Christ." I closed my eyes and caught my breath.

As he read scriptures describing battles with young men fighting like mighty warriors against the enemies of God, the terrifying reality of what Mark was saying dawned on me. He was talking about bloodshed not only for those who were found guilty of breaking God's laws, but for anyone who rejected Ervil's authority. And Mark considered himself a warrior.

Then he turned to a page in the book of Isaiah from the Bible: *"Behold my servant shall deal prudently, he shall be exalted and extolled very high....So shall he sprinkle many nations; the kings shall shut their mouths at him; for that which had not been told them shall they see; and that which they had not heard shall they consider."* Scanning down he continued reading out loud: *"He is despised and rejected of men; a man of sorrows, and acquainted with grief; and we hid as it were our faces from him; he was despised and we esteemed him not.*"

Mark paused and looked at me. "Don't you think that sounds like Ervil?" he asked reverently. I breathed a sigh of relief as he continued with his discourse without waiting for an answer. He went on to explain that eventually Ervil would be given miraculous powers that would command the attention of all nations.

I found myself breathing shallowly, staring wordlessly at Mark as he began to tell me about God's people ultimately living in luxury on the spoils of what was left after the religious wars and destructions were over. "Think of all the wealth that'll be left," he said with a gleam of excitement in his eyes. "It will be there for the taking by the courageous people who have fought for the laws of God." Then speaking in the tone of one bearing even more good news, he proclaimed with a triumphant smile, "And those loyal people will even be rewarded with positions of authority in His government."

I tried to appear neutral although a shiver ran down my spine. Mark didn't sound at all like Mark anymore. He sounded exactly like Ervil.

Numbly I realized why he had found the subject of the simple Israeli kibbutz lifestyle so uninteresting. It could in no way compare to the grandeur of the promises offered by Ervil. He had promised his followers not only complete happiness during his Godly reign, but he would share with them all the wealth and power of ruling the world - once they had conquered it for him.

For the first time, I sensed a very real danger in challenging my friend's words in any way. I kept my alarmed thoughts to myself as he continued eagerly sharing the insights he so deeply believed.

"You see Kim, people have to be educated about the truth - and if they accept it, it will set them free," he told me earnestly, now winding down. Then, leaning back in his chair, he quoted a verse from a song - a verse that I will never forget: "When you believe in things that you don't understand - you suffer." I stared dumbly, this time struck speechless by the irony of his words. But Mark gave me a comfortable smile. "'Superstition.' By Stevie Wonder," he added.

Mark rose from his chair and walked across the room holding a pamphlet in his hand. Sitting down beside me he offered it for my inspection. I struggled not to react as I scanned the cover bearing the title: "Hour of Crisis - Day of Vengeance" printed in bold letters. A vivid depiction of two hands grasping a raised sword seemed to jump out at me.

As I sat taking in the threatening words and image, I hoped that Mark, who sat silently waiting for my response, wouldn't hear the pounding of my heart. "I'll have to think about all this," I told him in a calm voice I heard coming from my own mouth.

"Kim, this is important," he told me soberly. "You understand how serious it is?" He shifted and looked at me intently. There was no hint of a smile in his eyes. All of the lightheartedness we had ever shared, seemed swallowed up in this moment. I was being warned.

"I understand," I responded looking directly back into his eyes. My mouth suddenly seemed very dry. "But I don't want to decide out of fear. I need some time."

Mark continued to gaze at me. Finally he nodded his head and sighed. "Okay," he said flatly. He rose and walked across the room to his briefcase where he slowly replaced the pamphlets and books before pulling out a notepad and pencil and scribbling something down. Then he remained standing as he tore off the page and held it out to me. "I won't be able to come here again," he told me with a look of resignation. "But this is a number you can call if you decide to join us. They'll know how to find me."

I took the paper from his hand and followed him to the door where he turned to face me. "Mark..." I began shakily. He stood looking quietly at me. "Mark, what you are talking about is scary." I hesitated before continuing. " What you are thinking of doing is....scary." He nodded.

I was afraid to confront him with how crazy I thought it all sounded - but I was too pressed by my fear *for* him, not to give him some sort of warning of my own. I chose my words carefully, "I hope... I hope for your sake that you will consider what could happen to you - how serious the consequences would be if you're wrong." I could think of nothing more to say. Although I had spoken politely, the air was charged with emotion.

To my surprise, his eyes softened and a look of complete tenderness settled over Mark's face. I could see that he was genuinely touched by my concern for him. He closed his eyes for a few seconds. Then he looked at me, shook his head, and smiled. "Don't worry about me, Kim," he said softly. "I'll be all right.You don't need to worry," he repeated as he reached for my hand to give it a gentle squeeze. Then he turned and walked away.

In Reply

In another time, in another place
I looked around and saw a face

The face of a friend I was soon to find
for I spoke with your soul
and conversed with your mind

Then months and years
held our friendship steadfast
and only destiny wept
for what she knew would not last

Through the simplicity of the time
we roamed side by side
'til enveloped by an ocean
at the change of its tide

In a later time, in another place
I looked around and saw a face

My heart leapt with joy
at the sight of my friend!
We spoke, my heart wept
for the beginning of the end

A warning was given
of the course I should take
and I answer you now
though my life be at stake

Words too shallow
for the importance of this
come straight from the heart
and fall from my lips

Friend, I rebuke you
and the words that you speak
from your teachings I turn
from your heart take my leave

For what I believe,
my own life I would give,
though my breath might be taken
I would not die, but live.

Kim Wariner December 1974
Written for Mark following our last visit

Twenty-three

Hour of Crisis
Day of Vengeance

In the days following his visit I contemplated Mark's warning. For years he had been like a kind and cheerful brother to me - was he now really capable of extreme violence in the name of religion? Two terrible questions loomed in my mind above all others: Would Mark actually kill for Ervil? Would he even try to kill me?

Rumors that Ervil's congregation had made blood covenants with one another, promising to carry out Ervil's murderous death threats, chilled my heart and filled me with dread. Residents of Colonia LeBaron, who had received copies of the same pamphlet Mark had shown me, took extra steps to beef up security there, yet weeks went by and nothing happened.

When Christmas Eve rolled peacefully around, I found myself happily celebrating the holiday at Kathy's place along with my parents, Judy, and her children. I was excited because with my own money I had purchased a portable washing machine that Mom and Dad could conveniently use in their small apartment. Leila's thoughtful grandmother had even sewed a custom vinyl cover to go over the top of it. Since the machine was much too big to wrap, my sisters had helped me plan a simple treasure hunt with Mom and Dad eventually ending up in Kathy's out-door storage shed where sat the little gold appliance with a huge red bow.

On the twenty-sixth of December I returned to Leila whose mother had just left after visiting her for a few days. That evening, before Leila's bedtime, the two of us stood together on our balcony, briefly admiring the long strands of Christmas lights strung up somewhere in the distance to create the image of a huge Christmas tree that could be seen from miles away.

The night was peaceful and quiet as I tucked the sleepy two-year-old in her cozy bed in the room that we shared. Then I sat down on the sofa to think. I realized I had not seen a single friend over the holidays. Everyone was gone - even Laura, who was still in Los Molinos spending time with her mother.

What I didn't know was that a friend she had met through Rhea and Donna at their new job in the L.A. area had joined her there for the holidays. Doug seemed to have fallen in love with the beautiful Laura - but Laura, who was deeply dedicated to our religion, regarded him only as a friend. Laura's three brothers were away, but her mother Charlotte and her younger sisters had graciously welcomed the attractive and friendly young man into their home.

That night as I picked up a book and settled down in bed to read in my silent San Diego apartment, Charlotte and her three oldest daughters were laughing and talking with Doug around the kitchen table in their snug home in Los Molinos. Because it was getting close to ten o'clock, the two youngest children of the family, Loretta and Natalie, were already sleeping soundly in the bed they shared.

Laura stretched restlessly in her chair and looked at her watch. The Monopoly game they were playing seemed to be never-ending, and she was beginning to wish that she too could crawl into her own warm bed for the night. It was then that she became aware of a strange intermittent popping sound coming from somewhere outdoors in the distance. Curious, one of the children looked out of the living room window to see a glowing fire at the far side of the colony.

The concerned family gathered around to get a better look at what was happening. What they saw stunned them. A pickup was slowly moving through the colony from one house to another as what appeared to be firebombs were thrown from the vehicle onto the roofs, leaving each house ablaze in its wake! Charlotte's family froze in horror. The popping sound they had heard in the distance was the sound of gunfire and - along with the pickup, it was coming their way.

Abruptly, the group sprang into action - running to wake the sleeping children before ushering them out into the cold winter night. It seemed like a nightmare come to life as they raced, tripping barefoot through the darkness into the weedy field behind their house.

Suddenly Charlotte stopped, "Doug's car!" she cried. "Let's get it to the back of the house in case we need it!" Not wanting to be heard or seen by the approaching gunmen, they worked frantically to quietly push the compact vehicle into the dark field where hopefully it would not be noticed by their approaching attackers.

There amidst the young olive trees the family had planted, they threw themselves down behind a berm of raised earth near the well. It hardly seemed high enough to hide them, yet there they waited breathlessly - shivering violently on the hard, cold earth. They didn't have to wait long. As the menacing pickup truck rolled to a stop in front of the house, the terrified family listened as sounds of gunfire and breaking glass erupted, filling the peaceful night with destruction. Three dark figures jumped out of the back of the pickup and darted around the house only three hundred feet away from their intended victims, firing repeatedly into every window of the now unoccupied home.

Still not satisfied with their devastating handiwork, the gunmen began to throw what seemed like an endless array of flaming Molotov cocktails onto the roof. Tears rolled down the children's faces, as the shelter the hardworking family had so painstakingly built - had been so grateful to have, burst into flames.

Seven-year-old Natalie - the youngest of the family - squirmed in the agony of her terror. What if the gunmen came just a little closer and saw them? Would the wicked attackers throw fiery bombs at them before showering her family with bullets? Even in her young mind, she knew that they made a perfect target - the seven of them huddled together helplessly there in a shallow ditch.

Her mother must have had the same thought, for as the fire began to spread across the roof of their house, the destroying angels sped away - and the family they believed they had just destroyed, now sat huddled together in the shelter of Doug's car watching them depart.

Using the back road that ran alongside Charlotte's property to exit the colony, the cunning attackers tossed nail studded boards from the pickup bed to delay anyone who might try to pursue them. As the sound of the pickup's engine faded in the distance, Charlotte's dazed family crept numbly out of the car and returned to see what was left of their home.

Although the roof of my friends' home was ablaze, their windows shattered, and ugly bullet holes covered the walls - they felt blessed. Not one of them had been hurt. Soon another blessing arrived in the form of the teen aged son of Irene and Verlan. Steven, Laura's younger half-brother, wasted no time in climbing onto the roof of the house where he bravely began to throw the flaming cocktails onto the ground. The fearless youngster eventually succeeded in putting out the fire and then, without stopping to rest, raced across the colony going from house to house to help others.

Steven was a hero that night - a rescuing angel who saved many of the homes from complete destruction. My parents' vacant house, located near the Chynoweth home on the opposite side of the colony where the initial attack took place, had been untouched.

Sadly, some of the other people in the colony had been terribly wounded. Ray Dambacher, who years earlier had transported my sister Kathy to the hospital in Ensenada, was shot in the legs so badly that he had to have help driving a pickup through the colony. His helper was Benjamin Zarate who had actually been shot in the head. Brother Dambacher worked the clutch, while Brother Zarate steered and used the accelerator and brake pedals as the two seriously-injured men slowly made the rounds, collecting the injured residents of Los Molinos in the back of the pickup to take them to the hospital of San Quintin.

The heartbroken families of sixteen-year-old Manases Mendez, and twenty-four-year old Edmundo Aguilar watched helplessly as the two young men eventually died from their injuries. Manases had been shot in the chest as he bravely battled the first fire, and Edmundo was shot in the head through a window after jumping out of his bed set ablaze by a Molotov cocktail. Fifteen other people were wounded.

Although devastating, the results of the attack could have been much worse. Charlotte later learned that the large fire her family had first seen was a two story tower on the far side of the colony that had been quietly set ablaze at the beginning of the siege. The cunning attackers then hid themselves in the surrounding darkness and waited as helpful, unsuspecting residents of the colony arrived to try to put out the mysterious fire. Then, when it seemed that no one else was coming, the raiders opened fire. They shot mercilessly at the confused and unarmed men, women, and youngsters before proceeding on a trek of destruction, driving the pickup to attack other houses of the colony.

There would certainly have been more fatalities and injuries during the first part of the assault if some of the victims had not escaped into the darkness. Others played dead, laying motionless near the burning tower after being wounded or shot at. As the pickup continued along on its path, its passengers succeeded in firebombing and shooting up more than twenty-four homes before attacking Charlotte's house and then disappearing into the night.

It was the very next day that news of the attack reached us in San Diego. "Kim, there was an attack on Los Molinos last night," Judy told me tensely over the phone that sad morning. "We don't have all the details yet, but someone said that two American women were killed," she added, sounding on the verge of tears.

Frantically, I searched my mind for the names of the American women I thought might have been in the colony. *Please God - not Charlotte or Lucy*, I prayed silently. And where was Irene? Wasn't she visiting someone in the U.S.?

The next few days were filled with fearful anticipation as we waited to hear the details. I eventually learned that no women had been killed in the attack. I also heard that survivors were naming some of Ervil's young followers as their attackers. The list of names they provided included Don Sullivan - the young man Mark invited me to sing for in San Diego, Mark's brother Duane, and Mark himself.

No - it can't be true, I told myself. Mark couldn't kill anyone. He wouldn't attack Charlotte's home where he had often spent time with us - his friends - singing, laughing, and playing games. He must have only watched, and inwardly grieved as others did the dirty work.

150

Yet if what witnesses later said was true, it was Mark himself who had been the one to fire the fatal shot into the chest of sixteen-year-old Manases who now lay in his grave.

Now lonely and miserable in my apartment, I struggled to understand as Leila played happily with her toys nearby. *I should be angry at Mark.* I was. I wanted to slap him in the face - punch him with my fists. *I should bitterly hate the man who attacked my friends - wounding and killing defenseless, good natured people.* But I didn't.

I knew that something beyond his own understanding had possessed my friend. Under the powerful influence of Ervil and others - perhaps most importantly his own mother - he had somehow become a pawn for a madman. He believed he was a warrior for God. Yet hadn't he somehow allowed himself to be deceived? I knew he was responsible for his own actions but... the Mark I knew wouldn't have done this.

Warm tears cascaded down my cheeks as I buried my face in my arms on the kitchen table. Although we had never become more than friends, Mark had still managed to break my heart.

The Butterfly - a Memory of Mark

"Oh, Lillie," I breathed in awe, "its gorgeous." I had never seen a butterfly so large and beautiful.

It was a lovely warm morning in Los Molinos. Mark and I peered into a large glass bowl sitting on the kitchen counter of Lillie's newly-built house. Through the transparent lid we could clearly see a dazzling butterfly, with large, stark-black wings brightly accented with deep orange bands sitting on the bottom of the bowl.

Mark shook his head in amazement. "Unbelievable," he marveled.

As we watched, the weakened butterfly began to struggle, fluttering about the bowl, dashing its delicate body against its glass prison. Mark grimaced and turned to Lillie. "Maybe you should just let it go."

"Let it go?" Lillie said in surprise. "Butterflies don't live long anyway," she reminded us, "and we'll never see another one like this."

We continued looking somberly at the exhausted creature now resting at the bottom of the bowl. "It's dying a slow death," Mark said quietly.

"It would be fun to watch it fly away," I murmured wistfully as the butterfly began to batter itself again.

Lillie stared at us - a bewildered frown clouding her blue eyes. Suddenly her face lit up in a smile. "Okay, you guys," she said with a tinkling laugh, "open the lid and set it free!"

And before we could move Lillie grabbed the bowl from the table. As she carefully lifted the lid the butterfly rose unsteadily from the container and began to flutter prettily about the room.

I looked at Mark in surprise, and the two of us began to scurry about the house, laughing like children as we chased the butterfly towards the front door that Lillie stood holding open.

Outside in the sunshine our laughter faded. Three good friends stood side-by-side happily gazing at the fading sight of colorful gossamer wings carrying the freed butterfly here and there in the fresh morning air.

Twenty-four

Close Encounters

Ervil was furious that Verlan had not been at the scene of the first fire. It seems that an important part of the bloody mission had not been accomplished that night. The master plan had been for the armed warriors to lure his uncooperative brother out into the open and kill him. We later learned that when Verlan did not materialize, Mark and the others had been forced to make an unauthorized decision, for they had been given strict orders not to open fire until Verlan appeared to help subdue the blaze. This was impossible, for our leader was traveling a very safe distance away from Los Molinos. In his search to buy land in Nicaragua, he had once again escaped the murderous plot of his older brother.

Disappointed with the lack of fatalities in what was supposed to be the beginning of his holy war on earth, the grim prophet decided to send yet another one of his henchmen to shed more blood. His victims were to be a group of weary Church of the Firstborners who had escaped with their lives during the first siege. Adding to Ervil's wrath was the fact that, these unrepentant "Joelites" planned to give testimony about the assault he had masterminded and bring criminal charges against those involved.

As they milled about on the sunlit sidewalk in front of the courthouse in Ensenada waiting for the judge to invite them in, Joel's hapless followers were stunned to see the tall familiar figure of former Los Molinos resident Raul Rios striding towards them. In his hand was a shotgun pointed menacingly in their direction.

Horrified, they realized that they were once again under attack, and this time there was no time to run and no darkness to hide them. As they watched, cringing helplessly, Raul moved closer as he aimed and prepared to fire. It should be easy to mow down these pesky witnesses - these avowed enemies of his leader and God's own servant.

What happened next was nothing short of miraculous - but it was not the sort of miracle Raul was expecting. For just as he pulled the trigger - he suddenly tripped. Instead of wounding his old friends and acquaintances, the shotgun blast peppered the sidewalk right next to their feet. Raul recovered and aimed again. He pulled the trigger....nothing happened. The gun was jammed.

Seeing that his intended victims had now decided to take the offensive, Raul threw down the shotgun and began running down the sidewalk with the small angry mob not far behind. He had only one hope of stopping them and accomplishing at least part of his mission. As he ran, he reached for a pistol hidden in his pocket and, still on the move, turned to aim yet again. He didn't have a chance to fire, nor did he see the telephone pole that suddenly seemed to jump up ahead of him - smartly knocking the gun out of his hand. The group closed in.

It was with dignity and restraint that the people who were supposed to be lying dead in front of the courthouse put their hands on their would-be murderer and escorted him to the police. Raul Rios was promptly thrown into jail.

The news of this event provided our church members with a surge of much- needed encouragement. But while we laughed joyfully at the description of Raul's unbelievable blunders, rumors of intimidating harassment by Ervil's followers surfaced in the San Diego area. Once again we were afraid

When my friend Laura called to tell me that she was now living with her family in San Ysidro, I took the first opportunity available to drive the used car my parents had given me to visit her there. I parked the car in front of the low-income townhouse apartments and knocked on the door. Before it opened, I thought I heard what sounded like something heavy being moved out of the way.

"Is that you, Kim?" I heard a familiar voice call nervously.

"Yep, it's only me," I answered reassuringly.

Finally the door opened and my friend stood before me. Laura was home alone. This was the first time I had seen her since the attack she had survived, and it was obvious that she had been extremely traumatized. I shook my head in amazement at the sight of the homemade booby traps she had placed under each window of the ground floor of the apartment. A nearly invisible string sagged under the weight of numerous pots and pans hanging across one large window. These were meant to not only trip a night time intruder entering that way, but to awaken the family with a crashing, metallic clatter.

I felt sorry for my friend. Didn't she realize that Ervil's people would not be interested in attacking a single apartment in the San Diego area? They probably didn't even know who lived here. Then again - the attack was still so fresh in her mind, I couldn't blame her.

"Come on up and we can talk in my bedroom," she said as she led me up the stairs. Once in her room, she locked the door behind us before we plopped down on the double bed where she began answering my questions, giving me a first hand account of all that had happened on that dreadful night, nearly a month ago. Over the next two hours, we talked - revealing our sense of loneliness and nagging worries to each other. I recognized that my friend was also feeling at least some of the loss of direction that I was experiencing. Neither one of us had answers to share.

When it came time for me to return to Leila, Laura walked me to the front door and hugged me before quickly locking it behind me. I stepped into the depressingly cold and deserted cloud-covered parking lot that late afternoon, anxious to be on my way to the warmth of my apartment. Taking quick purposeful strides, my long legs carried me the few steps across the narrow sidewalk to where I had parked a few hours earlier. I stopped abruptly and blinked. The parking space was empty.

Confused, I lifted my eyes to scan the area. And there - in the middle of the huge parking lot sat my little car. For a ridiculous moment, it seemed to be staring dejectedly back at me with its headlights, which were mysteriously on, while the driver's door hung unexpectedly wide open like a dangling injured wing.

I caught my breath and looked around. I saw many other empty cars parked neatly in their places, but no sign of a person. Was there a prankster hiding nearby? Keeping my eyes on my car, I backed slowly to the apartment door where I quickly turned to pound on it with my fist. "Laura! Open up! It's me - it's Kim!" I heard the bolt on the door slide open and Laura stood looking at me questioningly. "About my car," I told her dazedly. "It's been...moved."

"What?" Laura asked - just as confused as I. We slowly walked to the edge of the sidewalk to stare at it together. "Kim - it may have been Ervil's people," Laura said nervously with a look of fear in her brown eyes.

"I sure hope not," I told her grimly. I hesitated. "I guess I'd better do *something*." I began walking slowly towards the car with keys in hand.

"Kim - be careful!" Laura shouted tensely. "What if it's been rigged?" I stopped a short distance from the open car door. Raising my leg, I gave a firm shove with my foot and jumped back as the door slammed closed. Nothing happened. So far - so good. Now to try to start and move it. I slid carefully into the front seat leaving the door open beside me. My hand quivered slightly as I inserted the key and turned it. I held my breath, but the car started smoothly.

Although I now felt assured that my car wasn't really going to explode, I didn't completely relax until I was safely parked back in the original space. I climbed out to reassure Laura. "It was probably just some of the punk kids that we've seen hanging around here," I told her calmly. "Maybe they were bored, and wanted to stir up some trouble." Laura nodded hopefully. I tried to smile light heartedly. "That was weird, huh?"

Just then a large white motor home began moving our direction from the far side of the parking lot. As the cumbersome vehicle drew up beside us, it slowed to a stop. I sensed the tension in Laura's stance as I craned my neck to see the passengers who were obviously looking back at us. It was no use. The side windows were tinted and, from where we stood it was impossible to see who was driving.

I knew I should have been afraid - but for some reason I wasn't. I put my hands defiantly on my hips and glared. Who was in there? Arthur? Rena? Surely Mark would still be in hiding after what he did in Los Molinos. Slowly the RV began moving again, this time to the end of the parking lot where it disappeared after turning onto the road.

"Bullies!" I called angrily as I turned towards Laura... but she was already gone. Returning to the apartment I found her looking at a phone number written on a piece of paper as she dialed the wall phone hanging in the kitchen.

"I need to speak to Officer Collins, right away," she said clutching the receiver tightly to her ear. " This is Laura LeBaron. He told me to call anytime." Officer Collins must have answered immediately, for Laura quickly began to tell him about our nerve-wracking experience. "It was a white motor home," she said, anxiously describing the vehicle. "It had tinted windows and a sort of gold- colored W design on the side."

There was a pause and Laura turned pale. "He does?" she cried into the receiver. "Ervil has one like that?" Laura was on the verge of tears. "Isn't there anything you can do?" she begged desperately. "You need to send somebody. Please..."

"They can't do anything," she told me after hanging up. Her voice sounded hollow. "He wants me to call him if it comes around here again." The fear in my friend's usually-smiling face was heartbreaking. The nightmare she had lived through just wasn't going away.

We were relieved when, a little later, one of Laura's brothers arrived home from work. When I finally left them, I glanced repeatedly in my rear view mirror on the twenty minute drive back to my apartment. It was getting late. I swung my car into the semi-dark underground parking lot and held my key ready before scrambling for the elevator.

A few days later I had the opportunity to meet Officer Collins for myself when he and a fellow detective rang the buzzer to my apartment that afternoon and asked to talk to me. When the two men, dressed in dark suits, were seated in my apartment, the questions they asked were not about the incident at Laura's apartment, but about an old friend of mine named Mark Chynoweth.

"We heard about you from a woman in the Church of the Firstborn," one of them told me. "She said you and Mark were pretty close." I nodded. For the next hour or so I answered questions not only about

Mark - but about his family as well as my own. They were particularly interested in Ervil - probing for understanding and information - clearly fascinated with the mysterious dark giant who held such power over his followers.

When I told them about Mark's last visit they perked up. "Did you save the number he left with you?" asked Officer Collins.

"No, I threw it away," I answered honestly.

"Did Mark spend the night?" asked the other detective.

I looked at him in surprise. "Of course not - it wasn't like that. Mark wouldn't do that." Seeing the amusement in their eyes - I wondered how I could possibly explain to them that my old friend, who had just gunned down a colony full of defenseless people, would never take advantage of a young girl.

The officer broke into a grin. "Did he bring wine?" he teased.

I blushed and shook my head. "No."

"Aw - I hate it when a guy doesn't bring a nice girl wine."

"No - really. Mark wasn't like that," I repeated with an embarrassed smile. "He was married."

Twenty-five

The Decision

I had come to accept that I was different than the other young people that I met in everyday society. Always questioning life, I could never get involved with idolizing movie stars or worrying about fashion trends. Now the tragedies unfolding around me made the serious side of life weigh even heavier on my young shoulders. And I wondered where I belonged.

My parents loved me - but I recognized that, like me, they were confused. Mom would openly complain about the state of our church, while Dad was quietly uneasy. Looking back I realize that, as they both tried to fill some of the many needs of their grandchildren and older daughters, I was the only one who didn't seem to need their attention. Although they were always there for me to the best of their ability, the truth was - they were overwhelmed.

I had the admiration and respect of Leila's family - especially her grandmother, June. But in reality they didn't know me. As with Grandma and Grandpa Flowers, my real life was hidden from their view. Now, after living a double existence for most of my life, I was beginning to feel that I honestly didn't know myself.

Spiritually, I felt empty. Something important was missing, but I didn't know what it was. I asked God for help, but was unable to see any obvious answer. Finally, I even questioned my faith. What if the truth was something my family and I didn't know about? What if it was far away - maybe even in another part of the world? I needed answers. And I wanted someone to turn to for emotional support. I felt so alone. The only thing I was certain of, was that I needed to take a step in some direction.

It was while I was in the throes of this depression that Verlan reappeared on the scene and walked into my life yet again. He found me visiting at Judy's apartment one afternoon during my weekend off. "Will you take a little ride with me to the beach?" he asked with a friendly smile, his expressive eyes looking affectionately into my own. I returned his smile and went into the bedroom to find my sweater. "How's your family doing?" I heard his friendly voice asking Judy.

Verlan parked his pickup where we had a nice view of the ocean in the deserted parking lot of Imperial Beach. We had been here before. He reached for my hand, placed it over his heart and pressed it tightly against his chest. Then he began to tell me about his recent travels to Nicaragua. "Would you like to live there someday?" he asked shyly as he lowered my hand onto his lap and began to gently squeeze each fingertip.

The sun moved soothingly through the sky, its heavenly white light illuminating gray clouds in its descent towards the ocean. As I studied Verlan's by-now familiar features, a sudden thought presented itself to me: *Could it be that the answer to my recent prayers was sitting right beside me?*

I sat quietly and considered. Certainly if God had wanted me to find answers from another religion or in a different part of the world, He would have put me somewhere closer to those answers - or somehow brought them to me. Instead I was here, on a beautiful beach with a gentle and charismatic man who had sought me out for almost as long as I could remember. During all of the times of change I had faced, and in spite of the many pressures he endured, Verlan had always taken the time to find me. I believed he truly cared.

The ocean roared hypnotically, instilling in me a comforting sense of peace that I hadn't felt for quite some time. The sinking sun cast a pleasant glow on the side of Verlan's face - adding a dreamlike quality to my reverie. *Lord,* I prayed silently, *I don't know what to do with my life - don't know where to turn. I'm going to take this step in faith - believing that this is what you want for me. I leave whatever happens in your hands.*

I took a deep breath. "If we were to have a son together one day," I told Verlan quietly, "I would like to name him after my dad."

Astonished blue eyes stared at me. I realized then that my reply was both surprising and confusing - but since he had never actually come right out and asked me to marry him, I could not directly say yes. And I wasn't about to propose to him.

Verlan sat upright, squeezing my hand tightly. "What does this mean?"

Instead of coming right to the point, unknowingly I did what Verlan had sometimes done with me - I asked a probing question. "I read somewhere that marriage is happier if one of the partners makes the small decisions, and the other person gets to make the big ones." I hesitated before continuing cautiously. "If I were to marry you - could I make some of the small decisions and at least help with the big ones?"

At the time, I didn't realize how naive my question must have sounded to a man who was accustomed to making all decisions for his eight wives and their children, as well as having the final say on the important issues of the church. Not only that, but in my ignorance, I was thinking like a monogamist - as though our choices would involve only

159

the two of us as husband and wife. I didn't stop to consider that, even if Verlan's large family were allowed to vote on family matters, my vote would only count as one among many.

If he was surprised by my childish attitude, Verlan chose not to show it. Instead he smiled, and in the semi-darkness I could see that his eyes were shining. "Well, that sounds fair doesn't it?" he said with a warm laugh. He reached for my other hand, now holding both of mine in his. "Are you saying that you will marry me?"

The moment for being direct had arrived. I sighed and nodded my head. "I think it's about time for me for me to make a decision," I said matter-of-factly. "and I believe that you're the one I'm supposed to marry." Not very romantic, but honest.

I could almost see the wheels of his mind beginning to turn. "Let's get out and walk together," he said happily. "I can't stand to sit here any longer." Together we took the small uneven path down to the beach. Then, holding hands we trudged across the wet sand, a cool salty breeze puffing across our faces as the surf pounded beside us. Verlan was quiet. The busy man was making a plan. "I have to leave tomorrow," he told me absently. I wasn't surprised that he didn't tell me where he was going. "Before I leave, I'll ask your father for permission to marry you."

Suddenly he stopped walking and gathered me into a warm embrace. "Kim, you're a sweet girl," he said as he pressed his cheek against my wind-tussled hair, "I really do love you. You know I do."

I put my arms around his waist, buried my face in his jacket and nodded - not yet ready to say those words to him. Gripping my shoulders, he gently held me away from him, examining my face. "Shall I kiss you?" he asked tenderly. Not sure if he expected me to answer, I gazed passively into his eyes - trusting that he would make the right decision.

He seemed to be deep in thought as he stared over my head at the ocean, still holding my shoulders. "No," he resolved firmly as he pulled me close again. "No - I'll wait until I talk to your dad and we've set our wedding date." I shook my head gratefully. Things were happening so fast - being kissed by Verlan was something I was perfectly willing to wait for.

"When's your birthday?" Verlan asked as he put his arm around me and we resumed our walk.

"April first."

He laughed. "You're an April fool's baby?" Then serious again, "You'll turn nineteen?"

"Uh huh."

"My birthday's on April twenty-eighth," he told me jovially. "How about if we get married in April after you turn nineteen and before I turn forty-three?"

Even though he was quite serious, I laughed in amusement. With a twenty- five year age span between us - what would a few weeks in April really matter? Still the plan was fine with me. "Okay," I agreed pleasantly as I mentally prepared to discuss one more thing with him before finalizing our engagement. I needed to talk to him about Joel.

Waiting until we were back in the warm pickup, I turned to him a little awkwardly before beginning. "While you were gone, Jeanine talked to me," I told him solemnly.

"Is that right?" he responded uncertainly. "What did she talk to you about?"

"She brought up the idea of me being sealed to Joel." Verlan was silent. "I've been thinking about it," I continued boldly. "Would you still want to marry me if I decided to do that?"

"Yes. Yes I would," he assured me swiftly. "Only I don't think you need to worry about that part of it." He leaned thoughtfully back in his seat. " I know that the Lord is fair - and he wants us to be happy. If you will be sealed to me and, when we get to the other side, you decide to that you'd rather be with Joel - I believe that God will give you that choice."

I found this answer confusing. Wasn't there a reason for being sealed to one another while still on the earth? I immediately wondered if this was his way of dealing with the possibility of losing me and our children in eternity.

Then again, maybe he was right. I began to feel relieved about the idea of giving up worrying about the confusing issues of eternal marriage - some of which just weren't clear to me anyway. For instance - I had been taught that my kids and their posterity would belong to my husband as his heritage in heaven in his own spiritual kingdom. If that were true, I wondered what heritage would be left for our children in eternity. Was there an invisible line drawn somewhere, separating a man's inheritance from that of his sons'? I had heard my mother ask similar questions in relation to my sisters' families many times.

Suddenly I was perfectly willing to give up the burden of struggling to understand mysteries that seemed to be hopelessly over my head, and I resolved to take my place as a faithful adult in my religion on that night in February. As we drove away from the dark empty parking lot, I felt a new sense of purpose in my life. I had agreed to become the ninth wife of our church leader, Verlan M. LeBaron, and to be sealed to him for time and all eternity the following April.

Twenty-six

In My Grandparents' House

T he pain in my father's eyes tore at my heart as he settled himself into the chair opposite mine in the tidy living room of my parents' apartment. "Verlan asked me for permission to marry you today," he told me grimly. "He said that's what you want." Mom sat crying quietly on the couch nearby. "Is that true?" Dad's face was so pale that he almost looked sick.

I swallowed hard and nodded my head nervously. "I told him I'm against the idea," Dad continued sounding angry. "He already has too much responsibility to be taking on another young wife."

Mom blew her nose into a tissue. I sat in uneasy silence. "So you told him no?" I finally asked.

"I told him I don't approve of it, and I wish you wouldn't do it." Dad's tense shoulders suddenly sagged and he shrugged helplessly before continuing. "But I said that you've grown into a woman now, and I expect you'll do as you please."

I was almost paralyzed with discomfort and confusion. I hadn't expected this reaction from my parents who had raised me in this religion and watched my sisters marry into it. I didn't understand why they were now so gravely opposed to my decision.

As though she had read my mind, Mom decided to speak. "We've seen how hard it's been for your sisters and their kids, Kim," she said, her voice thick with emotion. "We don't want you to get into a mess." Then she asked imploringly. "Can't you see what you'd be getting yourself into? Why on earth have you decided to do this?" She sniffed and her face crumpled as two large tears rolled down her cheeks.

I didn't want to see my parents sad - I could hardly bear to look at their unhappy faces - but years of conditioning now hardened my heart. I had told God I would do this, and I needed to be strong. "Mom, I think things will be different with Verlan," I tried to console her. "I'm only trying to do what I think is right."

Mom shook her head and rolled her swollen eyes, "I have heard those words before."

A few days later I was relieved when Carolyn and Steve and their family returned from Israel. Not only were we happy to see them, but their arrival provided a welcome distraction from the unexpected rift between my grieving parents and myself.

After settling in an apartment a short distance away in the city of El Cajon, my sister and her husband were eager to share tales about the interesting experiences they had encountered in the Holy Land. Amazingly, besides already being fluent in English, French, and Spanish, my brother-in-law had now almost mastered the Hebrew language! A gifted conversationalist with intelligent brown eyes, he soon had us all imagining the lively democratic community meetings they had attended at their kibbutz, and picturing the busy member-owned chicken farm where he worked - almost as clearly as if we had been there alongside him. I listened with genuine interest; it all sounded so different from the strict authoritarian church-run society I was accustomed to.

Outwardly, Steven seemed to have adjusted to the fact that most of his other wives had remarried and started new lives with their families within the church without him. And now neither he nor Carolyn said anything about my decision to marry Verlan. Although Kathy and Judy were gently supportive, especially when I told them I thought I had been inspired, my oldest sister continued to remain strangely silent on the subject. I wondered if she hadn't heard the news. For some reason I wasn't anxious to tell her although time was passing quickly and in only one more month April would arrive along with my wedding day.

It was one day in March that my mother pulled me aside to talk to me about my grandparents. "Your grandma isn't able to walk at all anymore," she told me sadly. "She just never completely recovered from that broken hip. Grandpa is worn out from taking care of her by himself." She paused to let her words sink in. " Me and your dad are going to take a trip to Sacramento this month to help them out for a week or so." Mom raised her eyebrows, "Since you'd be leaving your job next month anyway, why don't you come along with us?" she suggested hopefully.

This was an idea that my parents didn't have to push. I knew that once I was married to Verlan, it would be harder than ever to visit Grandma and Grandpa. "I'd like to go see them with you," I quickly agreed. "When I go back to my job tomorrow, I'll have to talk to June and give her notice."

It was only one week later, with tears in my eyes, that I said goodbye to Leila, while June brazenly tempted me to return to them. "I wanted you to come to Palm Springs with us this spring," she coaxed. "You can go and visit with your family and be back just in time."

I smiled at her sadly as I stood by the apartment door ready to leave. Abruptly, she walked closer to me. "And I don't mean to be emotional or embarrass you," she said in a low unsteady voice, "but I've come to think of you almost as a daughter."

My brave facade dissolved as I sank into a nearby chair, covered my face with my hands, and cried. It was so hard to leave them. There was no way I could bring myself to explain to this modern Jewish woman that I would soon be the plural wife of a much older man, and that the new focus of my attention would be starting a large family - probably somewhere in Nicaragua or Mexico.

And how shocked she would be if she knew that an important part of my life now would involve trying to hide from that nice young fellow named Mark she had met not long ago in my apartment. How could I possibly share the stunning news that my old friend might just try to kill me? The terrible truth was that Leila would actually be safer with me gone.

Sadly, I couldn't even promise to return for a visit. The future would unlikely hold either the time or opportunity to socialize with old friends outside the church.

I stood shakily and returned to Leila to kiss her cheek, before quickly wrapping my arms around the short, tense figure of her grandmother. The room was strangely quiet as blindly I fumbled for the doorknob and walked out of their lives. On the very next day I would make a sort of pilgrimage with Mom and Dad to visit my grandparents as an unmarried woman for the last time.

~~~~~

My grandparents' home looked almost exactly as I remembered it in the quiet older neighborhood where it stood. We parked in the driveway at the side of the little yellow house, then strolled up the neat walkway surrounded by trimmed hedges and rosebushes to the already-open front door.

And there was Grandpa, standing as straight as an arrow. He seemed a little shorter and his neatly trimmed hair was now almost completely silver, but how I welcomed the strength of his hug - the firm clarity of his voice. I noticed with happiness that his step was still quick and spry.

In her recliner near the large picture window of the living room, sat Grandma with a small plaid quilt warming her lap. I took in the sight of her. She was dressed in a soft pale blue robe and her usually plump face appeared much thinner. Her striking blue eyes, looking at me through glasses as thick as the bottoms of Coke bottles, appeared startlingly huge and owlish. They lit up with a warm familiar smile as I bent to hug her.

Grandpa had already started his lunch in the kitchen. "You better get yourself in there and find something to eat before your grandpa eats it all!" Grandma commanded merrily. Then she added with a sad smile, "I'd get up and fix you something if I could."

Standing over the white enamel kitchen sink, I pulled out one of the shiny- colored cups I had used as a child. As I filled it with cold water from the tap, something inside me stirred. Here in my grandparents' house the cold numbness I had experienced since leaving Leila and June was beginning to melt, as overwhelming feelings of disorientation gradually diminished.

Before dinner as my elders sat visiting, I soaked and washed Grandma's neglected feet in a basin of warm water and carefully trimmed her long uneven toenails. She intently watched my movements. "That feels pretty good," she said with a grateful smile as I gently dried each warm pink foot.

"Thank you for doing that, Sis," added Grandpa who puffed on a sweet- smelling pipe as he relaxed in the recliner next to hers. "I can get your grandma into the shower, but I just can't see good enough to cut her toenails." He shook his head wistfully. "I don't want to hurt her."

It was humbling for me to realize how much this small deed was appreciated by these kind people. It really didn't seem like much compared to my grandmother's long life of serving and caring for others, or Grandpa's unselfish history of fulfilling the needs of his family, including his present devoted care of Grandma.

Later, before it got too late, I made the trip down the road and across a busy street to the nearby thrift store. I used to visit this place with my cousins when we were children - and now standing in quiet contemplation, I surveyed the clean familiar surroundings. There in the far corner were the friendly bookshelves I had once searched for something to read on one particularly hot and lazy afternoon.

Now my eyes fell on rows of pretty ceramic serving dishes and shiny glassware displayed in the center of the store, and I walked forward to examine them. Picking up a petite juice glass with a gold-painted rim and a tiny picture of a golden shaft of wheat on the side, I thought of how nice it would be to add this set to my hope chest - as a sort of last minute wedding present to myself. Soon I was toting the six matching glasses in a little brown bag back to my grandparents' house feeling almost like a carefree little girl again.

When it came time for bed, I helped Grandpa lift Grandma into her wheelchair. Standing on either side of her chair we slid one of our arms carefully under each of hers. When Grandpa gave the word, we gradually lifted as Grandma used what strength she had left in her legs to stand. Then we pivoted to slowly lower her into her wheelchair. I wondered how Grandpa had managed to do this by himself.

In my grandparents' bedroom, where a double bed once stood with a lovely old fashioned headboard, there were now two neatly made twin beds. I ignored the sad feeling in my stomach as we turned back the covers before working together to move Grandma onto her bed, finally lifting her legs onto clean white cotton sheets then pulling warm blankets up over her shoulders. Grandma was grateful but embarrassed to be on the receiving end of all this attention

"Thank you, Kim," she said meekly as I bent to kiss her goodnight on the cheek. "Maybe someday I'll be able to do something to repay you," she added with a weak smile. I managed a weak smile of my own before leaving her in the semi-darkness and making my way bleary-eyed back into the living room.

Grandpa had already put out fresh sheets, blankets, and a pillow for me to make my bed on the couch. Then everyone said goodnight as Mom and Dad retired to the guest bedroom, and Grandpa joined Grandma in theirs.

I spread out the sheets and blankets on the long, comfortable sofa, then keeping the volume down I squatted in front of the television cabinet to flip through the channels in search of some pleasant distraction. It was no use. The small figures moving about on the screen while meaningless voices chattered vaguely out of the speaker could not hold my interest. I turned off the television and snapped off the living room lamp before snuggling down under the clean- smelling covers.

I wished that I could have talked to my grandparents about my upcoming marriage. I felt like a hypocrite hiding this important part of my life from them - acting like a free-spirited child instead of a woman who would soon be married. I also knew the pain it would cause them if they knew the circumstances. They would never understand.

Before falling asleep, I pictured my grandma as an adventurous little girl walking and playing alongside the covered wagon that carried her family from Marble Hills, Georgia to the state of Oklahoma. Grandma had been the youngest of her family, and now she was the only one left. How her life had changed.

I sighed. No matter what the future held, I was grateful to be resting in this safe familiar place with the people I knew and loved so well. Here it was possible, at least temporarily, to abandon the spiritual struggle I had been immersed in for what seemed like a very long time. It seemed that on this peaceful night - it was okay to put all of my questions and fears aside. *Sweet dreams*. Isn't that what my parents and grandparents always used to say to me?

I believe I had been sleeping for several hours when suddenly I awoke with a vague feeling of distress. I sat up groggily as the sense of inner discomfort increased. I was...in pain. Not physically, but mentally - or was it spiritually? "Something's wrong," I murmured quietly.

As if in response, it seemed that somewhere in my soul, the gates of understanding were thrown open - and a flood of comprehension entered, waking me completely. The message was unmistakable and simple; something was telling me, without words, that if I went through with my plans to marry into polygamy - I would lose who I was.

I began to tremble as the disturbing realization persisted. Almost unaware of my actions, I stood and walked towards the living room window where I sank into Grandpa's chair. Now there was a coldness that seemed to clutch at my heart. "If I do this, I won't be me anymore?" I whispered out loud. I didn't know who I was asking - there was no one there.

I leaned towards the window and pulled aside the curtain to look out into the yard as I pondered what I was experiencing. Everything outside, like the living room where I sat, was still and dark - there were no answers there. But inside me I felt a convicting presence of truth. A wordless knowing filled my heart, leaving no room for debate or doubt: I was on the verge of marrying into a situation that would permanently alter my identity - forever changing the person who I was born to be.

I'm not sure how long the whole experience lasted, but it wasn't long before- gradually- the painful conflict began to fade until only the realization remained. I felt a tear slide slowly down my face as I made my way back to bed where surprisingly I fell quickly back to sleep.

It was still dark when I opened my eyes again later. This time instead of pain, I experienced a calm feeling of understanding. And instead of worrying over what I should do about the plans I had already made with Verlan - I simply accepted the fact that they were about to change. I didn't know exactly how or when, but one way or another they were about to change. For the time being I decided to keep my new understanding to myself.

Twenty-seven

Old Beliefs, New Understandings

I didn't know it, but while my sister Carolyn had been living away from us, she had become something of a liberated woman. At least by our church standards. When I returned to San Diego with my parents, I found that she had created quite a stir of interest with the first of several planned weekly women's meetings she had hosted at Judy's apartment. I was eager to go to the next one myself.

At that second meeting - which was attended by both women and some of the young men of the church - I heard ideas I had not considered before. Carolyn used scriptures to present her belief that married women were supposed to have their own open channel of communication with God. My sister reasoned that keeping this channel open was even more important than a woman's relationship with her husband.

I was impressed, for deep in my heart I recognized this to be true. But as I listened to the following discussion and debate, I learned that it was in the very roots of our religion that a woman was bound to follow her husband's instructions and decisions no matter what - even if it conflicted with her own conscience. I watched with interest as some of the young men argued against this idea, while a few others accepted it calmly as an obvious truth.

Then moving on to another subject, Carolyn brought out a Mormon scripture that referred to the people who would earn their exaltation and enter into the Celestial Kingdom of Heaven. In Mormon doctrine, as I was taught, this is the highest spiritual level in all eternity. According to the scripture being read to us, the beings who entered into that realm would be "equal in power and might and dominion."

"Did you notice that this scripture doesn't distinguish between men and women?" Carolyn pointed out. I was astounded. For in our church we were taught that in eternity men would be Gods who ruled their own earths. As for us women, to put it simply - in our quest for celestial glory, the more wives and children our husband had - the better it would be for us. And although we women would become goddesses, our husbands would certainly have absolute power and dominion. I had always kind of imagined myself as just being along for a timeless journey - making the sacrifices necessary to be included in my husband's kingdom in which he reigned.

Now, the funny thing was - I didn't care who had the power. I honestly didn't want it for myself. My idea of heaven would be living each day as a carefree little girl in some place like my grandparents' house. The point to me was: *the scripture we were supposed to revere, actually said something different than what we had been taught.* I was beginning to see that it was okay to allow myself to question. I no longer felt that I needed to implicitly trust in another person's authority. I believe that I was in the process of awakening to a God-given longing for my own understanding.

One day, not long after that first meeting, and without telling anyone - I sat down and wrote a letter to Verlan. In it I explained in one short page that I could no longer marry him because of the discrepancies I was beginning to discover between our church teachings and - there it was - *my own understanding.* I wished him well, sealed up the envelope, and mailed it to an address in Nicaragua he had left with me. I was certain that he would not be deeply disturbed - after all he already had eight other wives.

A few days later, unaware that I had already canceled my plans to marry Verlan, Carolyn decided to broach me on the subject. "Mom and Dad asked me to talk to you," she began gently, "about marrying Verlan...." She paused - seeming a little uncertain about where to begin.

"Kim, don't you think there's something wrong with the men of the church going around marrying these young girls when they already have all those wives?" she asked bluntly. "Irene claims that Verlan is actually thinking about putting his older wives 'out to pasture,' so he can have more time and energy for his younger wives." Now Carolyn was speaking heatedly. "You know what *that* means. There's a lot more to it than religion when a man starts getting ideas like those!"

I was shocked. Although I no longer had any intentions of marrying Verlan, I felt obligated to defend his honor. "Carolyn - don't be silly," I replied emphatically. " This is *not* about sex."

My sister stared at me incredulously for a moment before bursting into amused laughter. "Oh, ho, ho...so you think it's not about sex?" she asked dryly. Although she was still smiling, her eyes were sympathetic. "A man can have a different woman every night, and still keep adding young girls to his collection - and you believe it has nothing to do with sex?" She paused. "Tell me, Kim - who's being silly?"

I looked away in confusion. Could it be true? "You can tell Mom and Dad - you can tell everybody - that I've already decided not to marry Verlan," I said, my cheeks still burning with embarrassment.

One day not long after that, Mom dropped a bombshell on my lingering faith in Joel. "Did you know that it was Joel who had the furniture taken from our house in Colonia LeBaron when you were little?" she asked out of nowhere.

"Mom, that can't be true," I told her calmly, "it was probably Ervil." She must have heard a rumor from someone who didn't like Joel, I thought.

"Oh no," she said determinedly, "it was one of Joel's older sons that told me about it."

I was still not convinced. "Why would Joel have done a thing like that?" I asked sharply.

"To give our furniture to Magdalena," Mom insisted calmly. "One of her boys admitted to me and your dad that Joel told them to get into our house and take out the stove and bunk beds and some other things they needed," she explained in a matter of fact tone of voice. This was obviously old news to her. "He wasn't ashamed, because his mom needed them so bad and they weren't being used." Suddenly Mom seemed thoughtful. "I guess Magdalena really was poor," she admitted. Then she added angrily, "But that didn't give Joel the right to have his kids get into our house and take our things."

I wondered if I would ever overcome the disappointment I felt at that moment. Without permission, our prophet, whom we always regarded as a champion of the Ten Commandments, had taken the precious belongings we had brought with us all the way from Utah. He had given them to his first wife, and never even told us.

I found myself attending the women's meetings at Judy's apartment with more interest than ever. Kathy was enjoying every moment of them too. It seemed that all three of us younger sisters were thirsty for the freedom to find and know God for ourselves, and our oldest sister was leading us to believe we could do just that.

As we listened and considered the new ideas that Carolyn presented, her husband was busy writing and teaching about the communal lifestyle on the kibbutz, which he still believed represented the "United Order" spoken of by Joseph Smith. Steven was also outspoken about his opinion that the men of the priesthood held too much absolute power over the lives of others. He had grown accustomed to the kibbutz - where men and women were not only encouraged, but required to vote on almost everything.

The Silvers were getting plenty of attention from church members in the San Diego area, but not everyone was impressed. Understandably, Alma was furious that a man who had walked away from the church and his own families, should presume to teach anything to that same church! And he thought that the kibbutz idea was ridiculous.

But when Carolyn and Steven began telling me about opportunities enabling young people to visit the kibbutzim of Israel as students, I wondered if this was the direction my life should be taking. Caught up in the excitement of such an interesting notion, along with the other new ideas that had succeeded in creating something of a stir within the church, I was not prepared when Verlan came knocking on the door at Judy's apartment one day. I took one look at his worried face and my heart sank. The break up was not going to be as easy as I had thought. I was silent as he drove us to the same beach as before.

"Is there anything I can do to make you reconsider?" he asked hopefully as he turned to face me where we sat talking once again in his pickup. "Anything that might help you change your mind?"

I was distant but polite - just wanting the discomfort to be over. I began trying to tell him that I was not happy with the way things were in the church - that some things were wrong and *something* was missing. But how could I tell him everything? The harried church leader with his many wives and children was not able to understand what seemed to be the gripes of a willful teen aged girl. I only knew that I wanted the freedom to question and wonder - and I wanted the men of the church not to dominate their wives and children like tyrants.

I believed that, as in the past, Verlan just happened to be in the area on that particular day, and had decided to stop by and talk to me. What I didn't know at the time was that he had left his families in Los Molinos to travel all the way to San Ysidro for this encounter.

"Things could get better within the church," he tried to explain. "You know it takes time..."

"I'm not sure all of the leaders would really want that," I said quietly, thinking of Alma. "Verlan - I can't change my mind. I truly know that I can't marry you now," I stated anxiously. Was I being heartless? I felt that it would be futile to try to make him understand my experience at my grandparents' house. And I honestly believed that, because our wedding would have been just another one of many for him, my change of heart would not really be of much significance in this important man's life. I think both of us knew there was nothing else to say as we sat looking at each other uneasily.

I don't remember if we spoke at all as he drove me back to Judy's apartment where he left me in the parking lot. I know I wished him well. I realized that he would soon be busy with his many families, along with traveling and attending church and priesthood meetings - and that I would become a mere memory in his busy life. Although I had almost married him, I still felt that I hardly knew him. As I slowly walked towards Judy's door, I sadly turned to watch the good-natured man with the boyish blue eyes drive away.

Twenty-eight

The Meeting

One day, not long after saying goodbye to Verlan, Judy, Kathy and I unexpectedly decided to plan a trip to Colonia LeBaron together. This was to be a time like no other, because it would be just the three of us and Judy's two-year-old daughter. A trip just for fun - something unheard of before the three of us began experiencing a certain adventurous comradery since attending the women's meetings. I will always remember that journey, for not since childhood had I ever had this much uninterrupted time with my sisters without dealing with large numbers of children along with the pressures of day-to-day living.

After a pleasant trip that included small talk, laughter, and interesting conversation we arrived at the colony, where we split up to visit with our different friends. I eventually found myself at the home of Helen Leany, the widow who had married Verlan and had since left him. Her daughter, my friend Debbie, was one of the few single girls my age still left in the colony.

As we talked, Helen mentioned that she had heard about the women's meetings in San Diego. "Have you been going to them?" she asked with interest.

"I sure have - and I've been learning a lot," I informed her enthusiastically.

"Would you be willing to talk to us about what you're learning at a women's meeting here, if I organize it?" she asked. I took a moment to think about it. I still didn't like to be the center of attention - but sure - I could tell a group of familiar, friendly women about our discussions and share the scriptures we had covered with them.

It wasn't long before Helen got back to me with a time and place. The meeting would be held the very next evening at the home of one of Brother Jensen's wives named Ronita.

When the appointed time rolled around, Kathy and I drove over to Ronita's a little early to be prepared. I carried in my hand Judy's copy of the three- in-one Mormon scriptures with the proper pages book marked for easy reference.

Ronita's house was undoubtedly one of the nicest in the colony. It was newly built, and Ronita, who was both industrious and smart, had designed the unusual round house herself. The friendly woman welcomed us warmly. Once inside, I saw that the living room was at the center of the house and that, like the spokes on a wheel, the other rooms branched off to the sides.

Now that we were at the actual meeting place, I was beginning to feel a little nervous. I looked around at the extremely pleasant decor thinking that surely instead of an outhouse, this modern house would have a real bathroom. "Can I use your restroom?" I politely asked our pretty blond hostess. She directed me to a large room that not only had an inside toilet - but to my amazement had more than one sink! Instead of using the restroom, I stood in the center of the room and said a silent prayer - asking the Lord to calm my fears and to give me the right words to say to the women who would be attending the meeting that night.

When I reentered the living room I was surprised to see that not only had some of the women arrived - but a few of the men of the colony had showed up as well. There was Kimball's oldest brother Harvard, and along with my old friend Tina was her husband Joel Jr. As others continued knocking at the door, quickly filling up the large round room - I began to realize in alarm that, instead of speaking to a small group of women as I thought, I would be addressing what was turning into a rather large community meeting! Here I was - a shy eighteen-year-old with virtually no experience with public speaking. How had this happened?

Numbly I took the chair that Ronita had placed at the front of the crowd for me. I remember that someone opened with a prayer, but after that much of the rest of the meeting became somewhat of a blur. I had no choice but to take a deep breath - which I did - before boldly trying to quickly and clearly cover the points we had discussed in our more intimate meetings at Judy's small apartment in San Diego.

But this crowd was not a receptive one. I looked around. On the faces of some of my old friends I saw blank expressions, while on the faces of others there were frowns. I moved on to the scripture Carolyn had shared about being "equal in power and might and dominion," and there was a stir of confused consternation as the listeners understood my meaning. But there was surprisingly little argument. It wasn't easy to dispute the words of a scripture that everyone accepted as true - except to say that it was being misinterpreted.

I continued, carefully trying to convey the simple ideas that had captured my attention and now meant so much to me. But, instead of a warm welcome, or even animated debate, my words bounced back at me - and I felt only coldness and disapproval. I looked around for Kathy - she smiled at me encouragingly. Where was Judy? Had she even come?

This was hardly the friendly women's meeting I had expected. As people began to speak it became even more evident that to them I was not an old friend, wanting discussion on her thoughts about religion. Instead - most of them were seeing me as a religious heretic.

Just then Joel Jr., who had taken several wives since marrying Tina, stood up - his eyebrows furrowed in anger. "I want you to tell me," he demanded loudly, "what is a woman's relationship supposed to be with her husband? One, two, three!" He slammed a fist into his open palm with each count. I looked at him with wounded eyes. Joel and Magdalena's handsome, hardworking oldest son had always been my friend, and now it felt as though we were strangers.

I was flustered. "It's not that simple, Joel," I replied defensively. "I would have no problem following the lead of a husband who loved me the way Christ loves the church," I tried to explain. "But surely a woman should follow her own conscience if her husband is not in touch with his." I looked around for someone to agree. "A man can be corrupted!" I pointed out desperately. There was silence. "Think of Ervil and the wives who obey his madness," I begged.

I looked around again. Did I see a thoughtful expression here and there? If I did, those faces were certainly outnumbered by the stares of coldness, disapproval, and pity. I continued talking, listening, and arguing my point as if in a dream. I don't even remember how long the meeting went on or how it closed.

After the meeting, I walked numbly to Kathy's little car and sat in frozen anguish on the seat next to her for the ride back to Grandmother LeBaron's house where we were staying. "Don't you worry, Kim," she said cheerfully after a moment. "You should have seen yourself!" she declared, shaking her head in admiration. "It was plain to me that you were inspired." She glanced at me uncertainly. "You really were..."

When we reached the house, I asked to be alone for awhile. Kathy nodded in understanding and went on inside. Hearing the screen door slam shut behind her, I slowly climbed out of the car and stood staring into the large empty field across the dirt road from Grandmother LeBaron's yard. Darkness had fallen and a large silvery moon had been shining for some time - but I was hurting so badly, I couldn't appreciate the beauty of the quiet night. I had a sudden longing to run out into the open field, lay down and there cry out to God to help me!

But - no, that wouldn't do. Even in my present state of mind, I realized that the dark, weedy area was probably a home to scorpions and snakes. Instead I stood alone in the yard, frantically searching the twinkling velvet sky rising above the black silhouette of the mountains. My tears began to fall.

First there were only a few, and then they came faster and faster - until my nose was running and the little streams on my cheeks merged into a messy dripping flood. I choked back broken sobs and wiped a sleeve across my cold damp face. As the storm within me subsided, I tried to catch my breath.

"Just where do I belong now, dear God?" I quietly asked the star-strewn heavens above me. "Where do I belong now..."

Twenty-nine

Nicaragua

I was sleeping soundly when I heard the noise on the ground floor of the large house where I was staying. It was pitch dark in the second story room where I lay. My body tensed: *was that the sound of a door opening?* I froze in terror as I heard the creak of a window being carefully slid open followed by slow, quiet footsteps moving towards the staircase. And I knew that Ervil's people were here in the house, in the dark...looking for me. I heard them creeping closer and trembled - would Mark be one of them?

With my heart beating wildly, I forced my eyes open - afraid of what I would see - and gave a cry of relief. There was no two-story house with stairs to climb, no window to slide open. I was in a hot, humid room, laying atop a wide, flat bamboo surface that was the bed I shared with my four-year-old niece Leslie and three other girls. Across from us, on the other half of the room, slept six others on another identical bamboo sleeping area. I was in the rain forest in Nicaragua - about as far from Ervil as I could get.

A month earlier I had traveled for three days on the backs of mules and in dug-out canoes with Brother Harold's family to get here. We had walked along steep cliffs in the dark, trusting in the sure-footed mules who were familiar with the paths we traveled. We slept on the dirt floors of the homes of the friendly Miskito Indians who populated the area. I was responsible for my niece Leslie and eight-year-old Chris - children of Carolyn and Steven. My sister and brother-in-law planned to join us later in hopes that this might be a good place to establish a kibbutz.

Harold and his first wife Betty had liked the kibbutz idea, and it was they who invited us to travel into the Bocay River Rain Forest where Harold had bought extensive acreage and a banana plantation. There he and his older son had built a large three-room bamboo house on stilts. They had done an expert job, even weaving a waterproof roof from thatch that extended to the separate cooking area where sat a handcrafted woodburning cook-stove and oven. I soon learned why the large windows of that room were not covered with clear plastic as were the smaller windows of the house. The windows of that room were open to let the smoke and heat out.

The children were thrilled with the unusual adventure. Our large yard had been cleared of dense jungle growth that rose on all sides of it like a green wall that supported the blue square patch-of-a-ceiling sky. There were vines to swing on like Tarzan and Jane, and a river just down hill that was so pure you could drink from it. It would be our only source of water - our community bath, our laundering spot, our swimming hole.

Looking at it in a picture, a person might have imagined it to be a paradise, with its white-faced monkeys, colorful parrots, and toucan birds - but they would not have seen the tiny people-biting gnats that worked their way into our clothing, forcing us to wear long sleeves and tuck pant legs into our socks. They would not have listened to the wild cats roaring in the distance at night, or been warned of the feared "Barbas Amarillas" - deadly poisonous snakes that lived in our new world and drank from our river. We had been warned by Dón Sebastián, our closest neighbor a good day's walk away, to stay away from the river at dusk for that was when the jungle animals would come out to drink and refresh themselves.

On our first evening there, I had sat on the bamboo floor of the hut listening to Harold talking to his family about their new home "This will be the dining room and family room," he told Betty as they talked over the kerosene lamp sitting on the huge table he had built with long matching benches. "Over there can be the boys' room," he nodded to the left, "and the girls can sleep on that side." He pointed to the room on the right. "The tent outside can be my room to share with either you or Nanette until the rains come. I'll have to have something else built off the ground by then." Nanette was Harold's second wife who would be joining us soon. "I'll stay for a few days to help you get settled, then I'll go back for Nan," he explained.

As he spoke, something large and white flew past my head and smashed into the wall behind me. Then there was another and another. "What *are* those?" I whispered frantically to Harold's fair-haired daughter, Jill, who sat next to me. They were too large and ugly to be moths, but different than beetles.

My seventeen-year-old-friend smiled apologetically and whispered back, "They're cockroaches."

"But they're white," I pointed out incredulously, certain that she had made a mistake. "And they can fly," I added, hoping she would change her mind and tell me that they were something else.

Jill, who had been living in the Nicaraguan city of Jinotega for over a year, nodded and smiled sympathetically. "There are all sorts of roaches in the jungle," she explained kindly. I shrank back in disgust as another cockroach flew close by.

That night I overheard Jill begging her father to allow her to return to Jinotega with him where she could live with her oldest brother and his wife. "How can I meet anyone to marry someday?" she asked Harold woefully. "Everyone here is my family!" Seeing her point, Harold finally relented.

It wasn't long before Jill was gone and Harold returned with Nanette and her large family, and we settled into a routine. Mornings, Betty built a fire and made breakfast which was usually left-over beans which had been boiled to keep them from going sour. In fact, beans were almost all we had to eat besides rice and home-made tortillas.

After breakfast, Nan and I would head down to the river to wash clothes by hand. With two large families along with Carolyn's kids and myself to wash for, this was quite a job. We soaked each piece of clothing or soiled bedding in the river, soaped it up with a bar of laundry soap then wrung each item out, rinsing it in the flowing water of the river before spreading everything over the large rocks nearby. Later, Betty would bring us a cup of strong coffee made from boiled local coffee beans to enjoy as the the three of us worked together. Although our hands became red and sore, we would talk and laugh – watching as little yellow butterflies landed, clustering on our brightly-colored clothes.

Our bathroom was the jungle at first, and I found this to be rather traumatizing as I wandered into the thick greenery, watching out for bugs and snakes with a machéte in hand. Later, Harold put a sort of porta-potty with a bucket underneath in one of the sleeping rooms. Although I was afraid someone would push aside the sheet that hung in the doorway and barge in, it almost seemed like a luxury!

At first we all dealt with the inconveniences and the lack of privacy cheerfully. I would close my eyes and ignore the cockroaches that lived in the thatch roof and bamboo walls, and brush off whatever things crawled on me in the night. But as the months passed, I began to wonder when my sister and brother-in-law would arrive.

Then one morning as I sat up in our common bed to stretch, I was surprised to hear the children screaming frantically at me, "Kim, Kim! Get up! Get up!" Without asking why, I shot out of bed and quickly turned to see the reason for their cries. To my horror I saw a good-sized scorpion that had run out from under my pillow with its stinger raised and poised to strike.

"Mark, come and get the scorpion!" someone cried, as Betty's son rushed into the room.

Later that day, I sauntered into the cooking area to help with the dishes to find Betty carefully fishing drowned cockroaches out of the large pan of beans we would be eating later on. "It has to be done everyday," she told me bluntly, as she worked. "I've tried, and tried to

178

keep them out, but they always find a way under the lid." She looked at me and gave me a brave grin. "Don't worry, the cooking will kill the germs!" Maybe it would, but I wondered how many little cockroach body parts we had all been eating in the refried beans.

After that I took to carefully examining every bite of food that I took. This was tedious and nerve-wracking and I began to lose weight. Then came the boils that slowly began to appear on my legs, making it difficult to walk. Rising from a sitting position was excruciating and I would force myself not to cry out.

I knew that Betty was suffering with the heavy burdens of feeding and caring for so many people in such trying circumstances, but she and Nan always kept a positive attitude. One day Betty spoke to us about the necessity of caring for each other in ways that would help us to cope with our stresses. "Is there anything that you find especially hard to deal with?" she asked, looking at me. I thought about how I cleaned the kitchen at dusk as the cockroaches were pulled out of the beans nearby.

"Well," I admitted shyly, "I get depressed when I work in the cooking room at night."

"Then, that is one job you shall not have!" she told me emphatically with tears in her eyes. I realized then that the hard-working, smiling Betty had understood my misery all too well – and, like a mother, she wanted to protect me. Yet the long-suffering woman never suggested to any of us what we could do for her.

Then one bright day, all gloominess was unexpectedly lifted when there was a knock on the door. We had visitors! I was told that the very small, smiling, dark-skinned people we greeted were Indians – maybe Miskitos or Sumos – who had traveled for several days to meet us. It seemed that news had spread around the region, about the American family that was living in the jungle!

These gentle people brought us gifts of fish and meat from an animal they had hunted along the way. They were obviously very friendly, although I could not at all understand the language that they spoke which was some variation of the Spanish I had grown accustomed to in Mexico. Luckily, some of Betty's children were able to communicate with these kind souls. They had never seen Caucasians, and I'm sure that we looked very curious to them - tall women with varied coloring and clothing. Some of Nanette's children had hair of bright red with freckles, while Betty's were fair with hair as white as snow.

The Indian women wore simple home-made dresses and with their arms and legs exposed, I could see the callouses and scars resulting from the gnat-bites that they had apparently grown used to. Betty served them dinner from our humble kitchen, and later that evening before they left, we heated some unfamiliar tiny grains in a heavy skillet to make a jungle version of popcorn!

Although this was only one of many happy moments in the jungle, as two more months passed, I began to suffer from intense depression along with my hunger. At mealtime I would examine several large bites of food to keep from starving then push my plate away. The problem was that I really had found well-cooked, soggy cockroaches in my beans using this method.

I was thrilled on the days that Harold made trips to the plantation to bring back mules loaded with bananas of every shape and size, and how I loved the giant plantains that Betty would fry like potatoes, for I knew that they had not been invaded by nasty bugs.

One day my misery came to a head when we sat down at the large table to eat our evening meal of beans. I was so hungry that I was actually beginning to relax and enjoy the food, hardly examining the bites before putting them into my mouth. We were all talking and laughing, and I was just about to take another tasty bite, when a large cockroach fell from the thatched ceiling into my beans, landing with a splat. Everyone paused and stared. Then the children began to laugh hysterically.

I rose stiffly, allowing the blood to rush painfully into the boils on my legs, before slowly making my way into the sleeping room. I had to be alone – and it would be dangerous to go out into the darkening evening. But once in the room, I realized that there was no real privacy there either- someone could push the cloth door aside and enter at anytime. It was a room that over half a dozen people shared - and I needed a place to cry immediately! I sat down on my blanket, pulled a sheet over my head, and sobbed.

"Come here, I want to show you something," little Christopher whispered to me one evening as he pulled me to the front doorstep. He pointed to the deep blue sky where a brilliant star shone. "Sometimes, I look into the sky and see a really bright star like that one, and I make a wish that my mom will be here soon." I looked down at his face and saw tears in his handsome blue eyes. I held him close. He had seemed so happy swimming in the river, riding on the mules, and swinging on the vines, that I had not known how much he had been missing Carolyn.

Amazingly, it was only a few days later that Chris got his wish, when Steven and Carolyn arrived with their Indian guides. It really was wonderful to see them. And it only took a few days for Steven to assess the situation and pronounce that this was not the best place to organize a kibbutz. In fact, he informed Harold, he was arranging to have his family and myself guided right back out of there before the rains started! It was impossible, we were told, to travel along the Bocay in the rainy season. Horses had been known to drown in the mud!

I had forgotten what a long hard trip it had been into the Bocay, but I was to be reminded on the way back out. It was during the last day of the trip, as we rode the mules up and down steep hills, that the rain started and didn't stop. The wide sombreros we wore to protect our faces from the sun soon became drenched and drooped over our eyes as we rode along, soaked to the bones, too saddle-sore for words, and too exhausted to walk. Because the trail was narrow, we rode single file, and sometimes were separated by quite some distance between our mules.

I felt almost alone as, with a mixture of awe and misery, I lifted the soggy sombrero above my wet forehead to look at the breathtaking beauty of the green-hued hills around me and the cloudy violet-blue sky above. I still didn't know where I belonged

That was when I heard Carolyn's frantic voice, calling out behind me. My frustrated, helpless sister was methodically bellowing every curse word that she had ever learned in Spanish.

And although I felt like crying, I smiled.

Thirty

The Winds of Change

W here do I belong?" This was a troubling question that would follow me for years to come. After returning to San Diego, my parents and I decided to move away to a small farming town in California to be closer to Mom's relatives. There I attended a year of college and worked at my first job at the Good Shepherd Lutheran Home for the developmentally disabled. It was my duty to help provide recreational and physical activities for the disabled residents living there.

Although I liked my job, life was certainly different outside the church. It seemed that almost everywhere I turned, sexuality was the dominant theme of society. It was in the music I heard, the television and movies I watched, the magazines I read, and in the lives of many of my classmates. It appeared to me that people were being conditioned to behave in the opposite extreme of the people of my old church. There - multiple marriages were almost all that mattered and the responsibilities were overwhelming. Here - taking vows of promise and commitment before engaging in sex with someone was not even considered important.

I looked around in dismay as I wondered : Weren't women meant to be more than sensual playthings? And weren't men being programmed to be nothing more than greedy, lustful animals - lacking in responsibility and character? Although I made new friends and sometimes dated, I told no one about my past - and I still didn't feel that I belonged.

A year later, along with Judy and Paul's family and a few others, I made the decision to travel to Nevada to live in a modern motel where Steven and Carolyn felt inspired to establish a sort of American Kibbutz. Steven named this endeavor "Pilot Project" and promised that with God's guidance, we would learn to share each other's burdens and eventually be able to help others.

Our daily duties were divided up among the adults and rotated. On some days I would work in the community kitchen helping to prepare food for everyone. On others I worked in the laundry room washing, drying, and folding clothes before delivering them to each member's room. The most enjoyable job was to go shopping in a nearby town for supplies, for this guaranteed almost a whole day out - including a light lunch at a restaurant.

Eventually, Steven asked me to assist with teaching the younger children in our large community room. I enjoyed this time with the children as they worked on learning the alphabet, phonics, and did simple art projects. I was amazed by my brother-in-law's natural teaching ability and his ingenious ideas for helping the children to learn.

It was while on the "kibbutz" that I became acquainted with a tall, handsome, college student named Ron. I had met him before, for he was actually Paul's younger brother, Judy's brother-in-law. To our delight, Ron was very musically talented and provided our otherwise quiet world with enjoyable entertainment playing his guitar and singing us catchy songs he had written himself.

It wasn't long after he joined our kibbutz, that the two of us came under a shocking unexpected pressure. One evening, after asking to speak with us alone, Steven boldly claimed that he had been divinely inspired, and that it was God's will for us to marry. Although we were astounded, we trusted and believed him.

How could we have been so gullible? Amazingly, after being taught by Steven that people should not be dictated to by religious authority, and by Carolyn that each woman should have her own communication with God, I was unable to see the irony of our situation.

I believe that it was at least partly because we had been separated from society and were no longer participating in normal everyday activities - like visiting with others besides those in our commune, listening to the radio, or reading the newspaper. There was no television, and in effect we had actually been cut off from the outside world. In an attempt to be equal, we were even wearing matching plain blue work-shirts each day. With the exception of those living with us, all of our relatives were far away. We had lost our objectivity

Ron really was a nice guy, and we did like each other. That night we talked it over and agreed that, since we both seemed to want the same things in life, our friendship could eventually grow into love. Having grown to look up to Steven, who was one of the smartest people we had ever met, as our religious leader, we decided to agree to marry.

I was twenty-two years old, Ron was twenty-three. Our original wedding ceremony was a religious one performed by Steven in one of the motel rooms followed by a short honeymoon in Las Vegas. A few weeks later another simple wedding took place in the office of the Justice of the Peace. Both sets of our parents had traveled to join us, and a few other family members - mostly from our commune - attended this civil ceremony which Ron's mother had actually insisted on and paid for.

This point in time marked the beginning of a change in all of our lives at the commune. As months passed, the democratic meetings we had attended began to be replaced with other "inspired" edicts from Steve. In the months that followed, almost without realizing it, we were hardly allowed to decide anything for ourselves at all. Gradually, voting became nonexistent, and our democracy turned into a complete dictatorship with my sister and brother-in-law collecting all funds and in charge of all spending. Even the coveted purchasing duty became the sole responsibility of Carolyn.

Nine months later, I was eight months pregnant, miserable, and sick. Thankfully, Ron and I had been coming to our senses. We decided to leave the slowly evolving religious community, to make a life of our own where we would be free to make our own decisions.

After briefly consulting Carolyn and Steven, Ron put me on a plane to send me to my parents. Then, following a dramatic clash with Steven the next day, my determined young husband began hitchhiking in the cold November weather with only spare change in his pocket. A few days later he joined us safely in California. The time had arrived for us to begin thinking for ourselves.

With that decision came responsibility. It wasn't long before Ron found a job and we began to face the awesome challenges of marriage, including birthing and raising the child we had created. It wasn't an easy road for two inexperienced individuals who hardly knew each other. Unfortunately, our decision to completely abandon Steven's teachings ended up creating a rift between myself and my sisters, Judy and Carolyn, that never healed.

Kathy had not joined us on the kibbutz. Instead, she had chosen to remain in the Church of the Firstborn after being courted by a likable fellow named Lane. At some point, the new religious ideas we had been discovering together suddenly seemed unimportant to my widowed sister who had been on her own for several years since Joel's death. I believe that she was experiencing a powerful longing for love when she decided to marry the handsome man who was not much older than herself.

At the time he had only one other wife and even provided Kathy with a simple three bedroom unfinished house that had been vacated by a former wife. At first it seemed too good to be true, and I wondered if I should not have begged her so adamantly not to do it.

Our lives were on completely different tracks then, but the worst was yet to come. Lane, whose family had converted from the Short Creek group of polygamists that we referred to as Fundamentalists (short for the Fundamentalist Latter Day Saints, or FLDS), turned out to be not only a wife and child abuser, but a molester. Lane, whom I remembered as a friendly young man years earlier, was displaying the degrading behavior he had experienced himself as a child.

Sadly, the relationship between Kathy and myself deteriorated over the years as she refused to leave this mentally ill man and continued to "forgive" him, exposing her growing family to his horribly violating and dangerous behavior. I began to recognize the sad reality that an insecure woman, who has been deprived of love, will sometimes sacrifice not only her own reasoning, but even ignore her conscience to hang on to a partner who will offer her some semblance of caring.

To our great sorrow, Kathy's oldest daughter, Audrey was placed in a state hospital when she was but a teenager. Besides refusing to eat, to the point of starving herself, she talked very little and would not sit or lie down. Sometimes she became violent. One psychologist who examined her told my mother and me that some of her behavior was typical of a person who had been sexually molested. Ron and I tried to take Audrey for awhile, but at that point we were unable to reach her. We also realized that her violent outburts would be a danger to our unborn child.

On December 5, 1978, I gave birth to our first child - a son whom we proudly named Christopher Ryan and called Ryan. Since being on our own, Ron and I had become very close to my parents and Grandpa and Grandma Flowers who had moved into another small town nearby. Although Grandma was growing steadily weaker, she lived to meet our first son. Sadly, she died of heart failure while he was still a baby.

Over the next nine years, Ron and I had three more children together. First we welcomed Jacob, who was delivered by his father when the midwives were late coming. Then, five years later our family greeted Russell whom we would call Rusty. And only sixteen months later, I gave birth to our only daughter, Sarah. The joy we experienced at her birth was soon overshadowed by grief, for on the very next day - my father passed away.

Dad had been very sick with a blood disorder for most of the year, but his death came as blow to all of us. We mourned the loss of a loving father and wonderful grandfather. Ron was with him when he died. As I laid helplessly in bed, my thoughtful husband helped my grieving mother make the funeral arrangements.

Dad suffered terribly for leading his daughters into polygamy. And until the day he died, he grieved for Kathy and her children who had not left it. After Dad's death, Mom stayed with us for a few weeks before returning home to try to adjust to life alone.

Remembering my Father

"Hand me a nail, Kimmy." It was a warm summer day in Utah, and I was a little girl laying flat on my back on top of the chicken coop in back of our house where my father was working to repair the roof. I rose lazily and handed him a nail out of an old oil-stained paper bag. "Here, you can hammer it in for me," he urged handing the shiny new nail back to me. He showed me

how to hold the hammer and helped me get the nail started. I hammered carefully, sticking my tongue out of the side of my mouth in concentration. My arms and hands were getting tired and the nail still hadn't moved much farther into the wood. Dad watched quietly, a trace of a grin on his face.

Running out of patience, I suddenly gave the nail a few hard whacks. To my dismay, the nice straight nail was suddenly a bent nail. Dad wasn't upset in the least. He showed me how to turn the hammer upside down and watched as I maneuvered to pry the nail out. He coached me patiently as together we straightened the nail, and with a few swift hard swings of his own my father soon had it hammered neatly into place.

Then I stretched out beside him and relaxed once again on the roof of the old chicken coop. He showed me how to crook my arm and place it over my eyes to keep the sun out. I relaxed in the warmth of the moment on that morning, as I listened to the reassuring sound of Dad close by, rhythmically pounding nails into the roof.

Thirty-one

What Happened to Ervil

O ver the years, news had eventually reached us of the continued violence surrounding Ervil's church. Besides the murder of Rulon Allred, to which Rena eventually confessed, there had been others. We heard that Ervil had even ordered the killing of his own teen aged daughter - Lillian's younger sister named Rebecca. To my horror, it was said that one of the people who assisted in the teenager's strangulation, was Mark and Rena Chynoweth's brother, Duane.

The chilling thought of such an atrocity being committed by my old friend whom I remembered as an intelligent and likable young man, made me feel physically ill. And when we learned that Mark had been linked to the disappearance of another man in Utah, not only was I horrified - but I realized that we were all still in danger.

To our relief, Ervil was captured in 1979 and tried for conspiring to murder Rulon C. Allred. In 1980, he was found guilty and sentenced to life in prison in Utah. At last there appeared to be a measure of justice for the growing numbers of Ervil' victims. But, after mercilessly ordering the murders of others, it seemed that fate had been kind to Ervil. For, somehow, he had managed to escape receiving a death sentence himself.

But it was only a year later, on August 16, 1981, that the violent prophet was dead. Early that morning Ervil had been discovered by a guard in his prison cell, lying on the floor and clutching his throat. Although no one seems to be certain, there have been some reports that Ervil's death was caused by a heart attack.

It was only a few days later that Mom appeared at our door looking shocked and sad. "Kathy called from Mexico," she told me grimly. "She said that Verlan was in a car accident near Mexico City today." Mom's eyes filled with tears. "He's dead, Kim."

I walked into my bedroom and closed the door. I cried not only over the death of the man I almost married, but also for the loss of the father of many of my friends. As I sat pensively on the edge of my bed, I tried to understand the strange hand fate had dealt these two brothers. For years, Ervil had sought to have his younger brother murdered, while Verlan had managed to stay just out of his reach. Verlan never resorted to violence himself - he had only asked for justice in the courts of both Mexico and the United States. Yet in the end, both men had faced the end of their lives within only days of one another, and their bodies were returned to their families on the very same day.

The violence didn't end with the blood thirsty prophet's burial. Over the years we learned that some of those who had once been closest to Ervil were being murdered by some of his children. The list of people included Joel's assassin, Dan Jordan, and Mark's older sister Lorna, who was Ervil's widow. Then, in a violent struggle for power, Ervil's oldest son, my old friend Arthur, was shot down in cold blood by one of Ervil's converts.

It was years later that I stumbled across an article in the local newspaper while Ron was at work. The headline quickly captured my attention: *Four Die in Cult Style Murders in Texas.* Could this be about someone I knew? I continued reading, scanning the article for names, and suddenly they seemed to jump out at me. I gasped. The four victims, who had been shot to death, were Mark Chynoweth, Duane Chynoweth, Duane's eight-year-old daughter Jennifer, and Eddie Marston - Ervil's stepson with Anna Mae.

To hide my shock from my children, I walked out of our back door, and stood on the porch to continue reading. I learned that Mark had been shot in the office of the business that he owned in Houston; while not far away - Duane and his little girl were gunned down in the driveway of a vacant house to which they had been lured. Eddie was shot in another city about two hours away. All four victims, who had left Ervil's church years ago, were murdered at four o'clock in the afternoon.

Into the back yard I stumbled, finally stopping next to my favorite rosebush. As I stood next to the tall, fragrant plant covered with large pink blossoms, I silently bowed my head. There I remembered my old friends and grieved for the eight-year-old child whom I had never met.

That night I dreamed I was at an old vine-covered church house somewhere in the woods. Inside lay Mark's coffin. I began to cry as I realized I was at his funeral. And although I understood all too well that he was gone - I hoped that, somehow, he could know I was there.

In the days that followed, I learned that Mark had never taken another wife - and I thought about his widow Lillian and their baby named Brandon whom I had met so long ago. He would be a young man now, and would have sisters and brothers. I heard that Mark and his wife had joined a Christian church and had come to deeply regret following Ervil.

How I hoped that Lillian could someday overcome the tragedy of her past, and that she was not also in great danger. But only seven months later, the grim news reached us that she was dead - killed by a gunshot wound to the temple. It was not the hand of another that took Lillian's life. My old friend had committed suicide.

After Mark's murder, news of the blood atonements being carried out by Ervil's children stopped coming. Later we would learn that Ervil's group was responsible for over twenty murders, committed both before and after his death. Most of the dangerous family members were finally captured and imprisoned. Ervil's stepson with Rosemary, Doug Barlow, was eventually one of those linked to the simultaneous murders in Texas that ended Mark's life. Incredibly, one of the master minds of the murders was reported to be the oldest daughter of Mark's oldest sister Lorna whom I knew as a little girl named Tarsa.

~~~

Now grateful for our traditional American heritage, my husband and I settled into raising our family in the Christian faith we had embraced.

My sister Kathy, along with the other battle-weary members of the Church of the Firstborn, continued along in their religious journeys, hoping to say good-bye to tragedy at last and live their lives in peace.

Thirty-two

Summer of Sorrow

I was dreaming that there was a train coming. It was on its way *from Mexico, moving steadily down the tracks. As the powerful locomotive moved relentlessly closer, my heart beat faster for suddenly I realized that it carried something unbearably dark and ugly that I wasn't able to see. Now I was overcome with desperation - gripped with fear - as I saw that the train was almost here, and that there was utterly nothing that I or anyone else could do to delay its dreadful arrival. I wanted to turn away but, I knew it was not possible to escape the nightmare that this train was carrying.*

Groaning out loud, I awoke in the room where I had fallen asleep between my two youngest children. I let out a sigh of relief. I was safe at home - there was no train. *Thank God it was just a dream,* I thought as my pounding heart began to calm. But the memory of the dream troubled me for months.

July tenth of 1987 brought a warm beautiful morning to Lindsay, California. With windows thrown wide open, I worked busily around the middle-class home our family shared in the lovely old tree-lined neighborhood to which we had recently moved. The fragrance of orange blossoms from the nearby orchard wafted pleasantly into my kitchen.

Outside I could hear the laughter of Ryan and Jacob as my husband Ron sprayed them playfully with the hose he was using to wash Dad's old pickup we had inherited. Our toddler, Rusty, roamed the front yard in his baggy cloth diapers while in the shade of the house, baby Sarah watched the excitement from her infant seat.

It had been five months since Dad's death and it seemed that the intense grief Mom had experienced was finally turning to a more manageable level of sadness. But, for the first time in her busy life, she was alone.

Now, as I moved into the kitchen and began washing the dishes in the sink, the green wall phone behind me rang. I dried my hands on a kitchen towel and turned to answer it - expecting to hear Mom's voice on the other end of the line. Instead, my ear was filled with a crackling sound as a Mexican operator asked if I would accept a collect phone call from Colonia LeBaron. Surprised and concerned, I quickly agreed to accept the call.

There was a pause as I waited anxiously, and at last I heard the faraway voice of a woman speaking urgently over the static. "This is Lorraine, in the colony," she began quickly. I remembered Lorraine well, she was the sister of Ronita, and half sister of my brother-in-law Lane. "Micah's dead," she told me bluntly. I froze in horrified disbelief. It couldn't be true. Micah was Kathy and Lane's son who had visited at our house just six months earlier when Kathy had come to see our sick father. Micah was only five years old.

Before I could respond, Lorraine rushed on over the increasing noisy interference. "We called your mom, but we didn't tell her that Kathy's dead too!" she shouted - and then the line went dead. Now my head was spinning - my heart beating wildly. I grabbed the counter for support. "Kathy and Micah," I repeated numbly to myself. "Kathy and Micah..."

I don't know how, but I made my way out the front door, down the steps and into the front yard where I stood staring mutely at Ron. He glanced up and, seeing the look on my face, quickly dropped the hose and came to me. "What's wrong?" he demanded calmly.

I opened my mouth to speak, and the dreadful words spilled out. "Kathy and Micah are dead." A look of horror and pain filled my husband's eyes as he put his arms around me to pull me close. As the children watched with concern I buried my face in Ron's chest and wept uncontrollably.

"How?" he asked after a few moments.

"I don't know," I answered, sniffing violently. "We got cut off." I shrugged helplessly. "Probably a car accident," I said, remembering the dangerous highway between the colony and Casas Grandes. Just then the phone rang again.

"I'll take it this time," Ron said and he walked quickly into the house to pick up the phone. As we had thought, it was another call from Mexico. I sat with the children in the living room, listening to the sound of Ron's voice - numbly waiting to learn the details of the deaths of my sister and her little boy. Now Ron was raising his voice as he tried to be heard over the sound of returning static.

Then he was sitting beside me - grimly telling me the news I dreaded to hear. "It was an accidental electrocution," he said in a hushed voice. My mouth dropped open and I felt my body trembling. "I couldn't get the details because of the bad connection. I'm sorry," Ron said gently as tears filled my eyes again. "They want us to come as soon as possible for the funerals."

As we prepared for the ride to my mother's house, I felt myself growing calmer. I had to be strong for her sake - for I was facing the heart-wrenching task of telling Micah's already grieving grandmother that her thirty-eight-year old daughter was also dead.

It was Ron who accompanied my mother to the funerals. We had all agreed that it would not be wise for me to take five-month-old Sarah, who needed to be breast-fed regularly, on the quickly arranged flight to El Paso, followed by a hurried drive into Mexico. When six-year-old Jacob suddenly came down with a fever, the decision was final: I would stay at home with the children and Ron and Mom would leave as soon as possible - for it was not customary for people of the colony to be embalmed after death.

Alone with my kids, I tossed and turned that entire night as I grieved for my sister and worried about her children who desperately needed our help. Before he left, Ron and I had agreed that we would be here to assist Mom if she could bring them home. As I stared sleeplessly at the dark ceiling, I prayed fervently for the safe return of my husband and my mother.

The next day, Ron called to tell me they had arrived safely in the colony. And over the unusually clear connection, he grimly reported the ghastly details surrounding the deaths of my sister and her little boy. I was horrified to learn that they were not the only victims. "Estella's little boy was killed too," Ron told me sadly.

Estella was one of Lane's other wives. Her six-year-old child called "Lancito" after his father, had been Micah's half brother and playmate. It was Micah who had first grabbed onto the wire fence that had come in contact with a high voltage electrical wire. Lancito had tried to help him, followed by Kathy who touched the fence after coming out to look for the boys. Within a short time, all three of them had perished - killed by the electricity that their husband and father had carelessly run underground next to the fence. Lane had done his own electrical wiring. Although there had been other narrow escapes resulting from his faulty electrical work, he had never taken action to correct the problems.

Ron tried to be of some support to my mother as she tried to comfort Kathy's children. Putting aside her own pain, Mom worked to help fifteen-year-old Ruth care for the distraught family. At the group funeral, after looking in dismay upon the unnaturally swollen body of her daughter, and seeing the pain it was also causing the children, she requested that the coffin be closed. To their relief, her request was granted.

She held herself together at the very long funeral, even when Alma preached a lengthy speech about his religion - never once mentioning the dead. But later, Mom would tell me how proud she was of Ron when he stood up in protest and walked out. She could not bear to tell me of the trip to the weedy cemetery and the heart-wrenching burials of Kathy and the two little boys.

Before my mother and Ron left to come home, Mom and Ruth begged Lane to allow the children to return with them. How desperately they needed a place to be comforted and heal after their harrowing ordeal - but Lane refused, believing that we would try to keep the children once we had them. He was right - we wanted so badly to get the children away from him! But in the end he only allowed them to bring ten-year-old Aaron, his oldest son with Kathy, for a visit.

Ruth wept bitterly as she stayed behind with seventeen-year-old learning-impaired Luke, and her three little half-sisters: four-year-old Elena, two-year-old Leah, and six-month-old Holly. Kathy's oldest son, Lynn, was already living on his own and engaged to be married.

"Pray for us," Ruth cried to her Grandma and Uncle Ron as they were leaving. "Tell everyone I said to pray for us!" And we did.

Our prayers were answered several months later, when I once again took a call from Mexico. This time it was from one of Kathy's former sister-wives, a woman who had married Lane after my sister. "Kim, do you want these kids?" she asked me, sounding distraught. I held my breath in disbelief. "Lane's been molesting Luke," she quickly continued, beginning to cry. "I feel so damn bad," she sobbed. "If you want these kids you can take them." And we did.

After a hurried covert operation, the children were eventually delivered to their grandma's house. It all happened so smoothly, so fast; yet their lives and ours would be changed forever.

~~~

It was past midnight as I groggily made my way to the telephone in the kitchen. It had been a long and busy day - I hoped that the ringing would not wake my children, or Luke and Elena who had been staying with us. I picked up the receiver and held it to my ear. "Hello?" I said sleepily.

"Is this Mrs. Taylor?" a man's voice inquired.

"Yes it is," I replied uneasily. Who was this stranger calling in the middle of the night?

To my surprise, it was a police officer from our local police department. I closed my eyes and shook my head in exasperation as he quickly summed up the reason for his call. "I have a man here who claims you've kidnapped his children."

So began a long, complicated fight in the courts for guardianship of Kathy's children. Besides coming up against Lane, Mom and I also ended up battling with the local division of the Children's Protective Services who wanted custody of the family. To our horror, we discovered that it was their intention to offer counseling to Lane, and one day return the children to him.

We were prepared to fight that plan to the bitter end. Mom hired a prominent and skilled lawyer, and several months later, not long after the testimony of some of the children, we were overjoyed when Mom and I were awarded legal guardianship of all six children: Luke, Ruth, Aaron, Elena, Leah and Holly. The battle for their freedom was over- and we had won.

To our relief, Lane went back into Mexico. Time continued to be a blur of activity and sometimes confused teamwork as we tried to provide the children with the love, care, and security they so desperately needed. Traumatized and heartbroken, fifteen-year-old Ruth struggled with all her might to fill the tremendous void that the death of her mother had created.

Together, Ruth and I started a little craft enterprise in which we engaged the children. Our sorrows temporarily dissolved as we became absorbed in covering picture albums and frames with cloth and lace - while ordinary straw hats and wicker baskets became works of art covered with silk flowers. Finally we grabbed pencil boxes with lids and created lovely jewelry boxes upholstered with satin and ribbon before packing up all our handiwork to sell at craft fairs.

This experience turned out to be therapeutic for all of us, and to our delight, even some of the children's creations sold. As we worked together, I realized how little I knew about my own creative abilities. I sadly wondered about all of the wonderful talents that I knew Kathy and my other sisters certainly possessed that were never recognized or developed.

The years passed quickly, and at the age of eighteen with the help of a thoughtful family friend named Barbara, Ruth applied for a house through a special government program. Although there was a waiting list, it was only a few months before things fell miraculously into place. Mom provided a down payment, and on one fine day Ruth was granted a newly-built three bedroom home on one-half acre for herself and her three little sisters, which would require minimal payments. Aaron would remain with his grandmother until the age of sixteen, and Luke would continue to live most of the time with us.

It was during this time that I gave birth to our last child, yet another little boy we named Nathaniel. How blessed he would be to grow so completely surrounded by the love of our large family, his cousins, and his grandma.

Thirty-three

Where I Belong

I see you, Nathaniel!" Luke calls happily. He is concentrating on the screen of our son's new video camera trying to record him in our yard. The day is sunny and warm. "Now I don't see you. Where'd you go?" Luke sounds puzzled. Standing on his skateboard, Nathaniel had moved - but the camera had not. I hear Ron chuckle. We watch as our twelve-year-old son patiently shows his thirty-six-year-old cousin how to aim the camcorder, and keep it focused - following the action. "Oh, now I get it!" Luke cries jubilantly as Nate returns to his skateboard.

When Luke first came to us twenty years ago, he was a handsome, athletically built seventeen-year-old who functioned at the age of about an eight- year-old. He had been physically and emotionally abused for most of his life. Then, not only had he lost his mother and little brother, he had been molested by his own step-father shortly after their deaths. I dropped my head in sorrow on the day that Ruth explained to me that the scars I was examining on Luke's back were probably left from the bailing wire he had been beaten with by Lane.

For several years following Kathy's death, our lives were invaded with tension, as we tried to help Luke through his pain, and deal with his unexpected erratic behavior. Sometimes Luke's rage would boil so furiously that he would shout incoherently, or even tip over a piece of our furniture. But when he was in control of himself, we saw that he had a loving heart of gold. We noticed that he was always gentle with his younger siblings and cousins and kind to animals, and we knew that Luke had even endured abuse from Kathy's husband for trying to stand up for his little sisters.

It took awhile for me to realize that my husband seemed to have a calming effect on Luke, and I learned to simply back away without reacting to his angry encounters. I began to recognize that, instead of me lecturing him - or even attempting to soothe him with affection, my confused and tormented teenaged nephew needed a strong but patient father figure.

One day Luke behaved violently at his sister Ruth's house, and we hurried back from an out-of-town trip to deal with the family crisis. Back at our house, I left the room as Ron prepared to talk to Luke alone. It was beginning to look like we would have no choice but to look for

195

some sort of home to place him in, if Luke could not get control of his anger.

Sitting apprehensively in my bedroom, I expected to hear the sound of Ron's voice sternly correcting Luke's unacceptable and dangerous behavior - giving him a firm ultimatum. But, although he sounded firm, his voice was calm and even questioning. Then there was silence.

Feeling confused and curious - I rose and walked to peek around the corner of the living room to see what was going on. I froze in my steps, and tears rose in my eyes - for I had come upon a moving scene. There was Ron, gently embracing the trembling body of our distraught nephew as he stood sobbing on my husband's shoulder. Several times he tried to speak but his pain was too great to allow it. Then, "I'm sorry, I'm sorry," Luke began to repeat brokenly between sobs. After a while, his body relaxed and he let out a long sigh. "I just never had nobody that loved me," he whispered forlornly.

I believe that day was a turning point for Luke, for he never became violent again. Now, years later, with the help of a local agency, not only has Luke found a part time job - but he lives in his own apartment. On weekends, when he is not busy with Special Olympic activities, he spends the night at our house. That's when he and Nathaniel use the video camera, play games, and shoot hoops out in the driveway. In the evenings Luke listens intently to the different books that Nathaniel occasionally reads to him out loud.

Sometimes I marvel at the bond between our son, and the son of Kathy and Joel. So much has changed since their deaths. Except for Nathaniel, their children and ours have all grown into adults and moved out on their own. Ryan and Sarah have both married and Ron and I are now grandparents.

Grandpa Flowers lived in his own house until he was just shy of ninety-three years old - and it was there that he died surrounded by his family. Steven, Carolyn, and Judy's husband Paul have all passed away too. I was told that while only in his fifties, Steven died from a heart attack, while Carolyn, who had been suffering from high blood pressure, passed away from kidney failure just weeks before the death of our mother. Years later we learned that Paul had suffered a fatal stroke in Southern Mexico where he lived alone as a bachelor.

Mom has been gone for five years. I was blessed with children who, like their father, have musical talents that far surpass mine. Mom, who had a beautiful voice of her own, enjoyed listening to us sing. She lived with us for the last three years of her life. I cared for her as her heart failed, and she died in our home under the care of Hospice. Our family sang to her on the day she died.

The month before she passed away, Ron and I stood beside her bed in the presence of our family and Kathy's children to renew our vows on our twenty-fifth anniversary. Before the ceremony as I sat writing the things I wanted to say to my husband - memories of the past flooded my mind, and for awhile I was overcome with sadness. It seemed that we had spent most of our lives struggling and since childhood we had both experienced much pain. Had our lives ever really been easy? Although we had been together for twenty-five years, it seemed that we had not found time to really know each other, either before or after our marriage. We had faced so many problems, been so confused, and made so many mistakes. Inspite of our good intentions, we had not managed to do much more than survive. We still had so much to learn.

I began to struggle in my heart - wishing that I could turn back time. Knowing what I knew now - I would be a true companion to my husband, as I richly poured out my love and awareness over our beautiful children. Instead of being always busy, I would pay careful attention to all that each of them had to say. I would shower Kathy's sweet children with the abundant attention that they so needed and deserved, and I would appreciate my parents and love my sisters better. I would...I would love myself too. I began to cry. My frenzied thoughts faded as I realized that the past, with all its opportunities for joy and fulfillment, was gone. I had only the present. And I knew that I must receive it as a gift.

As I continued writing the things I wanted to say to my husband, I realized how much the two of us had grown, and I remembered happy times. I considered the power of forgiveness and accepted the gift of hope being offered to me in that very moment that God had created. Hope not only for myself - but for all of the loved ones with whom I would be sharing that special day.

And later, as I spoke the words I had written for my husband, I began to finally understand where I belonged.

I have a new understanding of the vows we renew today, for we have truly lived the meaning of the words we spoke to one another twenty-five years ago. It hasn't been the fairy tale journey written about in the books we read as children, or the perfect romance portrayed in the movies. We have been together in sickness and health, for richer and for poorer, through joyful times and times of sorrow.

We have survived moments of despair, even causing pain to one another, for these are the realities of marriage. But together we've also discovered hope and faith, and a longing to be better people. We have watched our children grow together, with sometimes indescribable joy. We have learned the meaning of forgiveness and love and come closer to the very meaning of life. We've taken each step together, for twenty-five years.

Thank you for always being there. For putting up with my faults, compulsions, and mistakes. Thank you for giving all that you have given to your family - for the hard work and selfless actions. Thank you for your generosity of spirit, your patience, and your thoughtfulness. Thank you for being a husband to me, a father to our children, an uncle to our nieces and nephews, and a son to my parents. Thank you for not giving up when times have been hard.

Through our marriage, I have discovered what is most important in my life. Being here as your wife and as the mother of our children are the two most important things on earth to me. In this discovery, I have learned to be a better daughter to my mother, and to truly honor the memory of my father. I wish he could be here with us to share this day. Although he is gone he is not forgotten. I would like to take this moment in time to express my gratitude to my mother and to remember my father as well as your mother and father.

I feel that this is a new beginning of our lives together. I invite God to be here with us today and for the rest of our lives.

And I pledge to you, my dear husband,
to stay by your side with love and honor,
as your helpmate and wife
through all that may come our way
from this day forward, til death do us part.

Photo
Section

Joel F. LeBaron, our prophet.

My sister Kathy and Joel on their wedding day.

Ervil and children from first wife Delfina.

The LeBaron Brothers: Ervil, Joel, Verlan, Alma, and Floren

The French Missionaries: Standing at far left is Dan Jordan in front of Steven Silver. Bill Tucker is standing in center and Bruce Wakeham is kneeling.

Kathy, and Judy holding me in Utah.

Mom, Kim, Kathy and Dad while visiting home of Grandma and Grandpa.

*Grandpa and Grandma Flowers with my
cousin's baby, Bryant*

*Me with older sisters Kathy, Carolyn, and
Judy in Utah not long before moving to
Colonia LeBaron.*

Colonia LeBaron

Kim's surprise birthday party in Los Molinos. Mark is holding the oil lamp.

Lillie and Kim not long after Lillie's marriage to Verlan.

Kathy, Dad, and Carolyn's son Chris in Los Molinos.

Rhea, Donna, and Mark playing a game at our house in Los Molinos.

*Carolyn, Kim, Judy, and Kathy at church conference in
Los Molinos*

*Rhea, Malinda, Kim, and Donna having fun with Mark
at the home he later attacked.*

Kim at Kathy's apartment.

17 year old Kim with Lynn, Luke, and Audrey.

Dr. Rulon Allred: Ervil's rival slain by Rena.

Rena Chynoweth: Ervil's thirteenth wife.

Jennifer Chynoweth: Duane's daughter slain by Ervil's children.

Duane Chynoweth: Slain along with his daughter after leaving Ervil's church.

Grandmother LeBaron with Kathy and Lane on their wedding day.

Kathy with her growing family in 1979.

Elena and Micah at Kathy's house built by Lane in Colonia LeBaron.

Kathy's family safe at their Grandma's home.

Kathy's family with ours. Mom is standing between Luke, and Judy's son Michael.

Tressie and Leo Wariner, my parents.

Ron and Kim with family in 1994.

*Luke receiving a gold medal for
Special Olympics softball.*

Kim and Ruth at a craft fair.

*The Taylor family sings at Sarah's wedding, accompanied by her new
uncle.*

About the Author

Kim Taylor resides in the Pacific Northwest with her husband Ron and son Nathan, the youngest of five children. She has two grandchildren.

Besides spending time with family and friends, she enjoys children and animals as well as working with the elderly. Healthy cooking has become a fun hobby, and she has a deep appreciation for the beauty of nature.

Marriage is a topic of importance to her, and recently Kim took up the challenge of creating an interactive pro-monogamy website and blog to encourage traditional American marriage. Readers are welcome to visit www.justonewife.com.

Made in the USA
Lexington, KY
19 February 2010